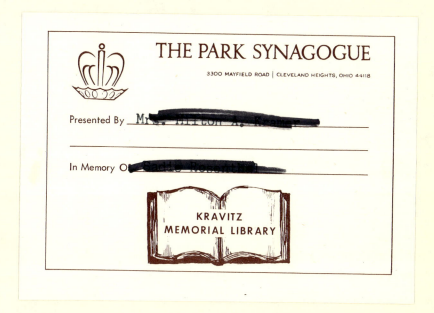

EXIT VISA

EXIT VISA

THE EMIGRATION OF THE SOVIET JEWS

PAUL PANISH

Coward, McCann & Geoghegan
New York

Library of Congress Cataloging in Publication Data
Panish, Paul, date.
    Exit visa.
    Bibliography: p.
    1. Jews, Russian, in the United States. 2. Jews in
Russia—Politics and government—1917- . 3. Russia
—Emigration and immigration. 4. United States—
Emigration and immigration.   I. Title.
E184.J5P275 1981   304.8'47'073   80-29320
ISBN 0-698-11056-0

Printed in the United States of America

Humbly and with love I dedicate this book
to those emigrés who, for my benefit, consented
to relive all that others are happy to forget.

Contents

Ah quanto a dir qual' era è cosa dura
  Esta selva selvaggia e aspra e forte
  Che nel pensier rinnova la paura
  Tant' è amara che poco è più morte . . .

A harsh task, to tell you how that was—
  that wilderness, those brute, savage woods—
  for in my mind they summon a terror back
so bitter, death itself is hardly worse . . .
                    —Dante, *Inferno*, I, 4-7

Preface

Although the emigration of hundreds of thousands of Soviet citizens to Israel and the West during the past dozen years or so has been the subject of much talk, the actual experiences of this emigration, the day-to-day histories of the emigrés, remain unknown. "How did you do it?" "What really happened?" "How did it feel?" These are the basic questions, the questions that are most difficult to answer.

The challenge of this book, therefore, is to uncover the real life of the emigration, to tease it away from the jargon and the slogans that surround it. Although *Exit Visa* is not meant to be a formal historical study, historical data have been introduced, wherever necessary, to create a clearer picture of the social, political, economic and cultural conditions that have helped to mold the characters and the fates of the emigrés, and that have given the world of this emigration its peculiar life.

In order to enter that world, and to follow the history and the circumstances of the emigrés, this book re-creates the emotional lives as well as the external conditions of several different families through their Soviet lives, their departures and journeys, and their resettlements. Each family experienced the emigration differently. They came from different social levels within Soviet society, lived in different parts of the Soviet Union, and settled in different areas of America.

Although the emigration of the Soviet Jews was initially assumed to be an emigration to Israel, by the mid-1970s more emigrés were settling in the West than in Israel. Historical realities therefore compel us to view this emigration as having two main prongs: the emigration to Israel and the emigration to America. There are also emigrés who have settled in Western Europe, Canada, Australia, and other countries, but these comprise only a small percentage of the total and are not dealt with here. This book concentrates on those who have come to America. To have given equal emphasis to those who have settled in Israel would have been impractical. The conditions vary too widely.

The Israeli experience appears in this book only through the eyes of those who had emigrated initially to Israel and then left to continue their search westward. This does not take into consideration the many thousands who have settled in Israel successfully, nor does it attempt to give a detailed and balanced picture of the Israeli situation. It is included here only as one more important influence on the lives and the psyches of the emigrés to the West.

The people portrayed in *Exit Visa* do not constitute a statistically "typical" sampling of the emigré community. However, after interviewing scores of emigrés in several cities, carefully and at length, after becoming well acquainted with many more than those who were formally interviewed, and after spending the past several years working on emigré problems with case workers and volunteer workers, we have come to feel that the experiences of these families are variations on a set of themes that recur in the lives of this emigration—and perhaps of all emigrations.

The people portrayed in *Exit Visa* are real; the book is not a fictionalization, though it re-creates actual scenes and even conversations, where our information permitted, and where that seemed necessary for an appreciation of the emigrés' experiences. However, certain factual details, which could serve to identify the people in the book, have been changed; those whom we interviewed were promised that their friends and relatives still in the Soviet Union would not be put in jeopardy by anything written here. To that end, all names have been changed and almost all professional titles have been altered somewhat, as have a variety of other details that could have served to pinpoint the actual people. The names and identities of the American and Western European case workers have also been altered to help preserve their clients' anonymity.

The emigrés who appear in these pages have taken a great deal of time away from their rushed and harried lives to assist us. It is to them that this book owes its primary debt of gratitude.

It would be misleading to give the reader the impression that the emigrés were the sole source of information for this book. In a number of cities, in Europe as well as in the United States, we were assisted greatly by volunteer emigré-resettlement workers, as well as by officers and case workers from the various social agencies that deal with the emigrés—the United HIAS Service, the American Jewish Joint Distribution Committee, the New York Association for New Americans, the Jewish Family Service—all of which are discussed in the body of this book. Many of these people spoke to us outside their official capacities, and were thus able to discuss with great candor the problems that they face in their work as well as their own perspectives on the experiences of the emigrés. In many instances the information supplied off the record by these agency personnel meshed closely with the stories told by the emigrés, and in some instances formed an important cross-check. Although these people, who spoke so frankly, deserve all my thanks, they will not be mentioned here by name as they have asked to be left anonymous.

Among those people who took time out of their very busy official schedules in order to help us understand the nature, structure and function of their agencies, I must mention Arthur Pruzan of the New York office of HIAS, Herbert Katzky of the New York office of Joint, Sylvia Friedman and Julia Desgun of NYANA, Merrill Rosenberg of the Vienna office of HIAS, Monek Einziger of the Vienna office of Joint, Yakov Kedmi of Sokhnut in Vienna, Evi Eller of the Rome office of HIAS, Loni Meyer of the Rome office of Joint, and Robert Price of the San Francisco Jewish Vocational and Career Counseling Center's Emigre Project.

The use of the first person plural throughout this preface is more than a literary convention. My wife, Anna Belle, who was the first to recognize the potential importance of a book such as this, worked closely with me at almost every interview. Her insight, compassion, intelligence and expertise ensured the success of those interviews and made it possible for this book to be written.

I would also like to extend my thanks to Zoya Veitsman, of the San Francisco Jewish Vocational and Career Counseling Center, who spent many hours introducing us to emigrés in a number of cities, and who was the first to help us find friends and supporters within the emigré communities.

A special word of praise should be directed toward my children, Joseph and Jennifer Panish, who have put up patiently with long periods of a topsy-turvy social life as we all became absorbed into the world of the emigrés. How many afternoons and evenings they sat through, hardly hearing a recognizable word of English! They are thus among the unsung heroes of this book.

I'm sure I will be neither the first nor the last author to thank Joseph Kanon, my editor, for his invaluable assistance, advice and encouragement in the preparation of this book.

Part One: ENDINGS

Chapter One:
Gorelsky

According to a Yiddish expression popular among turn-of-the-century Russian Jews, it was said of a man whose taste for the good life was matched by his good fortune: *"Er lebt vi Got in Odess,"* "He lives like God in Odessa," as though even God Himself was happiest there.

For several decades before the Communist revolution of November 1917, Jews had been flocking to Odessa, gaping at the stately gilt and marble buildings along her green boulevards and promenades, then crowding into tenements and courtyards that echoed the noise of the open markets and the Moldavanka hucksters. As a large city, Odessa seemed safer to the Jews than did their little towns, the shtetls, that were so terribly exposed to the marauding bands of Kossacks, drunken peasants and armed hoodlums who had been slaughtering tens of thousands of Jews in the pogroms. As a thriving port and mercantile center, Odessa was a city where one could live decently; there were goods to be sold and customers to buy them. What's more, Odessa was an intellectual center, a colorful, cosmopolitan mélange of peoples and tongues, a place where one could slip out from under the stern gaze of the rabbis and enjoy the pleasures of variety, the tang of the world.

Even after the Bolsheviks' Red Army destroyed the royalist forces in the Ukraine during those civil-war years of murder and pillage that ended in the early 1920s, Odessa maintained some of her color. Although her freewheeling élan was gradually muffled and regimented, Odessa seemed quite liveable when compared to the hungry cities and the demolished countrysides of heartland Russia to the north, relics of the years of industrial chaos, reduced trade and rural famine that followed the revolution.

And so the Jews continued to come to Odessa and to other cosmopolitan centers. Those who hadn't already run off to America or Western Europe soon discovered that moving to the big cities, entering Russian schools, and acquiring a profession were their best hope of survival, if not their only hope.

In 1917 Naum Gorelsky was a rabbinical student at a yeshiva, a Jewish seminary, in the Mogilyov district far to the north. Most Jews had been relieved, if not overjoyed, by the fall of the Tsar's government in March of that year, and many had nurtured hopes of a rebirth of Russian-Jewish life. There were demands for Jewish national autonomy, and when the so-called "provisional" government, in power from March to November, 1917, abolished all privileges and restrictions based on nationality or religion, the Jews began to feel that their day had come. But the Bolshevik overthrow of the provisional government, in November, changed the picture. In January 1918, Lenin's government enacted a decree that legalized the confiscation of religious property and prohibited religious instruction.

Toward the end of 1919, Naum Gorelsky and about a hundred other Jews were herded into the local synagogue. A bareheaded, clean-shaven young Jew strode forward and read to them, in curt, clipped tones, a decree from the new Commissariat for Nationality Affairs. This paper, signed by Yosif Stalin, declared the abolition of the *kehillas*, the associations through which the Jews had administered their social, educational, and community affairs. Many of Naum's friends, fellow students, even teachers, decided then that the wait-and-see period was over, and began to write to their relatives in America to send money for boat passage. But what good would that do, going to America? Naum had heard about the London and New York slums, the alien ways of America. What would he do there? Teach Talmud? More likely he'd end up running another man's sewing machine twelve hours a day, and on the Sabbath as well.

16

Part One: ENDINGS

The Bolsheviks were in power and the Party leadership wanted to divest itself of any taint of Tsarist anti-Semitism, yet large numbers of Jews found themselves classified once again as economic bloodsuckers. According to the new doctrine, only those with roots in the proletariat or the peasantry were politically and socially legitimate, but very few Jews fit this category. For generations, Russian Jews had been forced by Tsarist policy to scrape along as best they could, often to starve, as self-employed tradesmen and craftsmen. Now the newly hailed "dictatorship of the proletariat" declared that such people were the "class enemy," along with the old aristocracy, the landowners and the great merchants.

There was a time when some of the most dangerous anti-Semites in Russia could be found among those Jews who had converted to Russian Orthodox Christianity. Now that anti-Semitism was officially outlawed, Naum Gorelsky discovered that he had to be wary of a new variation on the old theme. Within the ranks of the Jewish socialists, before the revolution, there had been a small but vociferous number who not only rebelled against political and economic repression by the Tsar's regime, but were disaffected from all aspects of traditional Jewish life. They formed the extreme edge of a large spectrum of Jewish political groups that ranged from the socialists and the socialistically oriented Zionists, through democrats and liberals of all stamps. The most extreme group, some of whom were, or later became, Bolsheviks, were enlisted by the Communist Party to run its "Jewish Sections," and to see to it that Jewish culture, both religious and secular, did not propagate on Soviet soil. Through means both legal and illegal, these Jewish Sections joined with local authorities in closing Jewish schools and synagogues and in hampering Jewish religious observances. They also saw to it that rabbis, Talmudic scholars, the *mohalim* who performed ritual circumcisions, and the *shokhtim* who oversaw the kosher slaughtering of cattle for meat, were arrested and imprisoned in increasing numbers throughout the 1920s.

There were schools that taught Yiddish, but they had to adhere to the standardized Soviet curriculum, with its heavily atheistic, anticlerical indoctrination. They avoided any material that could support the students' devotion to Jewish culture, and therefore they lost appeal. When graduates of these schools discovered that their

17

lack of training in Russian hampered their professional advancement, they abandoned the Yiddish schools and rushed to get a Russian education—the only kind that counted.

Ultimately a moment of decision came for Naum Gorelsky: either get away from provincial towns like Mogilyov, where Party organizers were molding the angry street mobs into "politically educated" vigilante armies, or wait patiently for a delegation from the local Party committee—a grim little group, led, perhaps, by some Jew-hating Jew—who would stride into Naum's apartment and make shrill demands that Naum repent publicly for spreading religious "superstition."

The Gorelskys left Mogilyov, but not to cross the border. After all, Russia hadn't yet had a chance to recover her balance; perhaps cooler heads would prevail. The Jews had survived Tsar Nikolai, maybe they'd survive the Bolsheviks as well. Naum and his wife, who was pregnant with their first child, were on their way to join his relatives in the port city of Odessa, where he would soon be retrained as a pharmacist. In such times one finds ways to keep ahead of the Angel of Death.

And so, on a late winter morning in 1927, Naum Gorelsky hoisted his bag onto his narrow, bony shoulder and led his wife out of the Odessa railway station. They picked their way past those broad boulevards that led down to the sea—Pushkinskaya, Yekaterininskaya—and past the open markets, toward the old Moldavanka section. Naum paused for a moment to peer up at what had once been a church, its entryway now boarded up and heaped with rubbish, its golden cupolas gleaming incongruously above the political slogans scrawled across its muddied portals.

Naum Gorelsky's grandson, Alexandr, was typical of the bright, intellectually precocious Odessa Jew. He was addicted to the clever quip, something with a touch of wit and a bit of mischief. Inevitably this got him into trouble. In 1960, while walking through the schoolyard with some classmates, he had patted a bronze bust of Lenin on the head, and chirped, "Don't be so glum, Vladimir Ilyitch—*somebody* must love you!"

The other children did just as they had always been taught to do:

they informed the principal of the school, who decided on the spot that Alexandr had insulted the founder of the Soviet state, thereby disgracing himself and the school. Alexandr Gorelsky, at the age of ten, was expelled from school for "behavior unbecoming a Soviet schoolboy."

Alexandr did not become any easier to handle as an adolescent. Osip and Anna Gorelsky, Alexandr's parents, had an apartment that overlooked the kitchen window of Dora Markovna, who was Alexandr's social studies teacher as well as his class supervisor, the teacher in charge of all administrative and academic problems of the class. The Gorelskys did not yet have a telephone, and Alexandr's problems with teachers, or their problems with him, arose often enough to warrant a prearranged signaling system to save Dora Markovna the trouble of running up to the Gorelsky apartment every time Alexandr misbehaved. Late one afternoon, Dora placed a flowerpot with large crimson blossoms on her outer kitchen windowsill—the warning beacon.

The problem was not simply that Alexandr had disrupted the class, but that he had done it in a particularly undiplomatic way. Dora Markovna had been in the middle of a carefully prepared lesson on the ethnic makeup of the U.S.S.R., a very delicate subject, for the Soviet Union includes an even larger assortment of once-separate nations than the Tsars' Russian Empire did, and thus has a wider range of potential racial and ethnic problems. It is essential that these national minorities *not* see themselves as subject peoples of an imperial power. The official doctrine is that they are all brothers in socialism, all working together to achieve the ideal communist society, transcending petty nationalism and national identities. This doctrine of *druzhbá naródov*, "friendship among the Soviet nations," must be drummed into all Soviet students carefully and thoroughly, for it is an important counteractive to the latent desire for national independence that keeps cropping up in many of the Soviet territories.

Dora Markovna thus had reason to feel concerned when Alexandr raised his hand during her lecture, and asked why there was no mention of the Jews in a lesson devoted to nationalities of the Soviet Union. Aren't there Jews in the U.S.S.R.? And on their internal passports, carried by every urban-dwelling Soviet citizen over the age of sixteen, don't the Jews have to be listed as *Yevrei*, Jew, in the blank marked "nationality"?

Dora Markovna had to spend half the period explaining that Soviet power had saved the Jews; she pointed out that she herself was a Jew, and that she knew what problems her grandfather had endured under Tsarism; that now she was educated, had been accepted as an equal. Her husband, a sea captain, had once remarked . . .

"But your husband isn't a Jew," Alexandr interrupted.

"That's true, Alexandr; so what?"

"Do you know of many Jewish sea captains?"

"Well, I'm sure there must be . . ."

"I'd like to meet them, Dora Markovna, because *I* know that the government won't *let* Jews become sea captains anymore—"

That afternoon, Dora Markovna put out the flowerpot and urged Osip and Anna Gorelsky to do something about their boy before he created some real problems.

This behavior had more of adolescent spunk than political substance. At the age of sixteen Alexandr was far from being a Zionist, or even an enthusiast for things Jewish. In fact, he tended to accept Osip's attempts to explain away obviously anti-Semitic incidents as relics from a past age, as old pockets of infection that Soviet civilization would one day succeed in healing. Osip had preserved his own faith in the ideals he had once learned in school, such as the brotherhood and equality of the Soviet peoples, but the realities of Soviet life kept thrusting contrary evidence before his son's eyes.

Alexandr had always known that being Jewish made him different, and that the difference was negative, not positive. Several times, when he was a little boy, he ran toward a crowd of neighborhood children who were playing in the street, only to watch them dash away as they laughed and chanted the traditional refrain, "*Zhid, zhid, po ulitze byezhit!*"—"The Yid, the Yid, he's running down the street!"—as though Alexandr were some quaking frock-coated Jew scurrying to get out of the way of a band of mounted Kossacks.

But even at the rebellious age of sixteen, whatever skepticism Alexandr felt toward his father's faith in the ultimate ethical truth of Marxism, whatever glee Alexandr felt at the dramatically disruptive impact of his own outspokenness, he still basically believed, or at least wanted to believe, in Osip's wisdom. And although his behavior in school was unusually troublesome for a Soviet student, especially one who planned to get a higher education, Alexandr could feel more secure than most because he was somewhat protected by Osip's influential position as a mathematics professor of note in one of Odessa's major research institutes.

A year and a half later, in 1967, just after Alexandr graduated from high school, he was pleased to learn that a distant cousin—nineteen-year-old Isai, who lived in Lithuania—would visit Odessa in June, when the summer vacation began. Alexandr had never met Isai, but had always been intrigued by what he had heard about him. Isai was supposedly well brought up, very bright, a model of the cultivated young intellectual.

The Baltic countries—Latvia, Lithuania, and Estonia—had not been taken over by the Soviets until almost 1940, and shortly thereafter the invading Nazis pushed the Soviets out until 1945. From 1945 to 1953 that part of the Baltic intelligentsia that had survived the Nazi occupation was cruelly reduced by Stalin, but some of the old, Western-oriented academic and intellectual traditions survived, enough to be admired by many intellectuals raised in the Soviet Union.

Because the Baltic nations had not been Sovietized until the mid and late 1940s, Baltic Jews had been unaffected by those first two decades of Soviet rule in Russia, which had gone so far to destroy Jewish intellectual, cultural and religious life within the Soviet Union. As a result, as late as 1940, many Latvian, Lithuanian and Estonian Jews were well educated in Judaism, and were literate not only in Yiddish but also in Hebrew, the only language so thoroughly outlawed in the Soviet Union that not even Communist slogans could be written in it. After the defeat of the Nazis, some of these Baltic Jews emerged—some from hiding, some from the death camps—and began to reestablish themselves.

Alexandr knew little about that history, but fragments of it occasionally came up in conversation among his relatives, and lent cousin Isai, who, it was said, knew both Yiddish and modern Hebrew, a certain fascination. Anna had once mentioned that Isai's family had fled to the Soviet side of the border when the Nazis attacked in 1941, and that his father had died after spending years in one of Stalin's camps.

In 1963, when Alexandr was thirteen—about two years before Grandfather Naum died—he had overheard Naum talking about an aunt of Isai's who was living in Odessa. She had been imprisoned for five years for being a Zionist. Alexandr was amazed to hear the word "Zionism" mentioned in connection with a member of his own family, or with anyone else he knew, for that matter.

But what mattered, in that early summer of 1967, was that his cousin Isai was coming for a brief stay in Odessa, and that Alexandr would finally have an "older brother" to look up to. They would go sightseeing and swimming, Alexandr would tell Isai all about himself, and Isai would give him advice and admire his cleverness.

On the second day after Isai's arrival, Alexandr was busily rattling on about himself, while trying to get Isai to hurry and get ready for their trip to the beach. It was noon, half of this beautiful June day was wasted, and Isai was fiddling with the radio dial. He was thoroughly absorbed in hunting through the middle-wave band, not even half listening to Alexandr's self-revelations. Suddenly, as Isai combed back and forth through the loud hiss between stations, the speaker shook to the rhythmic, piercing *rat-tat-tat-tat* of radio jamming. Then, a fraction to one side of the jamming signal, barely comprehensible as it drifted through the noise, was the Russian-language broadcast of *Kol Yisrael*, "The Voice of Israel."

Alexandr told Isai to turn if off, or at least to make it lower. Osip didn't usually make a fuss about Alexandr listening to the "Voice of America," as long as it was kept very low so that the neighbors couldn't hear it. A number of Osip's colleagues at the institute lived in the Gorelskys' apartment house, and it wouldn't do to have them know that Alexandr listened to the "Voice of America." Listening to *Kol Yisrael* was more serious, and the radio was loud enough for Osip to hear in the next room. Besides, what about the beach?

To Alexandr's disappointment, Isai hushed him and listened more intently. Alexandr wasn't at all in the mood for filling his ears with that growling static, and he could barely make out the words of the broadcast, something about military action on the Israeli borders, and Israeli warplanes attacking Arab troop concentrations and Egyptian air force installations. As he reached out to turn down the volume, Isai snapped at him, "A war just started there. We could be wiped out by Nasser! Don't you care? Those are our own people!"

Our own people? There were Jews in Odessa and Israelis in Israel. What had one to do with the other? Certainly Alexandr knew that Israelis were Jews, and that there were Jews in America, Europe, and all over the world, but that was little more than an ethnographic curiosity to him. The idea that all Jews shared some special bond, a special destiny and identity as a people, was not something he would have learned from Osip. Perhaps Grandfather Naum might have had thoughts about it, but he had usually kept those to himself. In any event, Alexandr had never felt close to Naum.

When Alexandr was still a boy, Osip used to take the family on periodic visits to his parents, who lived at the other end of Odessa. Alexandr hated those visits. He hated the rickety, warped wooden steps that led up to his grandparents' small room; he hated the sour, sickly odor that crept out when they opened their door for him, a smell of dust and phlegm and large damp volumes. And he couldn't stand his grandmother's cross-examinations: "Sanya! You've been a good boy? You got good marks in school? You listen to your parents?"

Until his death, Naum had retained the archaic Jewish customs: winding the black *tfillin* straps about his left arm and hand in the morning; humming and mumbling the rites in Hebrew; reading from those large brownish books with the buglike letters. One Sunday, when Alexandr was fourteen, he walked into the room as Naum was putting his *tfillin* away. Alexandr peered at the two little black cubes with their narrow black straps—one for the arm and one for the head—and watched Naum roll up the straps and set the *tfillin* on a shelf. Alexandr pointed to them and asked what they were.

"Those are *tfillin*, *tfillin!*" Naum accented the word with impatience, as though the question itself, in its innocence, touched a raw nerve.

23

Alexandr was amused by the sound of the word, starting with *tf* like the sound of someone spitting: *tff-tffu! Tfui! tfillin.* Alexandr laughed and said the word back to Naum. "*Tff! Tf-fil-lin* . . ."

"Don't you talk that way!" Naum shouted. "Don't you dare! Get away!" He thrust the *tfillin* into their small velvet sack, shoved it into a drawer, and turned away from the boy in silent fury.

Alexandr's world had no place for this sour-smelling room with its tilted stairs. There were machines in the world, progress, Soviet achievements in science and technology, cars! Yuri Gagarin had already flown a space capsule around the earth, and the Soviet reporters had chuckled as they repeated the quip that Gagarin could find no god up there, above the sky, no god at all as far as the eye could see. And the entire Soviet population had laughed, and had cheered the triumph of Soviet science. The whole *world* had cheered. And somehow, right into the shimmering surface of that world of progress, of achievements, someone had driven a dark wedge, a small, musty room with small lives, and in one corner of it sat Grandfather Naum, a dry man with a shaved head, a narrow-skulled, birdlike, quietly tyrannical figure whose face had moments of unexpected intensity. He was strong-jawed, hairless, a stranger even to Osip and his other children; he loved them, though not demonstratively, and they obeyed him in all things; but they resembled him in no way, and they neither understood nor cared about his shamanistic mumblings.

"Our own people." It was a concept that Alexandr had learned about mostly from Soviet anti-Zionist propaganda, which, in the course of attacking Jewish "nationalism," presented some of its premises, though in distorted form. During the past year or so his skepticism of the Soviet system had grown. He could become bitterly angry over Soviet clichés about the abundance of products, the high productivity of Soviet labor, the "voluntary" nature of Soviet institutions, and especially over the anti-Semitism that he saw more and more frequently, but those things had never led him to embrace "our own people." And here was Cousin Isai, this newly arrived, newly acquired elder brother and confidant, putting "our own people" ahead of his own cousin Sanya! Out of pure frustration Alexandr, in a joking, but mildly angry manner, made a snide comment about wasting the day over the Zionist aggression against the innocent Arab peoples. Isai stared at him in horror.

The following day Isai left the Gorelskys to spend the remainder of his stay in Odessa with his aunt. Unfortunately, by the time Alexandr had an opportunity to spend a few days in Lithuania, in the early 1970s, Isai had already been imprisoned for "anti-Soviet activities." The two cousins never met again.

Within days of Isai's departure from the Gorelskys' apartment, Alexandr found himself increasingly curious about the war Israel was fighting. He had to get all his news from foreign radio broadcasts, because the Soviet press was releasing faked news about repeated Israeli defeats. One of Alexandr's friends kept a file of newspaper clippings about the war, and used to amuse their circle by recounting the discrepancies of the propaganda. Soviet news accounts of the number of Israeli planes shot down during the first four days of the war exceeded by several hundred the same Soviet newspapers' earlier estimates of the total strength of the Israeli air force. Finally, after describing serious Israeli defeats and retreats, day after day, the Soviet press suddenly revealed that Israeli forces had occupied large tracts of Arab border territory.

Alexandr and his friends discovered a certain pleasure in following the war news, discussing it, talking about "our" tanks crossing the Nile, "our" army occupying the Sinai. And while the Soviet Jews were basking in unaccustomed self-esteem, the Jewish jokesters began producing dozens of stories about the "Six Day War" that spread like wildfire from Jew to Jew, from city to city, over the entire Soviet Union. As Alexandr and his friends lay on the beach later that summer, one of them read aloud a *Komsomolskaya Pravda* article that attacked the Zionists—and, obliquely, the Jews—as "agents of world-wide imperialist aggression." Alexandr interrupted the reader with a story he'd heard the day before about an Odessa Jew who was talking to his friend from a public telephone. As the queue for the phone lengthened, the waiting Russians and Ukrainians started fuming with rage as they heard the Jew saying: "What's that, Avram? We've crossed the Nile? We're where? We're in the Sinai? Ai-ai! So many planes we shot down? . . ." Finally, the Russian at the head of the line yelled, "Hang up, you kike bastard! We all need the phone!" The old Jew looked up at him calmly (and here Alexandr tilted his head, looking up as though at a much taller person, lifted his shoulders a bit, holding them in a kind of shrug, with his hands spread apart, and said in a singsong Yiddishized Russian), "Listen, did I kibbitz you when you were beating the Germans? So don't kibbitz me when I'm beating the Arabs!"

Israel's victory in the Six Day War marked a subtle but vital change for many Jews throughout the U.S.S.R. After 1918, Jews, especially the young, could respond to the Soviet world only by joining what Communist Party theoreticians called the "progressive" historical forces. In Soviet terms this meant abandoning "narrow, nationalistic, parochial" values—that is, whatever was unique about the Jews—and embracing the new Soviet culture that would one day unite the working masses of the entire world. In practice it simply meant assimilation and conformity. So, by the 1950s, Naum Gorelsky was looked upon by many as a particularly fortunate man, for his children had assimilated successfully. Arkadi, the older son, was doing very well as a lecturer and a writer, and Osip had risen quickly as a mathematician. They were fortunate to have come along at a time when there were desperate manpower shortages in Russia. It was in part because of this success that Osip Gorelsky was never forced to abandon his faith in Marxism, and therefore in the official doctrine that anti-Semitism would ultimately vanish in the Soviet Union, for it was theoretically a by-product of capitalism.

However, Jewish assimilation, professional distinction, even military distinction during World War II ultimately did nothing to alleviate officially manipulated anti-Semitism, which kept reappearing in respectable guises. After Israel's sudden and unexpected victory, the mixture of shame and pride that Soviet Jews had lived with for decades underwent a change; their pride became a force. It was a force that nourished, and was nourished by, a new phenomenon in Soviet life: organized dissent.

By the mid and late 1960s, small groups of Jewish activists had begun to smuggle protest letters to the West, demanding a revision of Soviet policy toward the Jews and Jewish emigration. Forbidden, or at least unofficial periodicals, such as *Iskhod*, "Exodus," were being typed and circulated via *samizdat*, the literary and journalistic underground. Brief, public demonstrations held by activist Jews were quickly and brutally dealt with, but gave foreign reporters news calculated to increase external pressure on the Soviet government. Moreover, Jews had become an active part of the overall Soviet human rights and democratic movements, simplistically referred to in the West as the "dissident" movement.

All this added up to a constant embarrassment to the Soviets, and posed a growing threat to their public image abroad, even among foreign communists. Soviet Jews had never before succeeded in being so intractable, so independent. Something had changed.

And something had to be done about it. It was inevitable, therefore, that life again became more difficult for the Jews. At the end of 1966, after Premier Alexei Kosygin's landmark statement that those Jews who wanted to emigrate would be permitted to do so, there had been a slight rise in the number of exit visas issued. However, after the Six Day War no further exit visas were issued for about a year. There was also a sharp intensification of anti-Jewish propaganda calculated to convince people that the Zionists had organized themselves to spread fascism, Nazism, capitalism and counterrevolutionary sabotage. These propaganda policies were to some extent successful. The Soviet government had been able to justify, in the minds of many citizens, anti-Semitic quotas that were soon forcibly reducing the number of Jews holding important positions in the academic world and in the scientific community in particular.

Not long after the autumn of 1967, when he was already a student of mathematics at his father's institute, Alexandr became involved with the underground democratic movement. He helped type and circulate *samizdat* literature at the peril of imprisonment. As involved as he was with the movement, however, and as proud as he had been to feel a sense of identity with the Israeli victory in the 1967 war, Alexandr still felt a certain detachment from things Jewish. He was neither a Zionist nor the kind of enthusiast who hunted for underground or out-of-print Jewish literature. When he chanced upon books on Judaica, however, he read them with deep interest.

What was particularly painful for Alexandr, at this time, was his own impatience with his father's apologies for the Soviet regime, and Osip's blindness to the inconsistencies between Soviet life and Soviet theory. The more frustrating their arguments became, the more Alexandr remembered, with a kind of nostalgia, his vanished childhood faith that Papa would answer all objections, would defend both his own position and the social order, and would dispel all doubts and ambiguities.

In 1969, after spending two years as a mathematics student at Osip's institute, Alexandr decided to transfer to Odessa University to study history. Normally such transfers are unheard of in the Soviet system. Moreover, by the end of the 1960s it had become increasingly difficult for Jews to be admitted to any of the major universities in the European part of the Soviet Union. But Alexandr was fed up with mathematics, he was interested in history, and there wasn't much that Osip could do about it. For a Jewish boy not to get a higher education, especially a boy so talented, and most especially a boy whose family had the influence to get him admitted, was unthinkable, so Osip pulled strings and had him transferred.

Not long after Alexandr began his studies at the university, he married Ina, a tall, dark-haired, Modiglianiesque woman of twenty-four, almost five years his senior. Ina saw her marriage as a step up, for she had high hopes of entering the intellectual elite. Alexandr's parents considered her a social climber, however, and saw the marriage as a misalliance. Alexandr, after all, was of the professorial class, thanks to Osip's success. Well-placed professors have high prestige in the Soviet Union, and are often granted privileges that are unavailable to nonprofessionals. What is more important than salary or fame is the fact that they can effect their protégés' entry into valuable positions. Influence is an important form of wealth in the Soviet Union. People who can trade favors, such as professors, research-institute officials, and editors, form a kind of aristocracy, and to hobnob with them carries a certain amount of prestige.

Alexandr could sense hard times approaching. Jews were increasingly unwelcome in the academic milieu for which the university was supposedly preparing him. Although some of his professors thought very highly of his work, there were many influential people on the faculty who were determined to stop this show-off, with his questionable leanings, before he got out of control. Much to Ina's chagrin, Alexandr did nothing to assuage these professors' suspicions or hostility. His enemies knew only that he was a Jew who had already gotten too far, and that he was somewhat irreverent and unconventional. They certainly knew nothing about his retyping and circulating underground literature. It was at about this time that Alexandr began to amuse himself with the private little game of whistling a Jewish melody unobtrusively, as though unaware of what he was doing, as he passed a Jewish-looking stranger on the street. Any Jewish tune would do; there were plenty that were well known in Odessa. Sometimes—not so rarely, in fact—the stranger took up the melody, or whistled another Jewish song in response.

As proud members of the young intellectual set, Alexandr and Ina couldn't possibly miss the public screening of the new film on the life of Andrei Rublev, the great medieval Russian icon painter. It was a political as well as an artistic event. The Soviet government had delayed the film's release for a few years, presumably because in depicting the agonies of the Russian people, particularly of Russian artists under the Mongol domination, there was a hinted rejection of autocracy and an implied connection between ancient and modern sufferings. No thinking person could afford to miss a film that dealt with the burden of a harsh regime and the desire for freedom, especially someone concerned with the democratic movement.

As he watched the film, Alexandr was impressed by its beauty, but something very peculiar was nagging at him. He knew that all his friends were noting how this or that turn of plot or phrase bore on this or that contemporary problem; he knew that all their inferences and insights would be talked about for weeks ahead. These people would expect him to have strong opinions about the film; the writing, photography and acting were exceptional. But Alexandr was shocked at his own reaction, indeed, at his lack of reaction. His wife and friends were all utterly absorbed, were even weeping for the tragedy on the screen, and for the yoke that had never been lifted from this unhappy nation. Yet he was unmoved, uninvolved. It suddenly struck him that those people in the film—those Russians, ancient and modern—were alien to him and he to them. They cared nothing for his dreams and his grievances; they had, in fact, gone to some trouble to frustrate the dreams and to augment the grievances. So let the Russians worry about Russia's yoke and Russia's tragic history. As they themselves were in the habit of pointing out, Alexandr was a Jew, not a Russian. It was therefore none of his affair.

That evening marked the end of his involvement with the democratic movement.

The following year, in the spring of 1973, Alexandr went to Moscow to visit Beregov, an old school comrade of his father's. The man was a bit older than Osip—just past fifty—and he held a responsible post, from which he could use his influence to get Alexandr a job. As a non-Jew, he couldn't be accused of catering to his own "nationalistic" loyalties if he helped a Jew.

Beregov looked older than his age. His hair was almost white and his face was lined, but he had never developed the soft pudginess that Great Russians often swell into when they become successful. After a leisurely dinner, Beregov's wife left the two men alone, and Beregov poured good French brandy into handsome crystal snifters—luxuries enjoyed by the new elite.

Osip had considerable faith in Beregov. He spoke of him as a fair-minded, cultivated person whose success was not merely the result of back-room political maneuvers. Beregov was also not one of those upper-level Party bueaucrats who had spread tens of thousands of rubles around, accrued through years of influence peddling, to buy himself a Ph.D., as many undereducated officials had done. His degree was earned.

By this time it had become apparent to the entire Gorelsky family that Alexandr was not going to find a job he could accept. As usual, the placement committee, composed of university professors, administrators, and university Party functionaries, would appoint a favored few to the prize positions: teaching posts in Odessa and other major cities in European Russia. By 1973 such jobs were almost off limits to Jews, even to those few who had been permitted to formally defend their dissertations, and had thus been awarded a Ph.D.

Part One: ENDINGS

The next level down were those graduates granted positions in top-notch universities or research institutes off in the provinces, such as Novosibirsk in Siberia. Though far from the traditional cosmopolitan centers, the jobs were greatly sought after, but Jews had begun to be excluded from these as well.

The leftovers had to teach unwilling primary-grade pupils in backward villages, several days' journey from anything but mud; villages where the peasants of the collective farms lived in poverty and isolation, and where the teacher was essentially condemned to at least three years of deprivation and near-exile. Moreover, there was no guarantee that Alexandr would be permitted to return to Odessa at the end of his contract; it could become perpetual exile. Alexandr could refuse such a job if it were offered him, but then he would have to leave his field. There was one legal loophole, however. Ina was working in Odessa, and it was permissible to decline a contract in order to join, or to remain with, a spouse employed in the city. As Alexandr's final year of school was ending, a friend of the Gorelsky family, who was in the university administration, called Alexandr into her office and frankly, though sympathetically, suggested that although he had already published three fine articles on his research and was considered one of their top students, he should forget about the placement committee and take advantage of the loophole. Ironically, Ina had just decided to leave Alexandr.

So, on this pleasantly cool spring evening, in one of the newly built high-rises in Moscow, Alexandr sat over brandy with Beregov. As he answered Beregov's gently probing questions, he gradually sketched in the picture of his rather bleak situation: no career, no job, perhaps no wife. Alexandr avoided mentioning the fact that his relations with his family had become seriously strained because of his increasingly unsavory political attitudes.

Finally the moment came for Beregov to give some hint of his own attitude and his own course of action. At best, he might offer to help Alexandr find a position; at worst, he might demur modestly and make some excuse about the "present difficult situation." He merely stared out the window abstractedly, and then said, "Perhaps you should join your relatives in Israel?"

"My what? What relatives in Israel?"
"Mightn't this be the appropriate time to discover some?"

Osip and Anna were shocked at Beregov's comment, and tried to pass it off as a quip, but at least it was clear that he couldn't help Alexandr find a position. As Alexandr feared, his parents became feverishly worried about him; they knew he had already given some thought to emigration. He had defended the emigrés in several arguments with Osip, who lost no opportunity to disparage them.

Emigration was in the air. It was the summer of 1973, and record numbers of Jews had obtained visas in the past year; practically everybody knew somebody who had left. Right after the Six Day War, the Soviet government embargoed all emigration, but in 1968 a trickle of applications were accepted; and in 1969, about 3,000 Jews were permitted to leave. Although this increase triggered a landslide of requests for the invitations from Israel that were necessary before one could apply, only about 1,000 people got out in 1970, and the numbers were still very low in the first few months of 1971. In March, however, there was a sudden spurt in the number of exit visas issued. Departures in 1972 totaled about 15,000; the 1973 emigration rate was more than double that number.

Those who were out already were swallowed up in mystery. Cryptic letters were coming back, with odd, mixed reports. Images of disastrous inability to adjust were mingled with talk of freedom and comfort. With all the disillusioned letters, there was enough positive news and enough mystery to tincture this fearsome choice of emigration with a certain glamour.

Several weeks after his visit with Beregov, Alexandr sat on the edge of his bed thinking through the entire emigration dilemma. What did he know about Israel? Nothing, really. He knew that it was a parliamentary democracy, that the weather was hot, that the country was an armed camp because of the wars, and that it was difficult to live in. Still, in Alexandr's imagination there was an aura about Israel. He tried to be very hardheaded about it, to be scientifically critical and analytical, but there was always that slight glow about the Promised Land. What's more, he had just heard a rumor that there were ways of going not only to Israel, but even to America.

He needed information, answers to specific questions. The man to talk to was Misha, a former fellow student whose request for a visa had been refused over a year before. Like most "refuseniks," Misha made it his business to read all the letters from abroad. He listened to all the foreign radio broadcasts, and was in constant touch with the nationwide refuseniks' gossip network.

In Misha's room, Alexandr sat at the table with a cup of wine, and described his interview with Beregov, while Misha went through several bureau drawers taking out packets of letters, photographs, notes, and clippings. Misha's tall, gangling frame was dressed in what looked like hand-me-downs from shorter relatives. Only his jacket seemed to have fit him at one time, but that too was uncertain. It had lost its original shape from doing service in all weathers.

After they read through a few letters from recent emigrés to the West, Misha suggested they have their talk while strolling outside for a breath of air. The couple with whom Misha's family shared the apartment were due to return home soon, and they might eavesdrop. There were ways to foil human or electronic eavesdroppers without going outside. Alexandr and Misha could have used the Magic Slate, for example, but it was too nice a day to remain indoors. These Magic Slates were American children's toys that helpful tourists had been bringing to the Soviet Union. They were black waxed boards covered with a glossy gray plastic sheet. The dark letters, made by pressing the plastic sheet with a stylus, would vanish as soon as the sheet was pulled away from the board. All refuseniks had them, as did many other people who needed to converse privately.

As they emerged into a broad, tree-lined boulevard, Misha outlined the basics for Alexandr. When foreign pressure finally forced the Soviet government to allow the Jews to emigrate, the Soviets created artificial barriers to limit the emigration and sought to prevent a chain reaction of discontent among other groups that might want to leave. First, a Jew would be permitted to emigrate only to rejoin relatives; second, the relative must be living in Israel.

The first restriction—the need for an invitation from a relative—made it harder for a citizen to apply and easier for the Soviet officials to block or slow down the emigration process. Either they could intercept the invitation in the mail—a common practice—or they could question the validity of the relationship. The government's insistence that emigrés leave only with Israeli papers was meant to show the Soviet people that the only legitimate ground for emigration is a return to the "national homeland." No other Soviet nation would then be able to insist on emigration rights. A second reason, but one that gradually became useful to Soviet propagandists, was the desire to brand all emigration as treason. By this time, ordinary Soviet citizens had been taught that Israel was a militaristic, racist, almost neo-Nazi state. If all emigrés were Jews, and were pro-Israel into the bargain, then it would be easy to turn the word "emigration" into a synonym for treason. For that reason, several dissidents who were neither Jews nor Zionists, and whom the Soviet government exiled to the West, were forced to leave the U.S.S.R. with standard emigration papers to Israel. It was a propaganda strategy calculated to discredit dissidence altogether in the eyes of the average Soviet citizen.

The would-be emigré must first arrange to be sent an invitation from someone in Israel who would vouch that he was a relative. This could usually be arranged through emigrés who were about to leave, and who would give the would-be emigré's name, address, and other personal data to Israeli organizations—such as *Sokhnut ha-Yehudit*, the Jewish Agency—which would then pass the information on to people willing to act as the inviting relatives. Of course, the applicant might have *real* relatives in Israel, in which case he could try to get word to them to invite him. This wasn't easy, for all foreign mail to and from the Soviet Union is censored, and much of it never arrives at its final destination. This invitation must then be handed in at the local office of OVIR, the Office of Visas and Registrations, where the applicant would be given his application forms.

Then there was the catch that Alexandr knew would cause him the worst problems. OVIR demands that parents, spouses, even divorced spouses, who are to remain behind in the Soviet Union, write a declaration that the applicant is not in their debt. This is dangerous because it implicates these relatives in the visa applicant's "treason." Even elderly parents have sometimes been harassed by the KGB after signing these statements for their children. Alexandr expected no trouble from Ina, but he knew that Osip would refuse to sign such a statement, not because he was afraid, though it would surely be risky for him to be implicated in an emigration, but because Osip would see his son's emigration as foolhardy and self-destructive, and because emigration was a repudiation of the system and of the ideology that Osip had believed in all his life.

Alexandr knew that to ask his father to betray himself in such a way was an act of cruelty, yet he had no choice.

Although Alexandr's ex-wife Ina had become very much estranged from him during the last year of their marriage, her departure had left him with an aching sense of loss. Ina had removed the last of her belongings, and was living in Moscow with a friend, whom she planned to marry as soon as her divorce from Alexandr was final.

But recently, at a mutual friend's birthday party, Alexandr had met Zoya Vigdover, a quiet, brown-haired girl of about eighteen— pretty, in a wistful way, and rather reserved. She lived with her widowed mother, Ala Vigdover, a physician, and her grandfather. Since doctors are poorly paid in the Soviet Union, Ala's task was plain: she had to train her two daughters to be far above average in school, for without professional degrees their lives would be difficult. Ala herself had been thoroughly indoctrinated in the absolute need for higher education. Her father had risen from a poor ghetto village to become a dentist, and her mother had been briefly famous as one of the first woman law graduates in prerevolutionary Russia.

The compulsive zeal with which Ala and her father watched, fed, and tutored Zoya and her sister was intensified by the fear and stress the family had been living under during the years just preceding Zoya's birth. By the end of World War II, Zoya's father, Yosef Vigdover, had aged beyond his years. He had managed to escape from a Nazi concentration camp, and was found in the snow, starving, bleeding and unconscious, by some Ukrainians. He convinced them that he was one Ivan Vladimirov, half Russian, half Ukrainian, and he spent the rest of the war fighting alongside the Ukrainian partisans. Had they discovered that he was a Jew, that his name was Vigdover, not Vladimirov, they'd have shot him.

During the course of the war, Yosef became an intelligence officer, and after the Nazi armies collapsed he worked briefly in the Soviet administrative office in Vienna. After he left the army, however, Yosef was forced to pay dearly for having saved his life by adopting an alias. In 1953, while he was teaching chemistry in Odessa, he was already under some suspicion because of his tour of duty in Vienna. Stalin believed that Soviets who had had contact with the West were forever tainted. Then, as a Jew, he was automatically suspect, especially after the storm of anti-Semitic paranoia that Stalin had whipped up with his "doctors' trials." But then, shortly after Stalin's death, Party officials discovered that Yosef Vigdover had once used an alias. Their suspicions now compounded, they immediately fired him and forced him to leave the city of Odessa. For about three years Yosef and Ala lived in a desperately poor, muddy, verminous village near the city of Kharkov, to which Yosef traveled every day to give chemistry lessons. In 1956, when Khrushchev was beginning to "rehabilitate" many of those who had been persecuted by Stalin's terror tactics, Yosef was permitted to return to Odessa with Ala and their three-year-old daughter, Nina. Zoya was born shortly after this, and Yosef was allowed to start teaching again. Drained and exhausted by persecution, he was even further depressed when he discovered that although his accomplishments during the war had earned him the Order of Lenin, the highest honor the U.S.S.R. confers, the government now refused to recognize Yosef Vigdover as that same Ivan Vladimirov who had earned the award. Continuing anxiety, especially after rumors that Khrushchev's government was planning new show trials of Jews—this time in an attempt to link Jews with bribery and economic corruption—brought on a heart attack that killed Yosef in 1960, when Zoya was still a small child.

Zoya and her older sister had their course mapped out for them: Ala's job as a physician at the infirmary of an engineering institute gave her just enough pull to enroll Zoya and her sister as engineering students, despite the quotas, providing they did well enough through high school. One of the problems was that Zoya had long been a sickly child. She frequently had to be kept out of school for lengthy periods of time and then privately tutored for the exams. She always did well, but her frequent illnesses, which the doctors never seemed quite able to diagnose clearly, compelled her mother and grandfather to lavish special care on her.

Some of Alexandr's friends were struck by the contrast between his new girl friend, Zoya, and his ex-wife, Ina. Ina had seemed more a match for a fast-talking, self-dramatizing, assertively witty person like Alexandr, whereas Zoya was retiring, almost invisible at times, especially when she was with him. Alexandr himself occasionally warned Zoya that the emotional mauling of emigration might be the worst thing for her, but in her quiet way she continued to pursue him.

Later that summer, just as Alexandr was stepping out of his apartment house, he met his mother coming into the courtyard. He hadn't seen his parents in over a month, not since he had broken with them over his tentative decision to emigrate. Osip had been furious, though what he really felt was grief. Alexandr tried to avoid fighting with his father. The arguments left him feeling depressed and guilty, as though the anguish he caused Osip were something unique in the world. Had Osip ever caused Naum such pain as a young man? If so, Alexandr had never seen it. As a child, in fact, Alexandr had sometimes found himself wishing that Osip would get angrier at Grandfather Naum, would tell him off, break the old man's grip, and assert himself more.

Anna begged Alexandr to come home for dinner; she had just run into a friend who had a car, and who could give them a lift. Alexandr hesitated to go with her. He was worried that an attempted reconciliation, at this point, would either cause another battle or would result in his knuckling under to his father's authority, just as Osip had always knuckled under to Naum.

As Anna clutched his arm and coaxed him along the street toward the corner, Alexandr could see that she was nervous. She had always been upset by his arguments with his father, but now she seemed especially tense, and her smile looked unusually forced.

Alexandr reluctantly allowed Anna to pull him around the corner and up to a long, black Volga. When he was halfway into the car, he stopped. There were two strange men sitting in the front seat, and one in the back who was vaguely familiar. Alexandr remembered him after a few moments, an old friend of one of Anna's relatives, with whom they'd once shared a summer bungalow. Now he was a highly placed official in the Odessa branch of the Ministry of Internal Affairs. Anna squeezed into the back seat, so that Alexandr was wedged in between her and the official.

When they arrived at the Gorelsky apartment house, the driver and the other stranger in the front seat stayed in the car, while Alexandr, Anna, and their friend from the Ministry went upstairs, where Osip and Uncle Arkadi were waiting. For Alexandr, it was not much of a dinner; even though plenty of food was served, he couldn't eat.

Before the first course was finished, Osip and Arkadi took turns bombarding Alexandr with reaons for not applying for a visa, and with optimistic predictions about his career. The subject of anti-Semitism was delicately avoided in the presence of the Ministry official. Alexandr didn't argue. He knew that his parents didn't want him to debate with them, or to prove anything to them; they only wanted him to abandon his plans for emigration, so Alexandr refused to speak. He just smiled and nodded without offering either answers or counterarguments.

Uncle Arkadi began to press Alexandr to find out just how deeply he'd slipped into this emigration madness. Had Alexandr gone so far as to get an invitation from Israel? Ridiculous! From whom could he get such a thing? Alexandr simply sat and smiled, but in the midst of the hubbub raised by this question, the Ministry official rose from his chair and held up one hand. "Wait. I'll find out in a second." In the sudden silence this tall, light-haired man, so self-assured and so out of place in a room full of nervous Jews, went to the telephone, dialed a number, waited, spoke in subdued tones for a moment or two, then turned to the others in the room. "He has received two invitations. One from the Mairov family in Tel Aviv, about two weeks ago, and another from the Yariv family in Jerusalem, last week."

Stunned, they all stared at the Ministry official. Alexandr was as mortified as his parents. Both letters were lying hidden in Alexandr's desk drawer. He had told no one about receiving them and had not yet steeled himself to take the ultimate step of revealing his intentions by filing at OVIR.

In late December 1973, Alexandr was waiting his turn at the district OVIR office. It was an oblong room, with two large desks in front, and several dozen seats lined up in rows occupying the rest of the room. In front of each seat was a small writing table. Behind the two front desks were several doors, and over the doors, centered on the front wall, was a large dusty picture of Lenin.

The seats in the waiting section were almost all taken, but the room was silent. Outside, on the street, there were several small knots of people, talking excitedly. This was a place to exchange the latest gossip about changes in the emigration rules, all of which were kept secret by OVIR, and to ask others for advice. Here people traded letters from those who had already left, or spread whatever information those letters contained. But inside the OVIR office the people sat quietly, talking in whispers at most, with one eye on the expressionless policemen standing at the entrance of the room.

Those who were here to pick up exit-visa applications had brought their Israeli invitations in the original envelopes. Without the envelope in which it had arrived the invitation was invalid. One by one, shyly, the people handed their forms to the silent woman at the desk. She was wearing the stern semimilitary uniform of the Ministry of Internal Affairs—the MVD—which is responsible for the Soviet police, and of which OVIR is a branch. After she had accumulated a pile of the invitations and envelopes, she disappeared through one of the doors behind the desk for a few minutes, then returned with visa application forms. She barked out each applicant's name, thrust the forms at him, and rattled off the name of the applicant's inspector, who would thenceforth be in charge of his case.

When Alexandr's turn came he set his completed forms faceup on the woman's desk, so she could read his name on the top sheet, and explained that he was there to turn in his completed forms and to see his inspector, Comrade Bulgarina. "Wait there," she mumbled, and pointed toward a row of chairs along the left-hand wall of the room. After about an hour she shouted, "Gorelsky, Alexandr Osipovitch!" and pointed to the left-hand door at the front of the room.

Alexandr stepped through the door and found himself in a smallish room with a row of three tables stretching from right to left. The inspectors sat like blocks—icy, angry-looking women in MVD uniform. Both end tables were already occupied by applicants, hangdog and guilty before the just wrath of Soviet power, so Alexandr hesitantly approached the center place. Comrade Bulgarina looked up momentarily from her perusal of Alexandr's file, glanced at him with distaste, and mumbled, "Sit." After staring at his forms for a few minutes, without looking up she intoned, "Parents' permission?"

It was here that Alexandr was expecting trouble. Osip had refused to sign the required statement that Alexandr was not in debt to him, which left Alexandr's application incomplete. Incomplete applications will simply not be accepted for filing by the OVIR inspectors, so Alexandr was trying to force Osip's hand by a bold strategy. He had sent a telegram to his father stating that the sender, Alexandr Osipovitch Gorelsky, was in no material debt to the addressee, Osip Naumovitch Gorelsky, that a duplicate of the telegram was being routed to OVIR, and that if Osip wanted to claim that Alexandr was lying, that there *was* some debt, Osip should contract OVIR within three weeks. Alexandr handed Bulgarina his copy of the telegram.

"Have you received word from my father claiming that I owe him anything?"

"I see nothing like that here . . ."

"Then he agrees by default, as per my telegram to him, and my application is complete."

To Alexandr's amazement, she said nothing, slipped the forms into a folder, and dismissed him.

But Alexandr's stategy failed. After only two and a half weeks his request for a visa was refused. OVIR, as usual, gave him no reason for the refusal. They merely notified him to report to their office, told him verbally of their refusal, and said that he could reapply in six months.

Part One: ENDINGS

Now he was a refusenik, one who has been refused an exit visa, who has gambled all his chances and lost. As long as a refusenik remains in the Soviet Union—and some have been trapped there for ten or twelve years—he is effectively without rights or status. He must work hard and pay his own way, but is usually forbidden to work in his field. And even if he does find some menial position, the KGB might mention to the boss that he has a tainted record. The boss will take the hint and fire him.

Uncle Arkadi was in a particularly difficult position. It was his task to give lectures on current affairs to various workers' groups, lectures that were frequently published in the form of articles. Arkadi had been informed, within the past year, that lectures on political subjects should concentrate on denouncing the emigrants. The propaganda organs particularly valued such lectures and articles when they could be attributed to Jews. Arkadi obediently delivered his lectures to students and factory workers, and even wrote some articles on the subject, but for the first time in his career he miscalculated seriously. Instead of delivering hysterical denunciations aimed at inciting the latent anti-Semitism of the Russians and Ukrainians, he worked in a somewhat more sentimentally patriotic style that he thought might appeal to the Jews themselves. It backfired. The Jews looked upon him as a sellout and a traitor, and the Party men accused poor Arkadi of being too easy on the "anti-Soviet elements."

At the next meeting of the District Party Committee's plenary session, one of the local Party officials castigated both himself and the Party for having been too lenient in the past. He blamed the loathsome and dangerous burgeoning of Zionist propaganda on this lenience, and then publicly denounced and excoriated both Osip and Arkadi Gorelsky by name for their part in Alexandr's treacherous behavior.

This tirade was followed by the predictable demonstration of outrage at the moral failure and duplicity of people like the Gorelskys and, by implication, the treachery of the Jews in general. Both Osip and Arkadi were suspended from their committees, demoted in their jobs, and publicly humiliated. Even as hard years of career

41

advancement were being undone, rumors were being circulated to the effect that Alexandr himself had established an "underground kibbutz" for training Zionist counterrevolutionaries. This was a colorful way of forcing Alexandr to stop giving private English lessons to would-be emigrés, his only source of income.

There are no publicly available laws, regulations, or even administrative procedures in the Soviet Union governing emigration. Alexandr's only recourse was to make the rounds of the veteran refuseniks, to seek advice and information, to collar anyone who seemed to have experience, and to read and reread the letters coming in from those already in the West. Since most refuseniks are denied employment, or are fired quickly from the menial jobs they do find as soon as their status is discovered, they try to give some purpose to their lives by helping and advising other visa applicants. They are the recognized experts.

Within a few months of being refused a visa, Alexandr himself had a "case load" of about ten families. He helped them with applications and petitions; he advised them on dealing with recalcitrant parents and relatives, avoiding informers, packing, finding cars to transport luggage, and borrowing money. Many families even used him as a psychiatrist and a marriage counselor.

Alexandr had not had to accept money from his parents for years now, not since his marriage to Ina. Between his savings and Ina's earnings they had been able to afford a modest life style. Now that Ina was gone, and Alexandr was neither a student nor employed, the natural thing would have been for him to turn to Osip and Anna for help, but he couldn't—not since his decision to emigrate had rent the family into opposing camps. Alexandr's friends could never be sure whether he was pigheadedly refusing his parents' help or they were cold-bloodedly neglecting him in order to teach him a lesson. In fact, he refused to ask, and they were hesitant to encourage him to ask.

In the spring of 1974 Alexandr found his first job since becoming a refusenik, as a low-paid, unskilled laborer in a button factory. Alexandr's task had been to pull down the handle on an old stamping machine. The lever was stiff and was mounted over his head, so the only way he could operate it was to hang from it with all his weight. He was too light from his refusenik diet; the handle didn't move. He was fired after one week on the job.

There were other problems besides lack of money that caused Alexandr and the other refuseniks to worry about long-term unemployment. Since Khrushchev's day, in the mid-1950s, lack of gainful employment has been considered a crime in the Soviet Union. Since socialism theoretically eliminates the causes of joblessness, unemployed people who are capable of working are considered social parasites, and are punished accordingly. Throughout the 1960s and 1970s many "undesirables"—including quite a few who had defended points of view unpopular with the regime but who had committed no overt crime—had been imprisoned as "parasites," and were then exiled to collective farms where they formed a kind of slave-labor force.

One evening in August 1974, Alexandr and Zoya joined a small crowd of people in Misha's tiny room. The guests were of varying ages and backgrounds, but all shared that unmistakable, slightly tattered refusenik look. A small table at one end of the room held snacks and several bottles of wine. After a while, Misha stood up, towering over everybody, and began the proceedings by lifting his glass in the traditional dissidents' toast: "Friends—to our hopeless cause!"

There were several items Alexandr wanted to discuss with the refusenik council. He had recently noticed that he was being followed. Practically everywhere he went, even when he left town to spend time at a friend's datcha, he was followed, usually by a young man, perhaps twenty-five years old, with straight dark-brown hair and pleasant but unobtrusive features.

The others seemed much calmer about it than Alexandr, and told him that being followed by the KGB was something many of them had had to get used to. It took its toll on their nerves, though most of them saw it as the government's way of frightening off would-be helpers and sympathizers. They maintained that surveillance is a routine fact of Soviet life anyway, and that making it obvious is largely the regime's attempt at psychological warfare, a subtle use of terror.

There was also Alexandr's job problem. Since he'd lost the job in the button factory, Alexandr had held only one other position, on the truck dock of a workers' cafeteria in a nearby factory, and that too had not lasted very long. His boss, Petrenko, was a drunkard with the traditional attitude toward Jews: he started the morning mumbling about the *zhid*, the kike, and by the end of the day he was screaming at Alexandr almost nonstop. After a few days he simply fired Alexandr, yelling something about the "thieving Jews." Alexandr complained to the supervisor, who was about to give his job back to him, in fact, he was ready to fire Petrenko and give Alexandr *his* job. But as soon as he discovered that Alexandr was a refusenik, he changed his mind and backed Petrenko.

Alexandr finally came to the main problem he wanted to bring before the committee. Acquaintances of his family—people with semiofficial pull or official contacts—had been dropping hints to him that all would be forgiven if he were to repent, recant, and withdraw his application for a visa. There was nothing new about that line, of course, but he had just received a note from Osip saying that the head of Osip's institute wanted to see Alexandr. It seemed that there was to be a job offer in it somewhere. Alexandr was uncomfortable about the whole thing, and wasn't sure how to handle it.

The consensus of the meeting was that he should see the director as his father requested. As long as he didn't actually withdraw his application, what harm could it do to talk? And if the director were to offer him a job, what was wrong with that? It would be worth a try. Anyway, it would be interesting to see what *their* next move would be.

When Alexandr arrived at the office, the director, a thin man with wispy graying hair and a quick, nervous smile, sat back in his leather chair, placed both hands plams down on his desk, and peered briefly at Alexandr through thick glasses. Then he dropped his gaze, as though examining the backs of his hands, and said, "Alexandr Osipovitch, I'm not interested in what you've done, or what you're doing, or why. But we know your father here; we don't want to lose him. His heart is weak. I know. I've seen his medical report. I don't want to discuss emigration, or anything like that, just your job possibilities. Now, I've heard from a colleague and friend of mine, the director of one of the more prestigious research institutes in this area, and he has something for you. Go see him. Will you do it?"

Several days later, Alexandr arrived at the institute at the appointed time, and sat for about a half hour in the waiting room. Then the intercom on the secretary's desk barked, "Send him in."

Alexandr entered quietly. He assumed that the director would be occupied with the two men who had walked into his office a few minutes earlier, the head of the Institute Party Committee and the assistant director. As Alexandr entered the office, the assistant director walked out, leaving the other man sitting unobtrusively off in one corner of the room.

At the end of the long, narrow office, paneled in dark wood, there was a high, old-fashioned desk; behind it, a small, bald man was perched on what must have been a very high stool. The seat left for Alexandr was low and softly upholstered, so that he had to look up to speak to the director.

"What are you doing here?"

The voice was reedy, but incisive, and the director spoke without looking up from his scratching pen.

"I believe you asked me to come . . ."

"I didn't ask you to come." Then, still not looking up from his papers, he said, in a surprisingly mild, almost humorous tone, "You weren't invited, so why come? Good-bye . . ."

Alexandr began to push himself up from his chair, but the director interrupted him, slightly louder this time.

"Sit down. So? What are you doing here?"

"I'm looking for a job?"

"What kind of a job?"

"Whatever fits my training."

The director's questions began to fall into a grating and monotonous pattern, the pitch of his voice remaining level until the last syllable or two of the sentence, then rising a bit.

"Why didn't you find a job through the state? And what makes you think we have a job for you?"

"A mutual acquaintance . . . suggested that I discuss it with you."

EXIT VISA

The director put down his pen very slowly, as though it were primed with nitroglycerin and could be set off by the slightest jar. He clasped his chubby white hands, peered owlishly over Alexandr's head, and spoke quietly at first.

"We are aware of some talk that you've applied for emigration to the bourgeois-*fascist* state of *Israel*—" *Izz*-rael; his suddenly acid, biting voice hurled out that *Izz*, as though even the word "fascist" were insufficiently ugly to illustrate his contempt.

Alexandr paused to steady his breathing. He didn't want his voice to break from the dryness in his throat. "In . . . in fact . . . I applied to be reunited with my relatives in the state of Israel . . ." He was cut off by the director's shout.

"*Fascist* state of Israel! Listen to me!" Now he was leaning forward, staring straight at Alexandr, who could see that his eyes were pale blue, so pale they were almost gray. "I'm not talking to you from the nationality point of view but from the *class* point of view, and from the *class* point of view you're my *enemy!*" By now the director's face was nearly crimson, an artery was beating visibly in his temple, and his piercing voice was rising steadily. "If you leave this country, if you emigrate, and commit an act of treason against the working class and against all that I and many others stand for, as a Party member I'll tell you what I'd like to see! I'd like to see you shot, like we'd have done in the past! If I had the power—do you hear me?—If I had the power, I'd take a revolver and kill you myself, right where you are! Now *get out!*"

At the end of August, Alexandr submitted his second application. It still did not have his father's signed statement, but in his own way Osip had relented: appended to Alexandr's application, Osip had attached the following memorandum:

This is to certify that I no longer consider Alexandr Osipovitch Gorelsky to be my son. I refuse to recognize him as such, and bear no responsibility for his acts or actions.
(signed) Osip Naumovitch Gorelsky

In late September 1974, Alexandr and Zoya were married. They had planned to live in the same room he had formerly shared with

46

Ina, but a few weeks later Ina arrived from Moscow with her new husband and begged Alexandr to give her the room. She was in the midst of a medically difficult pregnancy and it was obvious at first glance that she was ill. She looked older, and was terribly weak; she spent a good part of the day lying down, and easily broke into tears. Since her mother's apartment was on the same floor of the building, only a few doors away, she was desperately anxious to live there, at least for the duration of her pregnancy. Alexandr and Zoya decided that it would be best to relinquish the room to Ina, and to move in with Zoya's mother, Ala. Since Zoya's older sister, Nina, had moved to another city with her husband, there should be room for Zoya and Alexandr. But at the last minute, after Ina had occupied Alexandr's old room, Ala told Zoya that Nina had suddenly become ill, and Ala had to care for her. She had come back to Odessa, and now there was no room for Zoya and Alexandr in Ala's apartment.

Living space, like most "consumer" items in the Soviet Union, is in short supply, especially in the major cities. Moreover, the apartment problem is complicated by the need for a *propiska*, an official police registration that permits one to live in a given city in the U.S.S.R. In order to prevent the farming population from rushing to the cities pell-mell, the Soviet government adopted internal passports in the early 1930s, and also instituted police registration of each citizen's residence. No one can move to any city without an acceptable reason. If a person can prove that he has been offered a job, and has a place to live, the police may then register him at that address. If he has no job but wants to move to the city to look for one, the police will not give him a *propiska* at any address within that city, and it is then illegal for the person to spend more than a few days there.

Since Alexandr was unemployed and a refusenik, and was now without an apartment, there was a danger that the police would deny him permission to stay in Odessa altogether, and that he would be exiled to some other area. At the last minute Alexandr was able to find an old woman who was willing to lie to the police and say that he was living at her place, though she demanded a large bribe to do it.

Alexandr and Zoya now found themselves without a place to

live. A friend gave them the use of his summer datcha, but when they moved in they found that it was unfit for winter use. By November the temperature was often below freezing both outside and in. There was neither electricity nor heat, and the one-room bungalow had become infested with mice. Each day, as soon as Zoya returned from the engineering institute, she crawled into bed and spent the rest of the day in a dazed, depressed half-sleep under layers of torn blankets that didn't keep her warm.

One day in early December, Zoya's grandfather came to the datcha and found his granddaughter—whom he had doted on from her infancy through her adolescence—shivering in the semidarkness under a heap of torn blankets, the floor around the bed whitened by frost. He sat on the edge of the bed and wept.

He did more than weep, however. He convinced Alexandr's parents to take the youngsters into their apartment for a week or so, until a better place could be found. Osip and Anna agreed, but they were terrified that people would discover that Alexandr, whom Osip had supposedly disowned, was in fact now living at his apartment, so he insisted that Alexandr and Zoya not leave the house later than six A.M. or return earlier than midnight. Sometimes, when Alexandr left the apartment, Zoya had to hide in their room until he returned. Several of Osip's fellow professors lived in the building and across the street, so Alexandr and Zoya were forbidden to go too near the window or onto the balcony. When Alexandr's parents had guests, he and Zoya were locked inside Osip's study.

Finally, they found a room in a communal apartment not far from Ala's place, a few weeks after New Year's Day, 1975.

On a frigid afternoon in late February, several weeks after his second visa application was refused, Alexandr ducked out of the wind into a metro station in central Moscow. He had just come from the Moscow headquarters of OVIR, where he had managed to wangle an interview with one of the higher officials of the Ministry of Internal Affairs. It was a brief conversation. The official at first shrugged off Alexandr's request for help, and said that his appeal was strictly a local Odessa affair, and was out of the Moscow office's purview. Alexandr dismissed that argument, and said that he

Part One: ENDINGS

was sure that Odessa would follow Moscow's hint, if the hint were only given. He went on to explain that he had always tried to be discreet, and to avoid getting his name into the sensationalist Western press, but that continued refusals would tempt his Western relatives to say something foolish to the newspapers. Alexandr left the office without any idea of what might happen, and with no particular hopes, but cheered that he hadn't been thrown out or insulted.

In the metro station he pulled off his ill-fitting, borrowed gloves and hunted through his pockets for the directions to the apartment of Misha's friends, Lyonya and Masha Goff. They had offered to let Alexandr stay the night at their place, and were not worried about associating with a refusenik under KGB surveillance, as they themselves had already received permission to emigrate.

Alexandr arrived about an hour and a half later, after losing himself thoroughly in a maze of identical, recently built apartment complexes in the Moscow suburbs. The Goffs were entertaining several other couples, all in various stages of application, who had come to help celebrate the Goffs' newly acquired exit visa.

Later, Alexandr was sitting in a corner, sipping his wine, and listening to one of the guests, Tatyana Levin, who had come to Moscow that morning to say good-bye to her uncle's family at Sheremyetyevo Airport. Tatyana was a Russian-looking woman in her late twenties, with light hair and rather high cheekbones. Alexandr vaguely remembered that a dark-haired, Jewish-looking man— Grigory Levin—had been introduced to him as this woman's husband, and at first assumed that she was a Russian married to a Jew, though it became obvious from her story that she was at least part Jewish herself. She was describing the way the customs officials at the airport had harassed the departing emigrés that morning. From what Tatyana could see, her uncle and his family had comparatively little trouble. The customs man did tear several pages out of her uncle's notebook, and confiscated some family snapshots as well as the aunt's old wedding ring, but basically they had gotten through unscathed.

What most upset Tatyana and Grigory was the treatment given the last family to pass through the customs barrier. They were a young couple with a little girl of about six years old, who was wearing a tiny pair of gold earrings, probably of little value. The customs inspector nonchalantly yanked the earrings off the child without undoing them, deliberately ripping open the little girl's earlobes. Then, while the girl doubled over and screamed, the blood running down both sides of her face, he simply looked at the father and smiled, confident that there would be no fuss.

Chapter Two:
Levin

Even at the Goffs' party, months after resigning his research position, Grigory Levin talked enthusiastically about the laboratory where he had worked. The staff had nicknamed it the "Jewish paradise," and Grigory had done research there for almost twelve years, but when the "Jewish paradise" began to collapse things quickly became intolerable for him.

Back in the 1950s two scientists had been authorized by a major Leningrad research institute to set up and manage this lab. Whether by pure luck or by some nameless official's design, the two scientists—Shuler and Naimann, both of them Jews—where able to hire the brightest young researchers available, without interference from the Party bosses. The result was a lively, intellectually effervescent staff, an island of enlightenment with a touch of Western-style sophistication. The staff members enjoyed one another, and they especially enjoyed the unique absence of Party busybodies, of informers, and of ideological crackdowns. About half of the scientists in Grigory's lab were Jews, hence the nickname "Jewish paradise."

The late 1950s were years of optimism. In 1956, when Khrushchev began to attack Stalin's crimes, people hoped for an improvement not only in their economic lives but also in their civic and intellectual freedoms. There was promise. Solzhenitsyn was permitted to publish his novel, *One Day in the Life of Ivan Denisovich*, which revealed some of the secrets of Soviet concentration camps, and previously censored Soviet writings were gradually being made available, as well as foreign literature in Russian translation. Khrushchev promised more consumer goods, more and better housing, and an improvement in agriculture to alleviate food shortages.

For many, this optimism vanished in the early 1960s. Literary censorship once again choked off Solzhenitsyn and other unorthodox writers, and most of the reforms that once seemed to presage some loosening of autocratic discipline were abandoned. Still, people could point to an improvement over Stalin's day, and many allowed themselves some hope.

In the "Jewish paradise," through the 1960s and even into the 1970s, Grigory and his colleagues could actually experience a touch of that imagined future liberalization. Since their staff performed essential research services for the parent institute, especially computer work, in which the Soviet Union has been so deficient, these men even began to think of themselves as immune from harassment by Party bureaucrats and ideologues.

The troubles began with Rubenshtain, one of the brightest young physicists in the lab. In the late summer of 1974, the administration of the institute received a letter from the KGB charging that Rubenshtain was the leader of a "secret underground Zionist cell." He had evidently been meeting secretly with some friends, at his apartment, to study Hebrew grammar and biblical history. The grammar book had been found by KGB agents during a search of his room. The institute administration insisted that Shuler and Naimann, the two chiefs of the "Jewish paradise," bring Rubenshtain before a meeting of the entire institute, and that he be forced to repent publicly. Ordinarily a person in Rubenshtain's position would suffer the humiliation without question, and several of his friends, including Grigory, assured him that there could be no way out of a public recantation. But when Shuler and Naimann called Rubenshtain into their office to work out the best strategy for his repentance, Rubenshtain, in his shy, hesitant way, insisted that he couldn't pretend to recant. "I can't swallow the shit down and I can't spit the shit up; it just sticks in my throat."

* * *

Part One: ENDINGS

The institute's amphitheater was almost full. In addition to several hundred employees, from technicians through senior scientists, there were representatives from the Party committee, and a few obscure gentlemen, not known to the scientists present, who sat high up in the back rows and observed the proceedings.

Down on the platform, Rubenshtain sat behind a small table, facing the audience. At the left and right ends of the table his two supervisors sat: Shuler, with his chin cupped in his right hand, his right elbow leaning on the table; and Naimann, staring at a sheaf of papers he was holding propped in front of his eyes.

Rubenshtain, hunched forward with both arms lying flaccidly in his lap, gazed at the tabletop and spoke almost inaudibly. Aside from occasional phrases that trailed up past the lower tiers of seats, only the motions of his lips showed that he was speaking.

". . . no intention to harm . . . only studying the ancient history . . . ancient Hebrew . . . culture of the nation . . ."

A voice from one corner of the audience suddenly snapped out. "We would *all* like to hear what you have to say, Rubenshtain. Speak up!"

". . . not true that we're connected with other study groups . . ."

The Party men were almost crimson with frustration.

"No, Rubenshtain! Stop defending our enemies! Stop justifying yourself!" one man shouted. "Tell us the truth!"

On the other side of the hall, several rows higher, a young man with closely cropped hair bellowed out, "Don't you feel your guilt? You refuse to admit your fault?"

Rubenshtain was not playing the game. A few formulas of regret, with no admission of guilt—this was not the Party script. The usual and proper scenario would have been for Rubenshtain first to make a fiery speech confessing, with shame, that he had become a tool of international Zionism, imperialism, and of the Israeli intelligence corps. Then, lyrically, he would thank the KGB and lavish tears of gratitude on them for rescuing him at just the right moment, for snatching him away from the filthy paws of the Zionist-imperialist conspiracy. Then, straightening up with pride, he would attack, in searing rhetoric, the conspirators' schemes to shatter the bond of friendship that unites the Soviet nations, in order to smash the entire socialist camp. Somewhat more humbly, then, he would urge all those present to learn from his delusions and errors, and to render unconquerable their vigilance against the enemy. Finally, and now with deepest humility, he would solemnly swear to bend the rest of his life and strength to the task of redeeming himself from guilt and of rendering himself worthy of his comrades' trust.

That was what the Party expected. Instead, Rubenshtain was giving them this mumbling, monotonous drone about not having realized that anything was wrong with Hebrew grammar or with ancient history. And, worst of all, he had the utter effrontery to conclude his statement with an almost inaudible formula about hoping that everyone understood his "desire to improve"!

Party men in various sections of the hall—mostly the younger ones, who had to show their zeal—shouted their anger and disapproval. At that moment, however, the chairman of the local union committee, an elderly man with a round, crimson face, rose from his seat and rumbled slowly, in a throaty voice, "What is that foreign word you call your little group of conspirators?"

"*Ulpan?* It's a Hebrew word. *Ulpan.*"

"Yes! *Ool* . . . what? *Ool-ban?* I can't even pronounce it!" As the other Party men chuckled, he deliberately mispronounced the word several times with an exaggerated, overacted, writhing disgust. "And you!" he continued. "You, Ru-uben-shta-ain"—again pretending to choke on the polluted, alien sound of this name— "How could you even become interested in Hebrew. Such garbage! Such rotten filth!"

Rubenshtain could only stare and gape, like a fish on land, as though something had made the air unbreatheable. After a moment, Naimann rose and gazed toward the upper rows of the audience. As one of Rubenshtain's superiors it was clearly up to him to conclude the meeting with a formal statement of his own.

"Comrades, we have all had occasion to thank our leaders for their vigilance against the Zionist aggressors, and once again we are thankful . . ."

Naimann went on, crying out against the Israelis, the Zionists, the fascists, and, with ever increasing ardor, he attacked the Zionist conspiracy. But the frustrated rage of the Party bosses was not assuaged, because Naimann's Russian was stained with the slight

54

but unmistakable rasp of a Yiddish accent that gave to his entire peroration an unwitting slant of parody. When he finished and took his seat, there was an embarrassed pause.

Cursing and grumbling, the Party men noisily stalked out through the double doors in the rear of the hall. Shuler and Naimann glanced at each other quickly, stood up from the table, and hurried off to hear the verdict. The rest of the staff filed out quietly.

Rubenshtain was lucky. He wasn't arrested; he wasn't even fired. But his name was henceforth never permitted to appear on any of his research papers and his low rank and salary were frozen without hope of future advancement.

Although Grigory had been able to hold his discontent at arm's-length as long as his research and his professional life went well, Tatyana had long felt strangled by the constraints of Soviet life. As they lay in their sleeper in the late-night train to Leningrad, after the Goffs' party, Tatyana was unable to rest. She was working out the schedule for the morning: first, pick up Lyuba, their six-year-old daughter, who had spent the past two nights at Grigory's parents' apartment; then get Lyuba off to nursery school, over an hour on the bus; then another hour or more until she and Grigory reached home to start work on their exit-visa applications.

The mere thought of her in-laws' apartment made Tatyana uncomfortable. It brought back those early days of her marriage, when they'd had to share those two rooms with Grigory's parents and his two brothers. There was nothing at all unusual about this arrangement; a large percentage of the Soviet people, especially those in the big cities, live in communal apartments split up among several families, sometimes five or six, who share a single kitchen and bathroom. These tenants often further subdivide their apartments by subletting a corner of one room, which is separated by curtains or a flimsy partition.

It was only within the last few years before Grigory and Tatyana's marriage in late 1967 that Grigory's parents, Olga and Zinovy Levin, managed to get out of a communal apartment and into their own place. The Soviet government regulates the amount of floor space to be allotted to each family, depending on its size, but most people live with much less space than the law suggests. Naturally, in a country where there is a perpetual shortage of living space, it is the usual thing for children to remain with their parents, even after maturing, marrying, and having their own children.

For the sake of privacy, Grigory's father and brothers used to set up curtain dividers every night, which transformed the living room into a series of narrow cells. As she lay sleepless on the tight berth of the Leningrad train, Tatyana felt choked merely recalling that tiny curtained-off space. After the first year and half of their marriage, Lyuba was born. At about the same time, Grigory's middle brother married and, naturally, had to move his wife into the apartment as well. That brought the population of the two rooms to seven adults and a newborn infant.

There was no choice but to move in with Sasha and Lyudmilla Petrov, Tatyana's parents. Their apartment was quite roomy and luxurious by Soviet standards, for Sasha was a Party boss. But Sasha Petrov was also a hard man to contend with.

Over forty years before, in the early 1920s, when he was fourteen, Sasha abandoned not only the Volga countryside's bleak poverty, but also its brutality, especially his father's cruelly punishing authority. Conditions in the local factory, where he worked for over two years after leaving the village, were even more filthy and degrading than on the land. But those two years had not been spent in vain: it was then that he had joined the Communist Youth League, Komsomol, and worked for them zealously. Komsomol repaid him by sending him to a preparatory school in Leningrad for civil-engineer training. After years of being beaten by his father and by his boss, and being intimidated by anyone else who was bigger or more important than he, Sasha was now a part of the revolution.

In 1927, three years after leaving his village, Sasha was still fired with optimism for his own future, and for the future of Russia, even as he sat munching his dry, black bread in the long, low, plank-walled workers' barrack in Leningrad, where he was trying to scrub the smell of the Volga River mud out of his pores. Conditions in this workers' barrack were hard. Dozens of men and boys had been crowded into this one long room. They slept on two rows of plank shelves attached to the walls. The place had no toilet, and not all of these newly arrived country people were fastidious about their personal hygiene, so the room was ridden with fleas, and the air stank. But Sasha had an instinct for trying to look and feel like something more than a peasant. He had no intention of spending his life in places like this.

What was far more discouraging for Sasha was his failure in the civil-engineering institute. He remained a believer in the vision and the ideals of Lenin and in the future of Russia, and he had fervently wanted to help build a new generation of socialist engineers. The Party was behind him, and he was legitimized by being from peasant stock.

Admission had not been a problem, but the competition was more than Sasha could handle. While his father had been teaching him only to kiss the rod that beat him, a lesson he learned better than he realized, the city boys had been learning how to study. Even many of the workers' children seemed to have a lot more book-learning than Sasha, and there were quite a few boys at the institute who had been admitted despite questionable class origins. For instance, there were numbers of Jewish students whose fathers couldn't really be called proletarians. They were poor, desperately poor, but then, who wasn't poor? Sasha's entire family still lived on the land, so he knew some things that couldn't be discussed openly about the poverty and famine that had killed millions within the past few years.

It was not Sasha's good fortune to become a civil engineer, but he had no intention of abandoning hope. Besides, some of his older mentors in Komsomol liked him. He was tough-minded, committed, and clever. It had been hinted that with his ability to organize people, his real future lay with the Party.

Tatyana's battles with her father had begun within a week after she and Grigory had moved in. Sasha, sturdily handsome even in his sixties, was standing by the dinner table, clutching a copy of *Komsomolskaya Pravda* folded back to an article condemning "Israeli imperialist aggression." Tatyana's mother, Lyudmilla, a small, tense woman with graying hair that showed few traces of its once lustrous black, was trying to clear away the dishes without making any noise. Sasha punctuated his words by smacking the newspaper across his open palm, his well-manicured fingers stiffly extended.

"I'll tell you who I'm talking about! That bunch of young cynics and complainers—traitors are what they really are—sneaking manuscripts off to be published in the West, sending letters abroad about their precious 'rights.' " Sasha tossed the newspaper onto a shelf. "You and your friends, you yawn when anybody mentions Lenin, and you'd scoff openly if you could get away with it." Turning to his wife, he shouted, "I'll tell anyone, Lyusya, *anyone*, that I'm not ashamed. I'm glad I can still have faith in a Soviet state with power enough to smack some of these troublemakers around!"

Tatyana stood with her back to the door, her face turned toward her mother. Her voice cracked with anger. "I'll tell you something about his faith! It's not for Lenin and the Party; it's that old-fashioned Russian cult of the clenched fist!" And turning toward Sasha: "Obey or be beaten, that's your faith!" She stormed out of the room, red-faced and trembling with frustration, as always after these tirades.

Still, it was Sasha who finally found an apartment for Tatyana and Grigory. Though semiliterate, Sasha had been able to become deputy director of his civil-engineering institute because he was a Party boss, and he was now able to use his influence to wangle a small apartment for them in a condominium his institute had built for its members. It was a one-room studio with a minuscule kitchen, but it was their own. It had less than the legal amount of floor area for a family of three, so they were permitted to put their names on the five-year waiting list for larger quarters.

Tatyana sat on the edge of her berth and listened to the clattering of the train wheels for a moment before getting up. It was dawn. The window was blurred by an icy drizzle. They had left the dry inland frost of Moscow and were entering the wet, rheumatic late-winter of that swamp that Peter the Great had chosen for his capital city. It was weather long familiar to Tatyana. She used to enjoy being in a warm kitchen when the days were this damp, especially at her uncle's apartment. Her mother had two brothers, one of whom Tatyana and Grigory had just seen off with his family at the airport. These aunts and uncles, the Jewish side of the family, had practically raised her. Tatyana had never been close to her father's side of the family; they all lived many hundreds of miles away, in the east of Russia. But her mother's family lived nearby, in Leningrad and in Moscow, and had always lavished Tatyana with affection. As a little girl she was everybody's favorite. In her aunt's kitchen, surrounded by the steady singsong of half-Yiddish, half-Russian talk, her aunt taught Tatyana how to cook Jewish foods, and occasionally even told her what foods used to be eaten on particular Jewish holidays, holidays alive now only in memory.

Thus, even though Tatyana inherited her father's handsome, strong-boned Russian looks, with his blue-gray eyes and straight, light hair, she always felt Jewish, and was deeply estranged from Sasha's Russia. Tatyana's Russia was that of the poets, the novelists, the musicians, the only Russia that can share itself with the world, that thoughtful, sensitive Russia that so many Jews find fatally attractive. This was not Sasha's Russia. His was the rough, demanding, imperious power that has always cut down her most brilliant sons.

The morning after their return to Leningrad, Tatyana was anxious to bring Lyuba to nursery school. She wanted to avoid an extended visit with the Levins; Grigory's mother was curious to hear all about how things had gone at Sheremetyevo Airport the day before, and whether Tatyana's uncle had gotten off to Vienna without serious problems. But if Olga were given a chance to start bustling about the apartment with teacups and cake plates, she was bound to ask about the progress of Grigory and Tatyana's visa applications, which would lead to a long discussion about the problem of Sasha's refusal to sign the parents' statement, and Tatyana simply did not have the stomach for that subject after a sleepless night.

Olga and Zinovy Levin sometimes forgot how shocked they had been a few years before when Grigory's youngest brother, Volodya, had first begun to discuss his own plans to emigrate. Now that he was already living in America, Volodya's emigration seemed quite acceptable, but originally his parents had thought it foolhardy to abandon a career and prospects. That might be all right for older people, or those primitive Jews from the Western Ukraine, perhaps even for the rough-and-ready underground merchants of Odessa or the mountain-village Jews of Soviet Georgia. But for well-educated professionals in Leningrad or Moscow? Unthinkable!

True, there were some professionals who had rediscovered their Jewishness, or had become enthusiastic over the dream of Zion fulfilled in Israel, especially since the Six Day War in 1967. One occasionally met such people. But the Yom Kippur War, in the autumn of 1973, frightened many emigrés. Obviously, a father was risking his son's life as well as his own in a place like Israel. The triumph of 1967 suddenly seemed less attractive to many Russian and Ukrainian Jews, who had already lost so many close relatives and friends in the war against the Nazis.

Few of the emigrés knew that they could choose to go anyplace other than to Israel; not more than three or four percent asked to be sent to any other countries when they arrived in Vienna. Only since 1973 did a substantial number of emigrés ask, and receive, permission to go to America or other Western European countries.

The idea of Volodya, their youngest son, going to a place like America seemed inconceivable to Grigory's parents. But America was the destination Volodya chose because the Levins had relatives there.

At the very time that Volodya was seriously weighing the possibilities of emigration, Zinovy and Olga Levin were visited by Yuri Gellman. Yuri was a nephew of Zinovy's who had been raised in the Russian-Jewish settlement in Harbin, China, and had gone from there to America in 1947. While in America he had lost track of his relatives in the Soviet Union. It wasn't until the late 1960s that Yuri was able to rediscover the Levins, and in 1973 he came to Leningrad as a tourist.

Yuri showed them color photos of his cheerful-looking family and his California home, and promised that he would help the family resettle should they decide to emigrate. Nonetheless, Zinovy and Olga remained skeptical. Would-be emigrés had to confront Soviet authority, a confrontation that was frightening and potentially destructive.

But when Volodya insisted, and began the process of acquiring an invitation from Israel, so that he could apply for a visa, Zinovy and Olga did not try to thwart him by refusing their signed statements. Their treatment of Volodya could never be compared with Sasha's treatment of Tatyana. They were like the majority of visa applicants' relatives, who, though frightened and saddened by what might well be a lifetime separation, would not stand in the way of their children's freedom.

In fact, Tatyana never did have the kind of clashes with Olga and Zinovy that she had with her own father. True, she and Olga had occasionally gotten on each other's nerves when they were all squeezed into the same apartment, but those conflicts were manageable, and the only time Zinovy had displayed exasperation toward her was when she changed her family name from Levin back to Petrov.

Tatyana had been married for just a few months and was about to complete her university degree, when one of her professors, a woman who had always praised Tatyana's work, beckoned to her as the rest of the class filed out of the lecture hall.

"When did Tatyana Alexandrovna Petrov become Tatyana Alexandrovna Levin?"

"A few months ago . . ."

"For fifteen rubles or so you can get your maiden name back. Go right down to the office and have it done."

"But my husband's name . . ."

"Your husband's name is Jewish, and you're a talented girl with a career ahead of you. Let me put it simply. Even when the Jews were getting ahead quickly, they were pretty well locked out of the humanities. 'Ideologically unsound' and all of that. Nowadays, with a name like Levin you'd have trouble being hired in any field, but especially as an English teacher. You may want to write, to publish—the doors will slam in your face. And don't worry about your husband. One day he'll thank me for talking you into it."

They avoided telling Grigory's father that Tatyana was changing her name back to Petrov, but a month later, when the official notification arrived, Zinovy saw it. For several weeks he avoided looking straight at Tatyana. At dinner, when they sat opposite one another at the small table, he averted his eyes, whether in pain, anger, or disgust she couldn't tell.

After all, what was left besides his name? When Zinovy was a small boy, several years after the revolution, his family had to cut short his religious education and place him in a Soviet public school. They comforted themselves with the thought that he had absorbed Jewish culture and values by their example, and that in a modern secular society, traditional Jewish learning was unnecessary. He would be a Jew without Talmud, without real Judaic study, but a Jew nonetheless.

Throughout the resurgence of anti-Semitism in the 1930s, which reached its peak when Stalin signed a nonaggression treaty with Hitler in 1939, Zinovy couldn't have forgotten that he was Jewish even if he had wanted to, but he and others like him in the Soviet Union differed from Jews in other parts of the world in one vital respect: those in America, or in Western Europe before Hitler's invasions, often turned to traditional Jewish lore and learning at will, or at need, even though they were not well trained in Judaica. At times of stress, or of anti-Semitic threats, even nonobservant Jews in the West drew sustenance from traditional Jewish philosophy, literature, and liturgy. Such support was not available to Zinovy and his fellow Jews in the Soviet Union. Perhaps it might have strengthened them in the years between 1939 and 1941, when Hitler was a "friend" of the U.S.S.R., when the Nazis were above criticism, and when Nazi persecution of the Jews was hardly mentioned in Soviet periodicals, or else was treated as a "progressive" attack on superstition. This inner support might have been useful at the time of the so-called "doctors' plot" in early 1953, when Stalin and his police were about to bring to trial a group of doctors, many of them Jews, on a trumped-up charge of murdering state officials.

For a while, it looked as though Soviet Jewry was about to be sentenced en masse as the government was preparing large-scale roundups and deportations of Jews to Siberian concentration camps. Plans for this Soviet "final solution" were dropped after Stalin's death in March 1953, but in the months before Stalin died, great numbers of Soviet Jews, especially those who held professional positions, were being fired from their jobs. Zinovy himself was fired and left without income, though he was then the sole support of a large family. What's more, Grigory, then thirteen years old, was being attacked and beaten almost daily by Russian boys, his former playmates, who easily detected what was in the air, and who scouted the courtyards chanting slogans about the Jews drinking Russian blood.

This was Grigory's only bar mitzvah lesson—this, and whatever lore he and his brothers learned at home, which was not a great deal. But Zinovy and the boys had always been Levins, and though the curse of an alien-sounding name could not be equated with the solace and support of a living tradition, the name's damning irrevocability somehow made it a symbol, a reminder. Now this new Levin, who might someday bear yet others, had suddenly slid back to being a *Petrov*.

But Zinovy was unable to remain angry at his daughter-in-law for more than a few weeks. He sat at the table one evening, his short, round frame hunched forward slightly. He ran his hands once or twice over the top of his bald, longish head, and thought: "Well, that's the kind of rotten world my children have to survive in." The crisis was past.

Tatyana had renounced the Levin name for her career. After all, what is as important as one's career? The hobbies, avocations, social activities, clubs and fraternal organizations that Westerners indulge in to divert themselves from the success game are almost nonexistent among Soviet professionals. For them, self-respect and respectability are almost exclusively dependent upon rank and success in the hierarchy. No one could deny that a minor emotional crisis in Tatyana's relations with Zinovy was a small price to pay for her career.

Tatyana had felt so fortunate to have a Russian maiden name to fall back on, and yet, ironically, she was almost broken both emotionally and physically by her very success in getting a "desirable" position, and especially by her two years of teaching in a military school. She earned the usual low pay: for twenty-five to thirty class hours per week she was paid a bit over a ruble an hour, with no consideration for time spent marking tests and preparing classes, for office hours, or for attending mandatory lectures on the international situation and mandatory political indoctrination classes. And that unbearable military discipline! Tatyana was addressed by her superiors at the school not as a colleague or fellow professional of junior rank, but in the harsh, barked commands of a drill sergeant. Every moment of her working day was rendered nightmarish by rigid attention to detail and harsh codes of behavior, by the endless bellowing of orders, by irrational rules, military rudeness, and humilation. To make matters worse, Tatyana was under pressure from her department chairman. She had tried to explain to him that the students from small rural towns could barely read or write, and had never heard of a noun or a verb. To put them into a traditional foreign-language course was futile. But the chairman, worried about falling behind in his "production norms," forced Tatyana to stand at attention before his desk, and shouted accusations of incompetence at her because students were failing the tests. Under this stress, Tatyana was developing chronic pains, which one of her friends, a recent medical-school graduate, diagnosed as stress-related heart and liver ailments. He gave Tatyana tranquilizers and other medications, but they afforded only slight relief until she left the job. Now that she and Grigory were applying for exit visas, her symptoms returned and she was again taking medication.

As they stepped into their bright, airy apartment and walked through the corridor lined with half-built bookshelves, Grigory was struck by a certain irony: five years of waiting and hoping had finally rewarded them with this three-room "dream palace" just as the rest of the dream was crumbling.

While Tatyana heated the teapot, Grigory took an envelope to the table and removed two stapled sets of printed sheets: their exit-visa applications. Each form requested the applicant's name, address, birth date, and place of employment, the same information for current and divorced spouses, and a list of the applicant's immediate relatives and their places of employment.

Tatyana's father had already made it plain that he had no intention of giving her a written statement that she was in no debt to him, lest he be accused of complicity. And there was her older brother, Pyotr, to worry about as well. He was a biochemist in a medical testing laboratory, and his consuming desire was to become the head of his lab. He was, after all, officially Russian, not Jewish, and his father was a retired Party man, so what could possibly stand in his way? Only Tatyana's emigration, which might mean the end of Pyotr's ambitions.

Beneath Pyotr's anger that Tatyana was endangering his career there lay a deeper resentment. He had always wanted to be like his father—the pure, native, patriotic Russian—and often wished that he himself were pure Russian instead of half Jewish. But whereas Tatyana, who felt a kinship with her Jewish side, looked very Slavic, Pyotr had a typically Jewish face, like his uncles. Since his boyhood he'd had to defend himself against street toughs who jeered at him in the streets and called him *zhid*. Now that he was a grown man with good prospects, his clean record as a "Russian" was about to be sullied again.

Pyotr was a nervous man, given to drink, and was as domineering as his father. Tatyana knew that he would do anything to stop her emigration, and she was especially worried that as long as he had Sasha's ear, he would sabotage any headway she might otherwise make in talking Sasha into releasing her.

Even as Grigory was reading the questions about his immediate family, he wasn't really thinking about the application, or about how Tatyana might solve the problem of Sasha's intractability or of Pyotr's childish resentment. He was trying to trace through his memory, back to that moment when he had first made his decision to leave. Was it after Rubenshtain's hearing? After that fiasco, Shuler and Naimann had been forced to hire a Party man, regardless of his qualifications, as soon as the next opening occurred. It didn't take long. A few weeks later, Vera, a young computer specialist, was the first in the group to apply for an exit visa to follow her family to Israel. The Party was now on the move. The "Jewish paradise" was coming to an end.

Tatyana interrupted Grigory's recollections. She was calling his attention to the list of required documents that was appended to the questionnaire, and to another paper that might well be a problem: the so-called *Kharakteristika*, the character reference from the applicant's last employer, necessary unless the applicant had been unemployed for six months or more. This reference was theoretically meant to show only that the employer had no claims against the applicant, but the requirement quickly became an excuse for harassment.

In Grigory's lab, as in many other places, the *Kharakteristika* would be given out only after a public hearing during which the applicant was personally vilified by his former co-workers. In retrospect Grigory realized that if any single event had forced him to face the futility of all his hopes, it was Vera's character-reference hearing. This meeting was held in their own lab, not in the institute's lecture hall, and the atmosphere was informal, but here too there were ambitious young Party men who ensured that the actors didn't forget their lines.

While Vera stood at one end of the room, her co-workers stood up, one by one, and called out their questions:

"How could you be such a traitor to your own friends, your own people, and run off to the aggressors in Israel?"

"What makes an educated person like you side with the Zionist imperialists? Here the Soviet people have given you everything and you're knifing us in the back."

None of Vera's co-workers refused to take part. Each one knew the rules, and it wouldn't have occurred to anyone to violate them.

After several hours of this kind of questioning, when everyone was utterly depressed and exhausted, the Party men were finally satisfied, and the meeting ended. Afterward, on the street, Vera's friends—those who had been abusing her during the meeting—clustered around her, and the crowd moved off toward Vera's bus stop. They all cried and kissed her good-bye, wished her good luck, and begged her to write and tell them what Israel was like.

After Vera's bus left, Grigory waited on the chilly street corner with Rubenshtain and a chemist named Natasha. He felt moved by the farewell, and was trying to describe his feelings. Like a bird, he was saying, like a swallow at migration time: restless, unable to sit still. The other two simply nodded. The next morning Natasha announced that she too was applying for a visa. Her hearing was scheduled for November.

If Vera's character-reference hearing demonstrated to Grigory the emptiness of his hopes, it was Natasha's hearing, one month later, that crushed those hopes altogether. Just after Vera's session, Grigory and Tatyana moved into their new three-room apartment. Like that wonderful laboratory, that "Jewish paradise," the apartment had a touch of extra comfort that made it possible for a person to close his eyes to Soviet problems. It was just the incentive that capitalists were always accused of exploiting, and yet it was the same force that propelled the entire Soviet system of state-granted privileges.

Grigory had borrowed a large sum of money to pay for the new apartment, and he had been spending all his free time and his last rubles on furnishings, and on building long rows of bookshelves in the hallway.

On a windy, frigid November evening, Tatyana, weighed down by a string bag full of groceries in one hand and a briefcase in the other, pushed through the door and winced. She had developed a blinding headache toward the end of her teaching day.

That fall she had received a coveted full-time English-teaching appointment at a technical institute, so she was finally able to leave the military school. The atmosphere in her new school was less harsh, but there were some problems there too. Some of the part-time teachers had put all their hopes on receiving full-time appointments. They constantly studied to improve their skills, and worked erratic hours at very low pay to prove their worth to the administrators.

The department chairwoman, a cultivated, pleasant, and sympathetic person, invited one of these part-time teachers into her office for a chat that day. A friend of Tatyana's, Nadya had been waiting for a full-time appointment for about six years, and had been passed over every year. From the adjoining office Tatyana heard the chairwoman say:

"Listen, Nadya, it's no mystery, is it? My hands are tied. Your father's name is Avram, your husband's name is Naum, your last name is Gershman. Now really! What can I do?"

On the way home, Tatyana had to struggle with a long line of aggressive, determined housewives and grandmothers, all trying to get to a store counter that suddenly had a stock of decent-looking vegetables.

As she walked into the new apartment after an hour and a half on jammed buses and trains, that nauseating clenched fist in her skull was augmented by the sharp crack of nails being driven into wood. Grigory, squatting in the hallway of the apartment, barely looked up from the long planks and the wood chips littering the floor. Tatyana reheated some of last night's supper on the stove. When she called Grigory to the table, he mumbled something, took a plate back to the hallway, and continued hammering. Just before midnight he put down the hammer, then stretched, walked to the stove, poured a cup of tea, and carried it back to the hallway. But before he could sit on the floor with his tools, Tatyana grabbed the teacup away. "Listen, Grisha, do you think you're living alone in this place?"

He looked around, almost dazed.

Tatyana's voice cracked; her cheeks were crimson and wet. "You want to nail yourself to the wall, Grisha? You want to fasten yourself to this apartment? Fine! But just remember that I'm here too. And I'm a human being, Grisha, human being! *Talk* to me!"

It wasn't until the next day that Grigory began to understand what was happening to him. The next afternoon was taken up by Natasha's character-reference hearing. The time was crawling by as one person after another stood up and intoned the prescribed formulas: "You are a traitor; You are unworthy of your country. . . ."

Grigory suddenly mumbled under his breath, "Bitch!" A lab technician sitting next to him looked up and grunted, "Who? Natasha?"

"Couldn't she just quit six months and a day before applying? Spare us all this torment? If you've been out of work for six months you don't need the character reference. She could have spared us all this."

"Maybe she needed the money, Grigory."

It was Grigory's turn. A number of faces turned back to look at him, roused from their gray, protective torpor by the acrid touch of anger in his voice. He hardly heard what he was saying, but he knew that Natasha had betrayed him personally, and all the Jews with him. It was people like Natasha who had smashed everything to pieces, who had destroyed the lab, destroyed Grigory's chances, destroyed his last hopes, his last illusions.

His throat felt ragged. The same Party slogans that they had all laughed at for years, that they had all recited with mock conviction at meetings like this, Grigory was now spewing out like bile. He stopped, and as he stood there in the embarrassed silence, his anger suddenly drained away. He nodded once, his face flushed, and sat down.

Later, as Grigory paced back and forth at his bus stop, he wondered about that warmth he had felt a month before, when they all wished Vera luck after her hearing, that love, that desire to join the flocks winging off to the lands of summer. Was it nothing but disguised envy? As he turned to shield his face from the cold drizzle blowing in on the wind, Grigory remembered something Rubenshtain had said after his public "repentance." "It's a hostage system. We're all hostages to each other," he'd said that day. "If one person tries to stand up straight, the rest of us pull him down. We have to. If we don't, we may be forced to stop being hunchbacks ourselves."

In the days and weeks after their one-day trip to Moscow, the Levins became more involved in the bureaucratic nightmare of preparing their applications. One of Tatyana's major tasks was to get her own character reference from the director of the institute she had resigned from several months earlier. People in directorial positions occasionally refused to take the responsibility of signing such a form. Their political reputations, hence their security, could be threatened by their names being associated with emigration documents; signing was seen as a subtle form of collaboration. Tatyana was frightened of asking the director, so she procrastinated. But there were others whom she was afraid to meet also.

She had been very friendly with some of the teachers, especially Nadya Gershman, the young woman who had been refused a full-time job because of her Jewish name.

In the Soviet Union few qualities are valued as highly as friendship. For generations, for centuries, children have been taught the virtue of informing the authorities about their neighbors' wrongdoings, but in everyone's life there must be a few people who can be trusted. These are the true friends.

It takes time and trials to learn whether someone is really a friend, but sometimes there is a natural sympathy between two people that quickly overcomes the barriers of suspicion. This was the kind of warmth that linked Tatyana and Nadya. For some reason that Nadya herself didn't quite understand, she trusted Tatyana more than the other faculty members, and spoke·with her more openly. When Tatyana was still teaching they used to ride the same bus to and from work every day, laughing, talking, joking.

One morning in December of 1974, Nadya mentioned a close friend of hers who used to teach at the same institute. "You wouldn't know her, Tanya. She went off to Israel a few years ago."

Tatyana tried to appear calm. She and Grigory had decided to apply, but no one was to know yet, and she couldn't afford to let Nadya notice her sudden interest.

"Israel? Oh, she had one of those visas, I suppose."

"Yes. Some business that was!"

"Oh?"

"It went off like a bomb; like a bomb filled with shit."

In January, several weeks after this conversation with Nadya, Tatyana resigned from her job. Her department chairwoman and her fellow teachers were shocked, but Tatyana told them that she was planning to have another baby, and that she had to stay home for her children's sake. What else could she do but lie? To have simply told her chairwoman that she was emigrating would have been unthinkable, a slap in the face.

"Yes," Tatyana thought, "she knows the rules of her game, and I know mine."

Weeks had passed since their return to Leningrad. Spring was now becoming noticeable through the icy, gray rains, though late March and early April can hardly be called balmy in Leningrad. Finally, Tatyana swallowed a dose of the tranquilizers she had from her military-school days, placed the bottle in her case alongside the application papers, and settled herself to see the institute director.

She arrived at his outer office without having met anyone from her department. One obstacle overcome. But she still had to get past the director's receptionist.

"What do you want to discuss with him? He's busy. He has other people to see today."

"It's personal business. I can only discuss it with him."

"What is it about?"

"It's an emergency. Just tell him I must see him immediately!"

The secretary scowled, shrugged, and disappeared into the inner office.

Tatyana sat on the edge of a chair. The tranquilizers weren't helping much. She tried not to think of the forms in her handbag. Perhaps concentrating on something else would help—that picture of Lenin on the wall, dusty, the glass cracked at an angle—

"You can see him now."

A thin, intelligent-looking man was sitting behind a large, polished wooden desk. He was well-mannered, almost refined.

"What can I do for you?"

"I have something very serious to tell you."

He stood up, showed her to a seat near his desk, and pulled out another chair for himself. He looked puzzled, a bit worried. Tatyana took out the papers and handed them to him.

"I have to apply for an exit visa."

His face was immobile. Polite, not overtly hostile, but immobile.

It's my husband. He wants to join his family in their national homeland . . ." Tatyana began to cry. "I'm a mother. What can I do? I can't stay here alone, raise my child alone . . ."

The director reached into his desk for a handkerchief; he brought her a glass of water.

Fifteen, twenty minutes: explaining, cajoling, making excuses, humbling herself. An act? The tears were real; the anger, and the fear, and the grief were real.

"I don't know if I can sign this. Come back in a day or two. And leave the papers with me."

Tatyana walked out of his office almost dizzy with relief. In the outer office, two women were waiting to see the director. Tatyana was too preoccupied to notice them. Suddenly one of them shouted,

"Tanya!"

It was Nadya, with the department chairwoman.

"Tanya! Are you coming back here to teach?"

"Well . . . no . . ."

"I'm about to get my promotion! Full time! The director's about to sign the forms right now! Don't go away, we'll be out in a second."

Grinning, red-cheeked with happiness and success, Nadya followed the chairwoman into the director's office. A few moments later they walked out. Nadya stalked through the waiting room and out the door. The chairwoman grabbed Tatyana by the hand and led her to the window. "What have you done? *What have you done?* You ruined that woman! She was already on the list for promotion, and now he's crossed her out. What have you done?"

The most valuable emotional asset for one who is applying for an exit visa is the ability to withstand endless abuse without losing control of one's nerves. Anger and the natural need to defend one's dignity must be reined in until the danger is past. Tatyana had to sit back and allow herself to be humiliated. Though the director of her institute had been polite to her, he refused to give her a character reference unless he was ordered to do so by the District Party Committee, which must then assume any future blame.

When Tatyana approached the receptionist at the District Party Committee office, the woman pointed out a short man with graying hair, standing with a small group of people who had obviously just come out of a meeting. They stood in the corridor, talking in low voices.

As the man walked past Tatyana, she stopped him and explained her problem in a polite, subdued tone.

The Party man drew himself up, elevated his chin slightly, and began lecturing Tatyana in a stentorian voice. As soon as he was positive that his first outburst had roused the secretaries in the reception area, the visitors and Party workers moving through the corridor, and any bureaucrats whose office doors happened to be open, he turned his back on Tatyana and stalked toward his office, allowing her to follow docilely as he continued to rail at her.

"I, for one, have no intention of lending support to those of the Jewish nationality who have chosen to strengthen the aggressor state of Israel. Don't ask me to behave in that fashion!" He spoke slowly and distinctly so that no one on that floor would miss a word. In his office, Tatyana sat quietly, eyes down, properly humble, as he bellowed on about how he wasn't going to sully his name or reputation, or the honor of the Communist Party of the Soviet Union, with Zionist collaboration. Nonetheless, Tatyana knew that he would ultimately have to call her institute director to tell him to give Tatyana the signed form. Refuseniks could be created only by higher decree, through OVIR, not by mere District Party Committees.

A few days later, after she had begun to get over the pains and the shortness of breath that had been bothering her since leaving the District Party Committee office, she went to her parents' apartment to try once again to convince Sasha to give her his signed statement. She took the tranquilizers along, just in case things became difficult.

When she walked into the apartment, her mother brought in tea and a plate of buns, but Pyotr just looked at Tatyana coldly and pointed to a place on the sofa. Seven years older than Tatyana, he was tall and strong-looking, with curly black hair, a prominent nose, and the large black eyes of Lyudmilla's side of the family, but now his handsome face was tightened in a scowl.

"Divorce your husband!" Pyotr stood in the middle of the living room, shouting at Tatyana, who was sitting stiffly on the edge of the sofa.

"Just divorce him! Grigory's a Jew, let *him* go to Israel. Or America, or wherever he's going. What's it all got to do with you, anyway?"

Sasha, leaning forward in his armchair, agreed. "Yes. Grigory can go, and you can stay home where you belong."

Tatyana leaned back in amazement. "But . . . but I'm your sister, your daughter! You mean you'd rather see me divorced? Raising the child by myself? Alone?"

Pyotr snapped, "We don't care, dammit! We don't care! Just don't ruin our lives!"

Shouting back didn't help. She yelled; she sent Pyotr and his career to hell until her throat felt like sand, but it relieved only a fraction of her anger and none of her grief. She leapt up from the sofa and lunged past her brother to the sideboard, where she poured herself a glass of water, trembling, and splashed part of it onto the tray and the floor.

Sasha wanted to be stern, but he was anxious to calm his family and to avoid more shouting. No need to satisfy the neighbors' curiosity.

"Pyotr, sit down. Be quiet. Tanya, stop yelling like that. And what are those pills? Are you still taking that crap? I've told you to throw it out! That medicine's poison for you."

Tatyana snapped back at him, shouting, "I *have* to take them! I can't eat or sleep. My life's a wreck—"

After weeks of these arguments Sasha evolved a plan of his own. He would appease Tatyana by giving her a statement certifying that he had no material claims on her or Grigory, but he would sabotage her application by adding the statement that, having been a loyal and true Party member for fifty years, he utterly disapproves of his daughter's self-destructive and disloyal actions, and that his signature indicates only that he has no material claims against her, and not that she has his permission to leave. He was afraid to use his Party connections to have Tatyana's application rejected, because that would only spread the word about this family scandal. Both Sasha's pride and his instinct for self-preservation kept him quiet. He had survived all those years under Stalin by learning how to be inconspicuous when necessary. During the last twenty-five years Sasha had seen many of his friends vanish: those who had worked with him, those who had trained him, those whom he had trained. They and tens of millions like them had disappeared into Stalin's camps. And what was to prevent it all from happening again? Sasha was well aware that many of the people who had helped run the system then were still around, some of them still holding their old jobs.

On sunny weekends on the outskirts of Leningrad, in areas not yet cleared for new housing complexes, groups of people can be seen, sweating and puffing, as they drag briefcases and bags stuffed with books off into the woods beyond the last bus stop. In a clearing hidden by a fringe of trees, small piles of books are laid out neatly on plastic sheets on the ground. This is the book black-market.

During the late 1950s, Soviet bookstores had begun to stock more literature of high quality than they had before: Russian classics that had not been reprinted for many years; some important twentieth-century works that had been censored since the 1930s; and translations of foreign authors. But these books vanished from the shelves during the early 1960s, leaving only propaganda pamphlets and Party-line junk. The good books were hard to get. New printings were sold out immediately, largely under the counter, for as much as five times the marked price. Those who wanted these books had to buy them here, in the woods. It was risky, however, because plainclothesmen sometimes came on harassment raids.

Grigory and Tatyana spent weekends dragging the best of their book collection into the woods. They needed cash, and they needed all they could raise. Getting out of the Soviet Union is expensive. It cost the Levins 40 rubles each just to apply for a visa. If the request were granted, Soviet citizenship would have to be renounced at a cost of 500 rubles per adult. The exit visas cost 360 rubles per adult, the airline tickets cost close to 300 rubles each, and the cost of luggage is high (few Soviet citizens do much traveling, so few of them own luggage). If Tatyana and Grigory received permission to leave, they would have to raise a cash amount almost equal to their combined annual salaries. This would not include money needed to live on between the time they left their jobs and their departure. There was no way to earn enough money for that period. Most of the emigrés, therefore, sell everything except absolute necessities.

On a Friday afternoon toward the end of the summer, several months after the application forms had been submitted, a telephone call came from OVIR.

"Please report to OVIR on Monday at ten A.M."

"What's it about? Did we get permission?"

"You'll have to come to the office. I can't tell you anything over the telephone."

"Were we refused? Just say *something!* Please! I'll come Monday, but just say if we were refused permission."

"You'll be told everything on Monday."

They arrived at the OVIR office early, to allow time for standing on long lines. Their fatigue was driven away by apprehension, just as their sleep had been driven away for the past few nights. Finally, the uniformed woman at the desk called their names, and sent them through a rear door to the small room where their inspector sat in silence, staring grimly at some papers. Tatyana and Grigory waited quietly for the inspector to acknowledge their presence. She looked up momentarily, shoved two forms across the table toward them, and mumbled, "Permission granted. Follow the directions on these forms."

After leaving OVIR, Tatyana ran straight to her parents' apartment. She was flushed, almost trembling, and hardly knew how to tell them the news. Lyudmilla opened the door partway and peered up at her daughter curiously. Tatyana could see Sasha coming up just behind his wife, looking over her shoulder.

"We just received our permission!"

Both parents stood in silence for a few seconds, while Tatyana waited outside the threshold, beaming and out of breath. Sasha, without saying a word or changing his expression, turned and walked into an inner room. Tatyana's mother stood motionless, expressionless, her hands hanging at her sides. She said nothing. After a few more seconds, Tatyana said, somewhat more subdued, "We'll see you next week, on your birthday."

A week later Lyudmilla's family gathered to celebrate her birthday. They sat around the dinner table, talking nervously, pretending that nothing unusual was happening. Those were Sasha's orders: "In my house no one may speak of this! I forbid you to discuss this business with my daughter, to kiss her good-bye, even to say good-bye! Just behave as usual."

After dinner, when Tatyana tried to sit close and whisper to Uncle Ilya, Sasha banged his fist on the table and shouted, "Ilya! I said that's forbidden in my house!" And the uncle, his eyes brimming with tears, half-whispered, "Sasha, be human!"

This was Tatyana's last chance to say good-bye to those uncles and aunts who had lavished so much affection on her when she was little, who had cooked Jewish dishes for her, and had taught her a few words of Yiddish.

Part One: ENDINGS

When Grigory and Tatyana got up to leave the party, her uncles followed them out into the corridor. They embraced, wished one another farewell, best of luck; they kissed and cried. Pyotr was sitting with his wife and child in the narrow kitchen, adjacent to the hall. As Tatyana passed, he slammed the door with his foot.

A few days later, Grigory and Tatyana went to Sasha's apartment to say their final good-byes. Tatyana tried to embrace her father and kiss him; *"Do-svidânya,* Papa"—"till we meet again"—but Sasha shoved her aside and said, "What a stupid thing to say! This isn't *do-svidânya,* this is *proshtchay:* good-bye! Finished! You got what you wanted. Go. I'm sure you won't be happy there, but that's your life. You want to make a mess of it, that's your business. Just good-bye."

From the moment the Levins received permission to leave, they rushed, and kept on rushing. From office to office, from desk to desk, proving this, signing that, they collected their certifications: no money was owed to the telephone service; the apartment had been properly cleared and returned to the government housing office (Tatyana, Grigory, and Lyuba were living with Grigory's parents again); no debts were outstanding to the bureau that rents out everything from pianos to typewriters, and all diplomas and birth certificates were properly translated into English and notarized.

Finally they went to the bank and paid the 360 rubles per exit visa for each adult in the family, and the 500 rubles each for renouncing their Soviet citizenship. Grigory added the signed receipts for these payments to the pile of certifications he had already gathered, and got on line with the batch of papers at OVIR. All the papers were checked carefully while he and Tatyana waited for some minor error to be found—real or imagined—something to trip them up en route to their goal. But they were lucky. OVIR accepted their papers, made them sign more forms, stamped their exit visas again, and confiscated their internal passports. Now Grigory and Tatyana Levin were nobody.

Nobody.

Because everyone over the age of sixteen has an internal passport. Without it one can do nothing. Between now and their departure date—perhaps two weeks—the Levins' only identification would be the exit visa, which marked them as an enemy.

EXIT VISA

The rushing wasn't over, nor was the expense. Rumors had come back, via letters from friends who had already left, that the emigrés must spend several months in Rome waiting for permission to enter the country in which they plan to settle. In Rome, the organization known as Joint—the J.D.C. (American Jewish Joint Distribution Committee)—supports the emigrés with biweekly checks. But prices are high, and the checks often don't even cover basic living expenses, and those 90 rubles (a bit over $120 per person) that a family is permitted to take out of the U.S.S.R. won't go very far. To be sure that they could survive in Vienna and in Rome, Grigory and Tatyana had to be prepared to sell items they had taken out of the U.S.S.R.: inexpensive Soviet champagne, linens, Russian folk crafts, tea cozies, cameras, ballet shoes—whatever they could buy and get past customs.

The Levins had to run from store to store with their remaining cash, looking for salable knickknacks for Vienna and Rome: more hours of standing on long lines, more shoving through angry crowds of shoppers, more store clerks' rudeness to swallow, more lugging of packages on jammed subways and buses.

They still had to go to Moscow for another frantic round of official errands—more frantic, this time, because they had no place to stay. They couldn't stay in a hotel without an internal passport, so everything had to be done in one day. Perhaps they could stay with some friends, but anyone they stayed with would feel uncomfortable; their very reason for being in Moscow marked them as an "anti-Soviet element."

Their visas had to be stamped by the Dutch Consulate (Holland represents the state of Israel, which has no diplomats in the U.S.S.R.); the Austrian Consulate (the first stop is Vienna); the Ministry of Justice; and the Ministry of Foreign Affairs. All were in widely separated sections of Moscow, each had its own problems, and all had unpredictable lunch hours. To negotiate this maze one must follow the plans charted by those emigrés who have gone before.

Tatyana and Grigory had a map and a plan, sent to them recently by the Goffs, from Rome. They arrived in Moscow at 5:30 in the morning, and followed their map, walking the route for hours to make sure that they could find this ministry and that consulate.

Part One: ENDINGS

It is illegal to take any official documents out of the country except for the officially notarized translations. But certain original documents, birth certificates and so on, can be sent through the Dutch Consulate. At the time the Levins left, emigrés often referred jokingly to the Dutch Consulate in Moscow as an unofficial branch of the KGB. According to the stories told by earlier emigrés, people were once able to bring their dissertations there to have them forwarded to Israel, but the Soviet government protested strenuously. Since the government forbids the taking of manuscripts and typescripts out of the country, it is dangerous to be caught leaving the Soviet Union with a Ph.D. dissertation. At best, the customs inspectors will merely confiscate it, but an unlucky emigré could be locked up and charged with espionage. According to rumor, the Dutch had had a confrontation with the Soviets a few years before. The Soviets accused the Dutch of assisting the emigrés to smuggle secret material (the emigrés' dissertations) out of the country, so the Dutch consul conceded that he would accept only diplomas, birth certificates, and the like.

When Grigory and Tatyana entered the room, the Dutch consul was sitting at his table, staring at his hands, sullen-faced. There was a Russian woman sitting next to him, who shouted at the emigrés like a Gestapo officer. Everyone cowered before her. Tatyana murmured to Grigory, "A KGB bitch!"

"What do you want from the consul?"

Tatyana spoke directly to the consul in English, which he understood quite well, but the "KGB bitch" continued addressing Tatyana in Russian, and repeating Tatyana's English to the consul as though she were translating.

Plan or no plan, map or no map, they simply couldn't complete all their errands in one day. The Goffs had sent them the names of some friends with whom they might be able to spend the night—pleasant, old-fashioned Moscow intelligentsia who lived in the oldest and loveliest part of Moscow, the Arbat, with its graceful wooden houses (now subdivided into small apartments), and large, beautiful trees in their autumn colors.

Tatyana and Grigory told the Goffs' friends that they had come to Moscow to see an editor about publishing one of Grigory's scientific papers. At one point in the evening, as they were having some coffee, Goff's name came up in conversation. The host set down his coffee with an impatient gesture.

"Now there's a fool!" he said, shaking his dead in dismay. "A great job, a fine career, and he goes and emigrates. Who and what will he find in the West? He's got a Russian intellect—he'll wither out there!"

. Grigory and Tatyana agreed: "Yes, yes, poor fellow, went off half-cocked—" Everyone at the table nodded sagely. The host and hostess were not Jews, of course.

The next morning, when Grigory and Tatyana left the house to finish their errands in Moscow, they were both struck by a wave of melancholy. Lovely old Arbat, early September, cold autumn sunshine. Tatyana said, "Look, Grisha! It's real Russia—those broad, trees with their autumn colors. And the houses! They must have been absolutely stunning when the Moscow merchant princes lived in them.

"Yes," Tatyana mused, "it's hard here in Russia, but at least we know each other, we know people of our own kind here, we can enjoy their society. God knows what we'll find over there, in Europe, in America. God knows . . . maybe we'll have to be strangers for the rest of our lives, with people who are different, who can't understand us. So different . . ."

Back to Leningrad. All furniture sold; almost all clothes sold; debts paid; visas stamped and ready.

On September 8, they took their pile of suitcases and dragged it all to the customs office, where a team of three or four officials emptied each case, felt the seams of every piece of underwear, ran wires through the hems to prevent Grigory and Tatyana from smuggling diamonds out, and counted all the pots, pans and utensils the Levins were taking for their cooking in Vienna and Rome.

The following afternoon, Tatyana's mother came to Grigory's parents' apartment to say good-bye. She didn't want to see them off at the airport because she was afraid the KGB would spot her. Zinovy Levin was in an expansive mood, he was already making preliminary plans for his own exit-visa application. He smiled at

Lyudmilla Petrov and said, "Admit it for once: Grisha and Tanya are doing the right thing."

Lyudmilla raised her eyebrows nervously, and spoke sharply.

"Wrong, Zinovy! I'll admit no such thing! I consider myself loyal to the Soviet state and to our Party."

Tatyana glared across the table at her mother. "Loyalty! You're scared. Your kind of people—you're just scared that you'll lose your little bit of paradise!"

"No! I'm loyal . . ."

"It's all damn hypocrisy, that loyalty to the state!" Tatyana was leaning over the table, staring across at her mother, and shouting into her face. "Hypocrisy! When the Party sent the two of you to Poland you were very cozy there, and you'd have been happy to stay *anywhere* in Europe rather than the Soviet Union. *Anywhere!* Damned hypocrisy and lies—"

"Stop it! You know I'm loyal. I won't listen to this!" She stood up very straight and turned to her granddaughter, Lyuba, who was sitting next to her. She bent down and kissed Lyuba's head, and whispered, "My sweet little girl, be happy in your new life—" grabbed her coat, and strode out.

In the moment of silence after the firm snap of the door, Lyuba looked around, then up at Tatanya.

"What new life?"

That evening, there was a going-away party at Zinovy and Olga's apartment. Grigory was exhausted; Tatyana was shaken from the battle with her mother. What will happen tomorrow? Will they suddenly be stopped on some pretext? Will the government suddenly change the rules? Several old acquaintances didn't come to the party. Too risky. But quite a few new people came, asking questions: How? When? Where? Who should we talk to? Write us! Show us the ropes! So, Tatyana thought, we're not the last to go through this hell.

On September 10, at 11 A.M., many friends and Grigory's family were at the airport, saying good-bye, throwing kisses, calling out, "Don't forget! Write! Tell us everything! Good-bye."

The plane was due to leave at 1:30 P.M.

Grigory and Tatyana walked past a counter for a customs check

81

of their carry-on luggage. Now they were separated from their friends only by that counter, but if they so much as reached across to touch somebody's hand the officers would grab them: they might be passing diamonds.

Grigory and Tatyana climbed the stairs to an outdoor balcony. In the strong, cold Leningrad wind, they looked down at the crowd of well-wishers, standing now outside the building. There was one friend with a guitar, yelling to them, his mouth wide, trying to outshout the wind. Scattered around the cluster of well-wishers were officers, KGB men, and armed soldiers. The bus driver called to the people to come in. Their friends began to sing, and fragments of their voices floated past the balcony. *Do-svidánya . . . proshtchay . . .*

Chapter Three:
Mendelyevitch

The mid-1920s. Alexandr Gorelsky's Grandfather Naum had been forced to turn from the scattered shards of the Moldavian and Ukrainian Jewish communities. All of his training—that intricate, delicate weft of Talmudic discourse; the clarity and breadth of Maimonidean dialectics; the daily, nightly rhythms of psalm and benediction—all of Naum's rabbinical lore and life were henceforth Naum's alone, private, unshared. In this new life, for friends and sons alike, he was simply an Odessan pharmacist.

Far off in the north of Russia, Zinovy Levin was in public school cramming math, chemistry, Lenin's speeches, Marxian materialism. The little Yiddish he had learned in childhood was becoming hopelessly confused with the German he had begun to study as a budding chemist-in-training, while textbook Leninism leached away the memories of his one brief childhood year in a Jewish religious school.

But others did not bend so easily. During this same period, in the late 1920s, on the edge of the city of Mogilyov, there was a small farming settlement where a Jewish widow, Nekhoma Mendelyevitch, did odd jobs. In addition to her small salary, she was given a bit of milk, cheese, and produce to take home to her children in the town.

Lenin was dead two years, and Stalin had not yet seriously begun the enforced collectivization of all Soviet farms. A few years later,

Nekhomah wouldn't dare go near the farmlands; teams of armed Party workers were sent to force the peasants to work communal plots from which the government exacted all the produce, leaving millions of country people to die of starvation, while millions of others were executed for resisting the "reforms."

But that lay in the future, and in 1926 Nekhoma was still able to bring home a little money and some food. The food didn't last long, because her oldest son, Nissen, was in the habit of feeding the *Shabbes* guests, the strangers he brought home every Sabbath from one of the few remaining synagogues in town. It was more like a hut than a synagogue; most of the shuls in town had been closed by the local Party committee, and those still functioning were under close surveillance.

Every Saturday Nissen returned from praying at the shul with a motley retinue, old Jews, young Jews, without jobs, without food, and no way of getting either. One Saturday, for example, he brought home a thin, graying, beanpole of a man named Shloymeh. Shloymeh wandered with his wife and children from town to town, where he did odd jobs for the local Jews. He earned barely enough for food, when he was lucky, and then moved on; in this way he kept his children out of the new Soviet public schools. He adopted this dangerously illegal itinerant life specifically so that he could be free to educate his children to be Jews. Attendance in the Soviet public schools was absolutely compulsory for all children, and the atheist indoctrination was designed to destroy what Shloymeh was determined to preserve. If Shloymeh were caught keeping his children out of school, especially to teach them religion, he would lose custody of them, and could ultimately be imprisoned or killed.

Every Saturday Nissen took his guests to the cold-cellar to give them some milk, cheese, a bit of whatever was there. It was a ritual that Nissen had started when he was thirteen years old, during the time of the civil war. In those days he had been known as a prodigy, a learned son of a learned father. He was a student of one of the leading rabbinical scholars, but his teacher had since disappeared. He had probably been shot.

Nissen still continued the family tradition of scholarship. He studied behind locked doors for part of each night and on Sundays, but on weekdays he went off with his Russian fellow laborers to work in a construction gang. They called Nissen by his Russian name, Anatoly—Tolya, for short—and knew him as a brawny guy who was skillful with his fists and had an easy laugh. He was a good worker too, even though he was a Jew, but he seemed to be a bit feebleminded. Well, not exactly feebleminded, maybe a bit silly in the head. Everybody was used to Tolya's lapses; sometimes they just couldn't get a straight answer out of him. Even the local Party committee representative used to shrug it off whenever he failed, and he always did fail, to convince Tolya to give up his Jewish superstitions. "You can't talk political theory with a halfwit like that," the Party man would mumble as he left the work area, shaking his head and chuckling. Not with Tolya Mendelyevitch nodding and grinning, and going on about how he might be superstitious but he was still building the Socialist Fatherland!

Nissen was especially preoccupied, one morning in 1927, as he trudged off with his Russian co-workers. He played cards with them over a glass of vodka, he sat with them and applauded the political indoctrination lecture that the Party man gave at the construction site, but his mind was on the rumors.

Earlier that year the government had arrested the Lyubavitcher Rebbe, the leader of one of the major groups of Jewish pietists, the Lyubavitcher Chassidim. The Chassidim were mystically oriented Jews who placed considerable emphasis on union with the Divine through joyous prayer. Although Chassidism was influenced by the Kabbalists, it was strongly populist in nature and had developed a large following through the past century and a half. There were, and still are, many schools of Chassidism, each of which organized itself around a spiritual master, a Rebbe, and was named after the town in which the Rebbe who founded the school had his headquarters. Since each of these schools of Chassidim had a master to whom it looked for guidance, the Chassidim, especially the Lyubavitcher Chassidim, were able offer the best organized and most successful resistance to oppression in Russia and Eastern Europe. Their underground had been active as far back as the first half of the nineteenth century, when Tsar Nikolai the First used to send raiding parties to Jewish villages to capture seven- or eight-year-old boys in order to impress them into the Russian army for twenty-five year terms. Few of the boys returned alive. The Lyubavitcher Rebbe of the time established a network of agents commissioned to contact the soldiers who guarded the children on their forced march to the garrison. The soldiers were bribed to hand the youngest boys over to these agents, and to list them as casualties of the forced march, dead of exposure or cholera. The agents then spirited the children off to be hidden among Jewish families.

These underground networks remained active all through the nineteenth and early twentieth centuries. After 1918, when Lenin's government forced the dissolution of all Jewish educational, charitable, and community activities, the Lyubavitcher Chassidim reorganized their underground for the purpose of secretly preserving and teaching the Jewish religious traditions. At that time, when rabbis, scholars, and teachers were running to the West to escape both the slaughter of the civil war and arrest for spreading religion, the Lyubavitcher Rebbe did not leave. He remained in Russia to see that his secret support system continued to operate, and to help the hidden Jewish schools, the hidden rabbis, the hidden students, and a thinly scattered invisible community. The regime hoped to end these activities by arresting him.

But now Nissen heard rumors that the government had released the Lyubavitcher Rebbe from prison, and would exile him to the West. They had planned to execute him, but international pressure had been brought to bear, and now it looked like they would force him to emigrate. This meant that the Rebbe would have to send his instructions from abroad, a slow and dangerous process. Nissen's constant fear that the secret police would arrest him and his family was alleviated only by his faith that whatever miracle saved the Rebbe would save at least a remnant of his people.

For many centuries, all over the Jewish world, certain basic traditions have remained. Several times a week the Torah scroll is opened before the congregation, and the chapter of the Pentateuch reserved for that particular week is chanted aloud. Since reading aloud from the Torah is a *mitzvah*, a commandment, which all male Jews are required to perform at least once, the honor of fulfilling this *mitzvah* is especially reserved for any young man who has just reached the age of thirteen. This is public testimony that, having become capable of reading and understanding the Torah, he is now fully responsible for fulfilling all the *mitzvos*, the commandments enjoined upon the Jews; he is now *bar mitzvah*.

But in the summer of 1961, when Nissen's son Izak—or Itchik, as they called him at home—reached his thirteenth birthday, there were no handsomely dressed crowds of Jews proudly strolling to the synagogue to admire the bar mitzvah boy's cantillation, as there would have been a half-century before. The angled, crowned calligraphy of the Torah scroll was utterly unknown to the vast majority of Soviet Jews, as were the prayer services, the language of the prayers, and the commandments themselves. As for synagogues, there were a handful still open in the Soviet Union, but who would take his son there for bar mitzvah, and thus demonstrate publicly that he had been flagrantly violating Soviet law by fulfilling the Mosaic injunction to "teach thy children"?

Yet there was the Chassidic underground, and therefore, in that summer of 1961, Izak was prepared for his bar mitzvah. Nissen had been teaching him all he could about Judaism, just as he taught a number of other young children. They met in each other's apartments, where that afforded privacy, and sometimes they would use somebody's one-family "hut" on the outskirts of town. Soviet cities had not yet surrounded themselves with vast apartment developments at that time, so many of these small houses were still standing.

As far as the neighbors were concerned, all the families of Nissen's students were ordinary working-class people. Like Nissen, these Jews avoided social and professional ambitions. Once a man begins to excel, to attain higher position and a more respected station, people are forced to notice him. They watch. The first rule of the underground: never excite curiosity. In the public school, the teachers barely noticed that there were a number of boys who seemed never to remove their frayed cloth caps. The classrooms were usually chilly anyway, and the boys were proletarians, from ignorant homes. Nobody cared much about them.

Izak's bar mitzvah was also carefully hidden. In a private home, where a *minyan*, a prayer quorum of ten men, met often for prayer services, Izak read from a Torah scroll, and a toast was drunk after the prayers. The celebrants were those same families whose children Nissen taught, the narrow circle of those who had mastered the art of invisibility.

Somehow, Nissen had gotten hold of a pair of *tfillin*, smuggled in from Israel, to give to Izak as a bar mitzvah gift, along with a prayer shawl, a *tallis*. As Nissen presented these gifts to Izak, he began to reminisce about his two years in the army, during the war against the Nazi invaders, and how he had never failed to put on *tfillin*, even during the battle of Stalingrad, and even though it had to be done in strict secrecy. One time, a shipment of ammunition had arrived at Stalingrad, and Nissen and the other soldiers had been unloading it for over twenty-four hours, with only a few minutes off to gobble some bread, or to run to the toilet. When Nissen was relieved on the loading line for a minute or two, he ran off to the train platform, where there were some buildings, and looked around for a hiding place where he could put on *tfillin*. He spotted a general standing near an outside wall, not far from the open door to his office, talking through a window to an officer in another room. Behind him Nissen could hear the sergeant calling, so he ducked into the general's room, hid behind his door, hurriedly bound the *tfillin*, prayed for a few seconds, pulled off the *tfillin*, stuck them back in his uniform, and ran out. The general was still there, gabbing by the wall, still oblivious to Nissen, who hurriedly sneaked back to the troops.

The day after Izak's bar mitzvah, Nissen went for a walk with Leib, an old friend of his, an elderly Chassid who had long been involved with the underground schools. Nissen was worried about Izak. He had taught his son as much as he could, but the boy was now at a difficult age. Nissen didn't want to send him to the Soviet public schools anymore; he didn't want the boy to hang around with Komsomol-indoctrinated Party-line atheists and with Russian girls. Something had to be done.

Leib was hesitant to commit himself. Izak was a prankster, full of mischief. He still needed a lot of discipline. It was risky. Of course there was no use talking to Nissen about risk, he was used to taking risks, but was Izak willing and able to take such chances for the sake of his cultivation as a Jew, for his *Yiddishkeit*?

That evening Leib dropped in at Nissen's apartment. He had just been invited to attend a wedding in another town and he was wondering if Izak would like to come along. It would be an old-fashioned Jewish wedding, the kind you don't see much anymore, and there'd be lots of young people around. Also, maybe Izak would like to spend the rest of the summer vacation there, with some families . . .

Why not? An adventure—

Izak lived with various people near Kharkov, in the Ukraine, for about a month after the wedding. Every week he stayed in a different home, ostensibly vacationing with children his age. Toward the end of the summer, Reb Sender, the father of the boy with whom he was staying, took Izak aside to have a serious talk with him. Izak stared up at Sender, and Sender couldn't help but laugh: there was an almost monkeylike, whimsical comedy in Izak's attempt to reflect Sender's serious expression. They all liked this boy, even though they called him *der vildeh*, the wild kid.

Wild or not, Izak learned well. He seemed willing to work, and he was anxious to emulate the best qualities in his new friends and playmates—their knowledge of Hebrew, Torah, and Talmud—and not merely their witty, snappy Yiddish, though in fact one's command of Yiddish was important. Russian was used only in the presence of non-Jews; within the group, Yiddish was the language of discussion and debate as well as of ordinary conversation, though the books must be mastered in their original Hebrew and Aramaic. The underground Chassidim were probably the last Jews in the Soviet Union to use Yiddish extensively. As a result, both children and teachers spoke a rough, uncultivated, provincial-sounding Russian, which reinforced the local non-Jews' impression that these were simply backward, ignorant, utterly unimportant people, not worth a second glance.

But the summer vacation was ending soon, and Reb Sender now had to ask Izak for a commitment: was he willing to enter the secret network? The dangers were obvious and real. Also, Izak wouldn't be living in a home, like an ordinary boy: he would always be hidden, passed from place to place, from town to town, an invisible one. There would be food, shelter, and a great deal of study.

Izak had no doubt about his answer. How could he choose otherwise than to join? It was that or become an ignoramus, a barbarian, knowing only Russian, reading only Russian, working only to stuff his belly, and able to teach his children only to stuff their bellies.

Fine. The underground schools would try him out.

"Not even your parents know where you are now, and they won't be told. The less known the better. From now on, if anybody asks, you're an orphan."

In a city in the Western Ukraine, Izak was taken to a small house near an area that had once been cultivated fields, but was now being excavated for an apartment complex. The house was occupied by an aged couple, Pesach and Channah, both in their seventies. Channah was small and wizened, always pulling twists of paper with a few raisins or little pieces of pastry out of her pockets, and offering them to the children. Whenever a new boy came through she would peer at him, ask his name, then offer him some goodies, along with a comment.

"Itchik? Hm! A Kossack, I can tell by the eyes! Here, take raisins—"

Reb Pesach was tall and very thin, with a sparse beard. He called Izak over, and stood straight and silent for a moment, looking at him sternly. Then he handed Izak a *Siddur*, the daily prayer book. He wanted to see how well Izak could *davven*—could chant the prayers—whether Izak knew the subtle rhythmic and medodic twists of the various prayers, and whether he was pronouncing the Hebrew correctly or skimming passages he didn't understand.

Izak opened the book and *davvened* as well as he could. The slight rise and fall of the chant went on for a minute or two, then Pesach interrupted:

"Half-and-half."

"Half-and-half?"

"Half the words you think are important, so you *davven* them. The other half you think are unimportant, so you mumble past them. But they're all important. Every letter is a mystery. Every dot is a fire. Good. Start *davvening* now, every single word clear and slow. You'll do this every morning for an hour or two until the whole *Siddur* flows from you like clean water. In the afternoons we'll study together. Agreed?"

"Agreed."

Part One: ENDINGS

Pesach was not only Izak's teacher, he was also his intermediary with the outside world, and his watchman. It was Pesach who occasionally gave Izak news of his parents and younger brothers, and it was Pesach who kept a careful eye on Izak's contacts and conversations with others in the town, on those rare occasions when they visited people or entertained visitors themselves. He taught Izak how to avoid talking and acting in ways that could give too much information to outsiders. Izak's ability to keep secrets was periodically tested. He soon learned to maintain his cover—that he was a visiting relative—with all but those who worked with him.

One day in October, while Reb Pesach and Izak were having their cold baked potatoes with herring, Pesach told Izak he would soon be handed over to another teacher, Reb Yossel Sheynes.

Too long in one place is dangerous.

About a month and a half later, in December, Yossel Sheynes arrived at Pesach's house. He was roughly the same age as Pesach, but he looked much younger. He was broad-shouldered, though a bit stooped, and had a round, florid face. As they walked toward Yossel's house, he bought Izak a glass of sweet-flavored soda, something Izak hadn't thought of since he had lived at home, and had rarely been able to afford even then.

Izak asked Yossel for news of his family, and Yossel told him that the public school had sent a woman to Nissen's place to ask why Izak wasn't in school. Nissen told her that Izak had been sent to live with relatives in Riga, Latvia. She simply wrote down that Izak was acounted for, and it seemed to have been forgotten.

"I'm still an orphan?"

"Don't forget."

It was dark, ice cold, probably near dawn. Izak felt something on his shoulder.

"Izak . . ."

Vaguely, in the moonlight filtering through the frosted window, Izak could make out a white shape floating near his pallet. Again he felt something on his shoulder. It was a hand, grasping him. He sat up stiffly, in one movement, almost a leap, but then he recognized Yossel Sheynes's voice, and saw that the white shape was Yossel's beard.

"Six o'clock, Izak. *Mikveh*."

Mikveh, the ritual bath originally commanded in the Torah, then elaborated in the talmudic commentaries, had always been a central ritual of the Jews. But those ghetto bath houses that had met Jewish religious prescription by being supplied with fresh water had vanished from the land within a few years after the formation of the Soviet state.

Only after total immersion in the *mikveh* was a Jew considered spiritually cleansed enough to welcome the Sabbath, on Friday evenings; only after such purification was a woman available to her husband after the menses. Many Chassidim had long been in the habit of beginning every day with immersion in the *mikveh*, so that their prayers, as well as the ordinary activities of the day, could be offered up in purity.

As Izak recited the preliminary morning prayers he wondered how they could have built a proper *mikveh* right under the authorities' noses. Then he followed Yossel Sheynes out through the crunching frost. It was just before first light, the motionless, hard, predawn cold of a Russian winter. As they walked along the banks of a stream, Izak was watching for the shape of some small building, the *mikveh*, well masked among the trees. Yossel stooped to pick up a heavy branch. A thin, glassy sheath of ice slid from it, like a stiff, crystalline snakeskin, and shattered on the stone-hard ground. Suddenly the old man hefted the stick over his head, not at all like a man in his seventies, and brought it down in a two-handed blow against the ice layer on the wide portion of the stream at their feet. The eastern horizon showed the first light now, and the blue-white ice sheet crazed, split, and tilted, exposing the glimmering dark surface of the frozen water.

"The *mikveh*!" Yossel said proudly.

Of course! It met the ritual requirements: it was clean, natural, moving water.

"In!" And dropping off his outer garments, Yossel Sheynes plunged into the burning-cold water. Izak jumped in after him, immersed himself for the merest instant, lifted his head to recite the blessing, and leapt onto the shore. Yossel sent him home to warm up and to begin his morning prayers, his *davvening*, but the old man himself stayed in the *mikveh* for a while longer.

* * *

Part One: ENDINGS

From December 1961 until the following March, Izak lived with Yossel. Every morning began with the *mikveh*. Then, at home, Yossel put on his *tallis* and *tfillin* and *davvened* for six hours. Izak had never seen anything quite like Yossel's *davvening*. For six hours Yossel would rock back and forth, concentrating on the words until his entire body seemed wrapped in the prayers, in the modulations of the chanted words, and ultimately in the melodies alone.

After lunch, Yossel usually had Izak recite a chapter of the Pentateuch, with some of the main commentaries, over and over until he had a good part of the chapter memorized. Later in the afternoon they read and discussed Chassidic philosophical texts. These works could not be printed, bought, or sold within the Soviet Union. Although they had been written generations, even centuries in the past, they expound mystical religious philosophy, and were therefore forbidden. Occasionally, the Soviet government has tried to appease religious adherents to Russian Orthodox Christianity by allowing some Bibles to be printed, or by allowing a priest to lecture, but such concessions have never been extended to the Jews. Moslems on Soviet territory—in Soviet Central Asia—have even been permitted to train new clergymen, a necessary concession to Arab sentiment in the Middle East. But mere possession of the Hebrew and Aramaic texts that Izak and Yossel studied could have resulted in prison sentences, especially since many of these books had been smuggled in from Israel or America.

A few weeks later, Reb Pesach unexpectedly came to Yossel's place late in the evening to transfer Izak once again. Izak and another boy would now be staying with a house painter and his wife, whose grown sons had long since moved to other cities. In case Izak or the other boy were spotted there, the story was to be that they were the house painter's grandsons. Every day two or three men, also ostensibly in the construction trades, would come to the house painter's place to teach the boys.

In addition to Pesach's usual admonitions to Izak that he stop fidgeting so much (". . .Maybe you'll sit still and quiet, like a real scholar. Why not? What's another miracle? . . ."), he had one serious piece of advice for Izak: "You'll be going to the stream with the other boy maybe an hour or so after Yossel breaks the ice. Don't just jump in and jump right out again. Some new neighbors are living near there, and they'll have to think you're one of those cold-weather-swimming fools. Athletics, you understand? The *goyim* believe in such things. So after you say the blessing the two of you can splash around for a couple of minutes."

Izak remained with the house painter for fifteen months. He was approaching his fifteenth birthday. On a mild June evening in 1963, almost two years after Izak had left his family, the house painter returned home with the news that Izak and the other boy would be leaving right after they'd had something to eat. He would take them to the *farbrengen*, the Chassidic communal gathering, and from there someone else would take charge of them. They'd probably go to one of the actual yeshivas. So far, they had only been receiving their preliminary preparation, but two things had been ascertained: they could learn, and they could be trusted.

That evening they were taken to a building with a large, windowless basement room, in which fourteen to fifteen teenagers and several dozen adults were sitting at three long tables arranged in a horseshoe. Most of the people were chatting, others were reciting Psalms or *davvening* quietly. Several older men, including Reb Yossel Sheynes and Reb Pesach, came in and sat at the shorter table forming the end of the horseshoe.

The room became noisier as more people arrived, walked around, dragged chairs from one spot to another, leaned on the tables to catch what someone several places away was saying, or excitedly quoted passages of the Talmud to one another from memory, arguing the text in the traditional back-and-forth recitative.

Barely audible in the skein of voices, Izak noticed Reb Pesach's dry, thin timbre in the first floating, almost keyless notes of a *niggun*, a traditional Chassidic chant. Within seconds, everybody was joining in the song, which had no words except *aya-a-ay*. But those sounds alone seemed sufficient. Izak had often heard Reb Yossel sing this wordless *niggun* in the first light of day, just before he *davvened*. On those mornings, Yossel's oddly boyish voice always seemed to find new adornments in the melody.

But now it was different. Some of the men struck the table, slowly and steadily, as they sang. Others swayed back and forth to the same rhythm, their eyes closed, their heads tilted slightly, their brows drawn together as they sang, as though each were trying to fathom some stranger's words in his own song. As the *niggun* rose out of this crowd of breathy, cracked, untuned voices, its trills and adornments were leveled away, and it became simple and strong. They sang it over and over until it seemed to lose both beginning and end. After a while, Izak couldn't say just how long, the voices quieted down, then stopped.

Yossel Sheynes leaned back in his seat, sighed loudly, looked around, and smiled. Everybody watched him. He leaned forward and pointed to the small cup in front of him.

"Everybody has?"

There were rows of these little cups on the table, and large vodka bottles were being passed around. Someone handed a cup of vodka to Izak, and all quickly recited the blessing that ends ". . . for all things came into being at His word." Yossel called out a toast: "*L'chayim!*"

"*L'chayim! L'chayim!*" echoed all around the room, and everybody downed the vodkas. As Izak fought for his breath, somebody shoved a cold baked potato into his hand. "The blessing—don't forget the *b'rocheh!*" Izak gasped out the proper blessing and swallowed a chunk of potato to put out the fire.

The room quieted down, and Yossel began to speak.

"About thirty-six years ago, when the previous Rebbe—may his memory be a blessing for us and for all Jews—when he was driven from Russia, he instructed us to be Jews in spite of everything. One of his oldest Chassidim told us we should be 'dry logs.' So all right, we knew what a Jew is, we can try to be Jews, but 'dry logs'? So he said that the founder of Chassidism, the holy Baal Shem Tov, may his memory be a blessing, used to say that you can't set a wet log on fire, but if the dry logs are burning right, they'll get the wet logs going . . ."

This was Izak's first *farbrengen*. He had heard many learned Jews giving lectures and discourses before. The underground Chassidim maintained the old Jewish tradition that no joyous gathering was complete unless someone stood up to speak a few "words of Torah," usually a brief analysis of some passage in the Scriptures or in the talmudic commentarial literature. But the *farbrengen* was a special invention of the Chassidim. Izak had been taught that in a *far-brengen* the singing, the vodka, and the snacks are as important as the speech of the wise, because they wrap his wisdom in joy.

He was glad that Reb Yossel would be the speaker. Although Yossel was a keen scholar, he preferred to reserve his talmudic analyses for other occasions. At *farbrengens* he concentrated on recounting tales of the *tsaddikim*, the righteous masters of the past. Izak had lived and studied with Yossel long enough to know his style. Yossel belonged to that old Chassidic tradition that revered stories and parables almost as deeply as sacred texts. According to that tradition, the stories of the great Chassidim could spark something in a person's soul.

As Izak mulled over the metaphor of the dry logs, he felt soothed by the embracing warmth of the image, even more than by his sip of vodka. But he pulled himself out of his reverie to listen to Yossel.

". . . Rabbi Levi-Yitzchok of the holy community of Berditchev, maybe a hundred fifty years ago, went to some Jewish merchants a few hours before Passover started. 'You have silk?' he asked. 'Sure we have silk.' 'You have bread?' 'What! Bread? On Pesach? Tfui! No bread!' And Levi-Yitzchok lifted his hands—like this—and he cried out, 'Oy, the Jews! Such a nation! The Tsar sends a hundred thousand soldiers and police to forbid us from trading in silk, and we have silk; the Torah says *no bread!* and there's not a crumb!'"

The men around the tables leaned back and laughed, and Yossel grinned broadly and nodded. As the people quieted down he went on:

"So, dry logs, another story from the Berditchever. Rabbi Levi-Yitzchok always saw the best in people. Once he came across a Jew smoking on the Sabbath. Smoking! So he says to the Jew, very quietly, 'Maybe you forgot that today's *Shabbes?*' 'No, I didn't forget.' 'Maybe you didn't realize that it's forbidden for a Jew to smoke on *Shabbes?*' 'No, I knew.' 'Maybe a doctor told you that you need tobacco to cure some serious disease, and so you *have* to smoke on *Shabbes?*' 'No, Rabbi, I'm smoking just for pleasure.' And the *tsaddik*, Levi-Yitzchok, looks up at heaven, again lifting his hands—like this—and he cries out, 'Oy, *look* at this Jew! No matter what I do, I can't get him to tell a lie.' "

Over the laughter around the tables Yossel called out, *"L'chayim!"* and the crowd responded, *"L'chayim! L'chayim!"* and dashed down another splash of vodka. One of the younger men, a few seats away from Yossel, banged his hand against the table and started singing another *niggun,* a more joyful one this time, and again everybody joined in.

When most of the men had quieted down, there were three or four at the far end of Izak's table who refused to stop singing. Yossel was about to start talking, but they began a new *niggun—aah-yada-daah—*banging on the table in unison. Yossel laughed and shrugged, and began to sing along with them, and then the rest of the men sang. Finally the room quieted down, and Yossel said:

"Nu? So, my dear dry logs, what's to be done? Is it possible to sing together if nobody else knows the song? So we teach others the song! And we study, and learn, as the Creator of the universe told us to do, but what's the good if we don't teach what we learn? In the Talmud, in the section called 'Chapters of the Fathers,' *Pirkey Ovos,* it stands written, 'If I don't do it for myself, who will do it for me? And if I do it *only* for myself, what am I anyway? And if not now, when?' That means, if I don't study the endless secrets of the Torah, who will study it for me? Because a Jew who doesn't study is like a man who doesn't eat. His heart will shrivel and die. No one else can eat for him. And then it says, if I learn only for my *own* learning, what am I? I'm a hidden loaf in a land of famine: I must teach what I learn or everything around me will blacken and rot, and so will I. And if not now, when? When? When all the children have joined their fathers in the grave? When there is no ear to hear? *When?"*

In the pause, someone came in and sat next to Izak. Most of the men hardly noticed him, but Reb Yossel leaned forward and half-whispered to him, "Mordechai, take a glass, make a *l'chayim."* The newcomer quickly took a cup of vodka that someone reached out to him, mumbled the blessing, quietly said, *"L'chayim,"* lifted his cup, and drank. The others murmured, *"L'chayim,"* a few of them lifting their cups to the newcomer, and then turned back to Yossel.

"So, my dear friends, my teachers, my masters, so, the Rebbe told us, thirty-six years ago, that we might soon be the only remnant. The others are gone, forgetting, forgotten."

There was another pause. Izak wondered why Yossel had allowed himself to be distracted so easily by the latecomer, Mordechai, just as he was getting to the most serious part of the sermon, for the storytelling had blended into the sermonic style that Izak knew well. Now that Yossel had come to the tragedy of their near extinction, which might still befall them at any time, he was obviously about to conclude by inspiring the assembled teachers and students to greater efforts, greater devotion.

But Yossel merely lifted his eyebrows, smiled an almost mischievously innocent smile, and began to sing a Chassidic children's melody, a traditional parting song. The whole room joined in but quietly, lightly, almost gaily, without the driving, dark force of the other *niggunim*. As they sang, Mordechai, the latecomer, turned to Izak and said, "Listen, Izak, after the *farbrengen* you'll come with me. Don't forget."

"Come with you? Where? Back to the house painter?"

"Sha! What house painter! He just got rid of a couple of grandchildren who visited him until he was blue in the face and sick of all such pests. Tfui!" And Mordechai laughed, "You're going to the yeshiva, of course, to learn to be a person instead of a monkey! Did you think we would abandon you in your condition of ignorance? Sing! Sing!"

A few days after the *farbrengen*, Izak was put on a plane to a city in Soviet Central Asia, to "visit relatives." There he lived and studied in a small house, with six or seven other boys. After several months he was taken to another town, thousands of kilometers away, in Moldavia. Here he lived with a handful of boys in a private house that had a long narrow backyard, which the boys used for exercise and fresh air, and a stream nearby that served as a *mikveh*. One day, almost six months later, Izak was going over a passage in the Talmud, chanting it repeatedly until he had it memorized, and was being questioned by another boy on the logic of the *shayleh*, the talmudic question at issue, when Shura, the man whose family occupied the house, opened the cellar door and whispered, "Scatter!"

Izak froze for an instant. The other boys were out the door already, heading toward the back fence, pulling on their coats. Izak's heartbeat was a quick, rhythmic roaring in his ears. As he ran the first few strides from the house he heard loud voices from inside. Shura and his wife were calling out to each other, from room to room:

"Isn't that someone at the door, Shura?"

"What's that? You heard a knock? Can you get it, Ida?"

"I don't have my shoes on."

Izak ran at a crouch, in case the neighbors were watching, and pounded toward the back fence. He saw the last of the boys disappear over the left-hand corner of the ridge of the fence. He took the right-hand corner, which was hidden from the outside by a thicket of bushes. The branches would still be bare at this time of year, but if he could lie still on the dark, snowless ground, he wouldn't easily be spotted. If the searchers, whoever they might be, were knocking at the door already, they might have someone watching the grove behind the fence.

As Izak approached the fence, his throat and lungs were burning, and it seemed to him that his rasping breath could be heard by all the neighbors. He grabbed the corner of the fence ridge and hoisted himself over without letting his shoes bang against the slats. He tried not to look around—he felt somehow that to see would mean to be seen—and tumbled straight to the base of the fence. His face and the back of his neck were stung by stiff twigs, and he found himself huddled on his right side on a layer of half-rotted leaves, surrounded by the stalks and twigs of a mass of wild-grown privet. He closed his eyes, and lay there as still as he could. All he could hear were the stertorous rasp of his breathing and his roaring, pounding pulse.

After a few moments Izak opened his eyes and tried to look around without moving his head. If he peered down along his nose and slowly lifted his gaze toward his eyebrows, he could see the beginning of the woods and the back fences of several houses that lay at right angles to Shura's house. The area seemed completely deserted. The other boys must have been well hidden among the trees. The corners of the fence were not within his line of sight, and without moving his head he couldn't tell whether the police—or whoever the troublemakers were—had sent people to look behind the house. Izak wanted desperately to look. He began to suspect that a certain dark blotch, just a fraction of a degree beyond his range of vision, might be a KGB man leaning against a tree, vastly amused at this half-grown Yid, not even sixteen, who thinks he's invisible. Izak had met enough survivors of round-ups and arrests to know how it was done: at any moment the shadow would detach itself from the tree, move toward him with a rapid stride, and a shoe would smash into his face, half lifting him off the ground, as the sharp shout rang out, "*Ruki nazad!*" "Hands behind your back!"

Izak clenched the muscles of his neck to stop his head from moving to look at the KGB shadow, until finally his neck and shoulders were trembling. Maybe they're like snakes, he thought. People say that snakes can't see their prey if it doesn't move. Maybe the shadow is only a shadow, or a tree trunk, or anything but a *ka-gey-bist*, a KGB man.

Two figures suddenly entered Izak's field of vision, about fifty feet away. Every muscle in his body thrummed for an instant, even before he realized that anything was there. As he stared through the latticework of privet branches rising crookedly out of the ground like long, jagged wheel spokes, his first impression was of two squat, moving sacks topped with angular black shapes.

Two middle-aged women with black kerchiefs walked through the rear gate of one of the neighboring houses, cut across the near trees, and passed within twenty feet of Izak, arguing about something in the local Moldavian dialect. The only words Izak caught were some family terms: "—Aunt Maryasha . . . husband . . . stupid son-in-law—" Then they were gone. The shadow had not moved, nor had the women glanced at it. It was just a shadow.

Izak knew that if this were a real raid there would certainly have been men at the back. Still, those things were unpredictable. Best to lie still. Say *tehillim*—the Psalms of David. Izak lay still and started to chant the Psalms soundlessly, though he tried to imagine the voice and the chant clearly as he moved his lips. As the hours passed he used this exercise to avoid thinking about the painful cramps in his muscles, the shudders of cold passing through his body, and his swollen bladder.

Before nightfall was due, the low cloud cover that darkened the sky combined with a wispy fog to render almost everything indistinguishable. Suddenly, Izak heard Shura's voice. He seemed to be talking quite casually with is wife, Ida. Their voices became louder as they approached the back fence from inside the yard.

"Ach! It's lucky we've got a warm stove in such weather! No use standing around out here, Ida." And the voices drifted back toward the house.

All clear.

Izak rose slowly from behind the bushes, painfully climbed into the backyard, and limped like a hunchback into the house. Soon the other boys came straggling in furtively, shedding clods of half-frozen mud and leaves as they came.

"Eat quickly, boys. Eat quickly and say the blessing. Tonight we bury the books."

Shortly before midnight, the moonless dark of the yard was pierced by a single point of light, a small candle lamp balanced on the edge of a large, deep hole not far from a tangle of bushes. As the almost invisible figures of two or three men, standing near the hole, put their shovels aside quietly, Shura tapped the rear window of the house, and the boys began to haul out the cartons they had been packing all evening. Each sealed box contained religious books— Bibles, prayer books, commentaries, philosophy—well wrapped in waxed paper. After the last carton was tucked into the ground, and the hole was filled, leveled, and camouflaged with sod and dry leaves, Shura gathered the boys together in the house.

"Tomorrow you'll be split up into two groups and taken to two different houses. We don't want you here if anybody comes back to do more investigating. Today a couple of plainclothesmen came to the door to find out who's living here. They asked a few questions, but I don't think they found anything too suspicious. Meanwhile, in case they're on to something, you'll be gone. After a week or two we'll get most of you out of this town for a while, but not until we're sure that there's nobody keeping watch at the stations."

The next day, Izak was brought to a cellar used for storing fruit, in a small house in the same town. The boys' usual teachers stayed away—the decision had been made to lay low, to wait and see—so the boys had to study by themselves.

There were four boys in this cellar, from fourteen to sixteen years old, and they began to find it difficult to sit still after the first day of studying without their teachers' discipline. On the second day, Izak found a box of apples that were being stored in the cellar. He took two of them out of the box and started to practice juggling.

On the afternoon of the fourth day after the raid the door to the basement swung open, and two men entered and stopped in the open doorway. They were graying, but muscular, and were dressed in heavy, grease-stained workmen's coveralls. Both of them were experts in Talmud, and taught the older students. Two of the boys, who happened to be sitting across from one another, suddenly began debating a talmudic question. At that instant, the third boy began to recite slowly, from memory, a passage from the *Likutei Amarim*. The men in the doorway hardly noticed these three boys. What caught their attention was Izak diving toward an empty chair with a volume open in front of it, while three apples seemed to hover five or six feet off the ground for an instant, then fell through the space Izak had just vacated. Before the first apple had bounced twice, and just as the second apple was about to thunk against the hard dirt floor, Izak's voice was already singing out: "Rabbi Eliezar explains the passage as follows . . . "

Several months later, after Izak and the others had been scattered to other yeshivas in various parts of the Soviet Union, Izak was returned to Shura's house. He was sixteen now, and was teaching the younger students, as well as studying. There was soon another close call.

Menachem, a fifteen-year-old, had left to spend a week with some people in Vitebsk. When his scheduled time to return had passed, and he was over a half-day late, the others became concerned about him. Shura warned the boys to be ready for trouble. If the police had become suspicious, and had picked up Menachem, they might have forced him to talk.

Part One: ENDINGS

That night, Yeshaya, a sturdy, white-bearded man of eighty-two, came to Shura's house supporting Menachem on his arm as though their ages had been reversed. Yeshaya, a man to whom command came quite naturally, walked Menachem toward the sofa, and lowered him on to his back while calling for a pot of tea and a coverlet.

The old man leaned back with his cup of tea, and waited for everyone to gather in the room before he spoke. When everything had quieted down, and Menachem seemed to be resting comfortably, Yeshaya told them that a militiaman had come to his door that noon and had ordered him to the police station to identify his goods and his "messenger." He didn't know what it was all about, but he went along without saying a word. At the station he saw Menachem, practically dead with fear. They had obviously just finished searching Menachem's valise, and had found his *tfillin*. When the police demanded that Menachem account for the presence of those *tfillin*, he said that he was bringing them as a gift to Yeshaya from an old friend of Yeshaya's in Vitebsk.

As soon as Yeshaya understood the game he had no trouble falling in with it. The captain made the mistake of chastising Yeshaya for violating the law on transporting religious articles, which could have landed the boy in prison for three years, if he were one year older, and for following medieval superstitions. Yeshaya immediately saw his opening, and flew into a rage. Shura and the students began to relax, even to laugh a bit, as Yeshaya re-created the scene for them:

"I got good and mad then, and I opened up a mouth to that captain, I can tell you! I gave him such an earache, he'll go through two liters of vodka tonight to kill the pain! Didn't I, Menachem? Didn't I? Wrap the boy up tighter and give him some warm water to drink. He'll be all right."

Yeshaya took a moment to peer at Menachem, whose teeth were chattering audibly.

"Well, I turned to that captain and I told him, 'Look here, Balabanov, don't you dare to lecture me, a man three times your age! I was building this country when no one knew if there'd be a country to build. What have you ever done for Russia? One day we'll probably be hearing that you've been sent away for taking bribes, so don't lecture me! A little respect for an old man!' And then I said to him, 'You plan to lock me up or not? You gonna put an eighty-two-year-old man away? Because if not, I'll take this boy off your hands right now, *with* my *tfillin!*' So the young hero of a captain, he doesn't know what to say. He turns to his lieutenant, and he says, 'Tell the old man we've got to confiscate the illegal religious articles, and get him out of here; this isn't a rest home for the senile.' Hah! Two hours later I went back there, slipped the sergeant a packet of rubles to spread around, and left with the boy's *tfillin*. They're in my coat pocket."

He took a sip of tea while holding one hand up for silence, just in case anyone tried to get a word in while he was sipping. He looked over toward Menachem, who had meanwhile begun to regain a little color in his cheeks. Yeshaya put down his cup and turned to Shura.

"Menachem told me he took a copy of the *Likutei Amarim* with him. He thought he had it in the valise, wrapped up in a shirt, but it wasn't there when they searched him. Whether he lost it or left it home isn't the point. You shouldn't let the boys walk off with books smuggled in from America. I've seen that edition, Shura. It's got "Brooklyn, New York" printed right on the front page. You want those tax-paid assassins to yell 'anti-Soviet' and slap criminal charges on everyone in sight? It wouldn't be just a case of a crazy old man anymore. They'd have a *real* investigation. Be more careful."

Menachem rested in bed for two days, during which he hardly said a word. On the third day he recovered. After lunch, he sat on his pallet and unpacked his valise. His panic of the past few days had lost its force, and he could look back on it with a measure of detachment. He still felt a bit breathless after the shock of seeing everyone safe at Shura's house. When the police stopped him at the railroad station and ordered him to come with them, he thought, "That's the end of it. They must have grabbed the whole yeshiva, and now they've got me too!" And while they were searching his belongings, shaking out each article of clothing, prodding and squeezing everything, he kept thinking of that book. He was sure it had been in his valise, folded into one of his shirts, but he must have left it in Vitebsk. If the police had ever found that book, there'd *really* be . . .

Menachem suddenly yanked his hand out of the valise, and almost leaped off his mattress, as though he'd touched a live wire. Slowly, he reached back into the valise, and took one corner of the rumpled shirt. Yes, it was too heavy. As he lifted it out, carefully, a brown book with imitation-leather binding tumbled out onto the floor. He recognized it by the characteristic worn spots, and there, on the front page, "Brooklyn, New York."

It was a clear, autumn Sunday morning. Izak was now beyond the Soviet compulsory school age. He had his own internal passport and a job, and could now move back with his family. Izak and his parents had just spent their first *Shabbes* together in over seven years, and now he and Nissen went out for a stroll and some talk.

Nissen could see that his son's face had lost a good deal of that immature, elfin quality. His features had sobered somewhat, and had begun to develop more manly lines. But still, when Izak smiled his ears seemed to stand out, as the midpoint of his upper lip lifted a bit, and Nissen could see the old prankish ragamuffin sparkling behind that bookish pallor.

Izak had found a job in a factory, running the machine that stamped serial numbers onto the engine blocks of trucks. After a while he was able to arrange a position as a go-between, or "pusher." Because the Soviet Union has a fully controlled economy, factories produce what—and how much—the government tells them to produce. If there is an increased need for a given product or a given piece of raw material, the suppliers cannot step up production to meet demand on their own initiative, nor can they stop turning out items that are already oversupplied without getting the government to alter its plan. In order to meet the production quotas, factories must constantly be on the lookout for items they need but cannot obtain in sufficient quantity through normal channels. For this purpose industrial managers use go-betweens, people who arrange trades between their own factories and others. Izak's job, then, was to locate industries that were oversupplied in materials or equipment that his own boss needed, and to get it by bartering whatever his factory had in overstock that the other plant needed. It was a job that demanded skill and discretion, because such bartering deals are illegal. They weaken the government's control over the flow of goods, and are seen by Party ideologists as insidious out-croppings of capitalism. Nonetheless, the practice is necessary and common.

But to Izak this job was a gift from heaven. Since he had to spend at least several days a week traveling, he was able to observe the Sabbath and the religious holidays without his absence being no-ticed. Because the Soviet Union operates on a six-day work week, fulfilling the Torah's injunction against working on Saturday poses a constant problem for those Jews who are determined to be ob-servant. Each one must find some gimmick that leaves him free from Friday evening to Saturday evening, and the one excuse they cannot offer is that they are keeping their faith. As Izak and Nissen strolled along the street on this Sunday morning, Nissen's first questions centered around that very topic: how serious were the risks Izak had to take in order to live up to his real obligations, and what did the Rebbe have Izak doing? Directly or indirectly, each person involved in the underground yeshivas felt that he was under the personal command of the Rebbe.

To the various schools of Chassidim, their Rebbes are not simply chief executives, administrators or teachers; they are considered men of special spiritual power and responsibility. The Rebbe's dis-ciples feel that he knows the mind and history not only of each of his followers, but of every Chassid and even every Jew, in the entire world. Indeed, the present Lyubavitcher Rebbe, like his predeces-sor, managed to maintain his communication lines to those Chassid-im in the U.S.S.R., and had long been actively involved in support-ing the underground. It was even possible for some of the under-ground's local issues to be referred to the Rebbe for decision. Therefore Nissen's question—"What does the Rebbe have you do-ing?"—was meant literally.

Here too, Izak's mobility was especially useful. He had to visit a prescribed circuit of *melameds*, those who tutor the smaller children just as Nissen used to do. He checked on what they were teaching, what problems they had, and what they needed to keep functioning safely and effectively.

Izak and Nissen paused in their walk to sit on a bench, so that Nissen could rest his lame foot. Nissen pondered in silence for a few moments, and then asked the question he had been saving for last: "What about leaving?"

To religious Jews such as the Mendelyevitches, Israel is the real native land from which they have been exiled for millennia. Russia, Latvia, Lithuania, the Ukraine, America: these are the lands of the Exile. To Izak, his family, his teachers and his friends, the Land of Israel (not the state, but the Land) is in fact more than a *native* land, it is the *true* land; just as Yiddish-speaking Jews refer to the soul's place of enlightenment after death as the *emesseh velt*, the true world, Israel is the true land, the hidden reality that underlies that illusory geography, that transient and ephemeral scenery through which they have been passing for centuries.

Now that Israel had been established, the Land was solid, real; it was theirs again. The time to partake of the miracle had come, and partaking of it was more than a preference, it was a *mitzvah*, a commandment, and a deed of cosmic import. And since the Soviet government had finally begun to show signs of letting people go, it was beyond choice or convenience; it was their duty to go. But there were conflicting duties. As long as there were still Jews in the Soviet Union, somebody had to stay and teach, and so Nissen rather hesitantly asked, "What about us?"

"The Rebbe sent word back that I shouldn't try to get out until I have a replacement to continue my work. Those of us who can teach, and who can get around a bit, are stretched pretty thin. It could take a few years, Papa. Do you and Mama want to go first?"

"No!" Nissen stood up from the bench. "No, we'll all go together. I'm not leaving any of my children here. As soon as you're able, we'll all go to Israel together."

By the end of 1968, Izak's replacement had been trained, and the handful of students for whom Izak was directly responsible had either emigrated or were applying for visas. At that point, Nissen contacted his relatives in Israel for an invitation. His mother-in-law had been one of a few elderly Jews allowed to emigrate in the late 1950s, and his brother-in-law had already been smuggled out of Russia by the underground. There were said to have been over fifty-thousand visa applications by the end of the 1960s, though only a few thousand visas were actually granted.

In the autumn of 1969, after they had received permission to leave, and had gathered practically all the necessary forms and signatures, Izak suddenly heard Nissen shout from the entrance to their apartment, "We've got to be out of here within a week! Get the tickets. Finish with OVIR—"

Izak couldn't understand what had happened. So far their departure had been attended with less fear and fuss than usual. They were considered to be expendable. Izak was classifed as a semiskilled laborer; his brothers were unskilled, or still of student age; his parents were on pension. Izak's boss had even contrived to keep him on the job throughout the application process.

And now, Nissen was suddenly panicked.

Izak found Nissen limping toward the stove, trembling, his shirt-front dark with sweat. Without speaking, he thrust an envelope into Izak's hand. It contained a small folder that resembled a passport booklet, and an official letter. It was a draft notice ordering Izak Anatolyevitch Mendelyevitch to report for induction into the Soviet army in three days.

Izak had met young Jews who had been taken into the Soviet army in recent years. The more identifiably Jewish they were, the more they had been harassed during their two years of service. Those who had been caught trying to live up to any of the Jewish religious obligations were punished, even imprisoned. And after they were finally discharged from the army they weren't allowed to apply for an exit visa for at least three more years.

Izak had never seen Nissen frightened before. Nissen was pale, his eyes dilated like those of a terrified child. He took the papers from Izak.

"It never happened, Izak." His voice was cracked, dry. "It never came. Understand? Now, we've got a few days to get on that plane."

Part One: ENDINGS

Nissen held the papers over the stove until they began to blacken and flame; he dropped them into an empty metal trash can, added a few drops of lamp oil and a handful of papers, and stood silent, staring motionless through the greasy smoke until nothing was left but shapeless gray-black ash.

Chapter Four:
The Terminal

Roughly three months had passed since Alexandr Gorelsky's visit to the Goffs' apartment in Moscow, where he had met Grigory and Tatyana Levin, and another three months were yet to pass before the Levins would receive permission to emigrate. On this warm May evening in 1975, Misha was groping his way up an ill-lit flight of steps to Alexandr and Zoya's room, where he was to give them some advice on packing. It was now their turn. A few weeks earlier, at the end of April, Alexandr had been called in to OVIR and given his permission to leave, and now Zoya had just received her exit visa.

At the top of the steps Misha found himself in a dingy foyer. There was a small communal bathroom off to the right, a dark hallway leading straight ahead, and another to the left. He turned left and walked down the poorly lit corridor. Several doors to individual rooms opened off the corridor, and at each door the width of the hallway was pinched almost to impassability by the heavy wooden wardrobes that the tenants kept outside their rooms to save a few precious square feet of living space.

Misha had to duck and weave his head to avoid the shirts and linens hanging from the laundry lines stretched across the hall. Toward the end of the corridor he found Alexandr and Zoya's door. Inside, on the edge of a narrow bed, Alexandr was sitting, hunched over, with his elbows on his knees and his cheeks propped on his hands, staring at a great pile of books in the middle of the room. To the right of the heap of books was a minuscule stack of dingy underwear and several pair of unmatching socks. As Misha walked into the room, Alexandr's face brightened in anticipation of some good stories. Misha always managed to pick up something amusing on his rounds. This time it was a new rumor: a woman had told him, with absolute solemnity, that when her cousin arrived in America the year before, he was able to trade a cast-iron frying pan for a used Chevrolet in good condition.

Alexandr laughed a bit nervously. How could there *not* be such rumors, when there was no legitimate, responsible source of information? The Gorelskys, Misha, and thousands of others were passing rumors, intrigued and amused by rumors in the same way children tell stories about sex. There was a driving need for information.

Up until this point Alexandr's emigration had been a shadow of the mind, and had at best the assumed reality of a stage play. It had all *seemed* real—the anguish of the initial decision, the conflicts with Osip and Anna, the humiliation and fear in living as a refusenik—but when Alexandr looked back on it, there was a touch of fantasy about that whole period in his life. What made it even more dreamlike was the fact that Alexandr had experienced the feeling of freedom. The refusenik has so completely failed all expectations that nothing further is demanded of him. He is absolved of all obligations. It is the freedom of the prisoner.

But now Alexandr and Zoya had a future, and that future was making demands: the first, that they decide what to pack, and to pack one must know something about one's destination. So again, that lack of knowledge lent tremendous importance to rumors, for rumors might have a germ of truth that could spell the difference between success and disaster.

Misha had come to help them pack. Some things would be needed as soon as they left, and must be in their hand-carried luggage; other items could be shipped; the rest of their belongings could be sold or given away in Odessa. Obviously, as soon as they arrived in Vienna, where they would spend the first week or two, and then during their several months in Rome, they would need standard survival items, such as clothes, a few cooking utensils, perhaps some medicines. Letters from earlier emigrés had warned that the agencies that assist the emigrés in Vienna and Rome do not always provide enough money to live on, so it would be necessary to transfer funds out of the Soviet Union by taking items to sell in the flea markets of Vienna and Rome. And what should be shipped? They would need pots and dishes no matter what country they settled in. Most of all, Alexandr would need his books. They were the tools of an academic's trade.

Misha's expertise was particularly valuable when it came to the arcana of shipping crates. Even in a big city like Odessa, large pieces of wooden planking had to be bought at a handsome price on the black market. A complex and highly sophisticated science of crates had developed among emigrés. For instance, the black-marketeers who supply the wood might palm off unseasoned lumber on the naive, frightened purchaser. This green lumber would warp during the months spent in transit. One of the current crate rumors maintained that Soviet customs men and shipping handlers expressed their contempt for emigrating Jews by pissing into open knotholes or warp spaces in the packed crates. Nobody could prove it, but to some people it seemed well enough within the realm of possibility to be taken with some provisional seriousness.

In fact, there were rumors on both sides. Most of the non-Jews had heard, and many believed, that the Jews had been hoarding heaps of diamonds, which were stuffed into hollowed out spaces in their furniture, and that those Jews were even using iron-coated, solid gold nails to hammer their crates together. Thus, the worsening economic problems of the Soviet Union could once again be blamed on the plundering Jews.

Misha was able to put Alexandr and Zoya in touch with a man named Yasha, one of Odessa's top crate experts. For a fee, he would come to an emigré's apartment, and just by looking at the belongings he could tell how many crates would be needed, what size they should be, and so on. Misha also contacted a fellow who worked at a lumber yard that prepared planking and scaffolding for construction sites. He would prepare the panels that made up the crates. All that was left was to make an appointment at the customshouse in the freight yard, and then to track down someone with a van, who would hire himself out as a driver—another illegal way that people make money in the Soviet Union.

The appointment at the freight yard was made for the last week in May. About four families arrived just as the yard opened, each trying to be the first in line. The customs inspectors take hours with each family, and there is always at least one group left uninspected at closing time, and told to go home and make a reappointment.

By six A.M. the van was loaded, the wood panels were strapped on top, and dozens of cartons and plywood tea cases were stacked in the rear. As the van pulled up to the waiting guards at the gate of the freight yard, Alexandr craned forward from the rear of the van, where he sat perched on the edge of a heap of boxes, to lean out over the driver's shoulder and identify himself.

"Gorelsky. We're due at the customs office."

"No vehicles without official passes. You'll have to leave."

"We've got an appointment. Gorelsky. At the customs office."

Alexandr had to keep clear of traps. The refusenik is almost a criminal, in Soviet eyes, and he cannot afford to make any mistakes.

Ordinarily, the guard might simply be asking for a bribe, but if Alexandr tried to slip him ten rubles the guard could properly have him arrested. The guard ignored Alexandr's arguments, stepped into the road, and waved two cars through, both crammed with emigrés' belongings; neither one had an "official pass." It was getting late. Maybe that was the ploy: harassment, to prevent Gorelsky from reaching the customshouse altogether. At half-past eight, most of the other families were assembled at the customs shed, but Alexandr was still trying to get through the gate. His clothes were wet with sweat, even though the morning chill was still in the air. After hesitating for a few minutes, he leaned over and spoke to his driver.

"Look, they're not interested in making trouble for *you*. Why don't you just saunter over to the guards and gab with them for a few minutes, and when you're done, see that this ten-ruble bill stays with them."

Ten minutes later they were through the gate, and were pulling up at the loading ramp of the customs shed.

At 9:30, a half-hour late, they heard the click of a bolt, and the long steel portal of the loading dock began to rumble open. A uniformed customs agent stepped out onto the ramp, glanced at a sheet of paper, spit off the ramp into the mud, and called out:

"Gorelsky here? Bring your stuff in."

Alexandr found himself unable to move for a moment.

"Are you bringing your stuff in here or not?"

He broke out of his numbness and started tossing boxes out of the van and dragging them into the customs shed. The agent who had opened the door stood there, hands on his hips, a cigarette clamped in his teeth, and watched. Alexandr was panting and sweating.

"How much stuff you got?"

"Much as I need."

The agent spat the cigarette out and stared at Alexandr for a few seconds before he spoke.

"Don't get wise here, you've still got a long day to spend with us."

Alexandr tried to think clearly for a second, then continued to drag the boxes into the shed. He was conscious of only one clear sensation: the fear that he had just alienated the agent. He hauled faster, if only to drive away the mounting apprehension that there must be at least one KGB operative among the four nondescript customs workers standing in the open shed. How easy it would be for them to plant something forbidden in his goods, and then to "discover" it, and haul him off to jail. It wouldn't be the first time . . .

"Open 'em up."

Box after box was opened, dumped onto the table, sorted and examined. Most of the boxes were packed with books.

"You can't take these books. They're printed before 1951. Not permitted."

"Wait, I've got special permission to take these particular books. See? They gave me this signed permission . . ."

"Shit on your permission. Toss 'em aside."

Book after book, box after box, bed sheets, pillowcases, dishes; everything dumped onto tables, some things put back, others set aside and disallowed.

One of the men let out a low whistle and lifted up a bag of charcoal. The four of them stopped work and stared at Alexandr. He explained that when he bought the samovar, the charcoal for heating it was included in the price, and he thought there just might be room . . . But even while he babbled on about the samovar, he could see that the customs men were convinced there were diamonds hidden in the briquets. Now they would have a bit of fun. The chief inspector pulled out one of Alexandr's newly purchased bed sheets, spread it out on the table, dumped the entire five pounds of charcoal onto the sheet, and began to pulverize the briquets with a wooden mallet. At first he was hammering with the same slow, lazy rhythm with which the whole inspection had been carried out, but within the few minutes the speed and energy of the hammering increased, and soon all the men were pounding at the charcoal as fast and as hard as they could. It was noon already, the air was hot, and the men worked up a sweat from their frantic hammering. Soon their hands were black with pulverized charcoal, and whenever they wiped the sweat from their faces, they streaked their brows, hands, and clothes with black smears. After ten minutes they were finished hammering. The chief inspector loosely folded the sheet full of charcoal—being sure not to dump the black dust on the floor—and tossed the sheet and the charcoal dust into the pile to be crated.

"All right boys, pack it up."

The carpenters began assembling the wooden panels, while Alexandr helped them to arrange the boxes so that everything would fit without breaking. Meanwhile Zoya set out the vodka and cheese they had brought along as an "encouragement" to the customs men, and the men leisurely packed and hammered as they became steadily drunker. Alexandr was unable to drink or eat anything. He was too anxious to see that everything was packed properly, and didn't end up in the pockets of the customs men.

By 2:00 P.M., the men were drunk and tired. The chief inspector reopened the steel door and stood out on the ramp, looking down at the three families who had been waiting outside for six hours.

Part One: ENDINGS

Alexandr and Zoya trudged out, exhausted, and shoved back into the van the ten crates of items that the customs men had disallowed. Most of these items were textbooks and literature printed in the 1940s or earlier, but there were also some dishes and other small valuables that the customs officials considered "antiques." Behind them the next family could be seen—an elderly couple dragging their possessions into the shed through the hot sun. As the van bounced along the rutted freight-yard roads, past the guard box, and toward Alexandr's apartment, he mumbled, "So they'll piss in it . . . !"

Early June: the last day.

Alexandr and Zoya were exhausted by the unremitting hysteria of the last-minute rush. The train was due to leave at 5:20 P.M. At 1:45 they were still not finished packing everything into their five old-fashioned, heavy suitcases, and Zoya's mother arrived with a carton full of medicine bottles, which she insisted that they take. Zoya relented, finally, and dumped it all into one valise, including a half-liter bottle of ether that had been sitting untouched in Ala's office for years.

Meanwhile, Alexandr found that he had twenty-five rubles left over after setting aside what little cash they had for the trip. On a moment's urge he rolled up the bills and stuffed them into the lining of his necktie. The Soviet government allows each emigré to convert ninety rubles into dollars and take them through customs, so Alexandr and Zoya could take something over two hundred dollars. But between departing from the Odessa railroad terminal and passing through customs on the Czech border they would need extra cash.

It was 3:00 P.M. Less than two and a half hours were left, and groups of people were starting to troop into the apartment. The first to arrive was Misha, who brought several friends—those who still acknowledged the Gorelskys' existence. Naturally, many former acquaintances had vanished from their lives, some because of the fear of guilt by association, but many because the emigré's life and thoughts are alien to those who have no plans to leave. When a person receives an exit visa—even earlier, even when he first applies—his relationship to the world changes, and he sees it with other eyes; ordinary Soviet life begins to seem insubstantial and dreamlike to him.

But there were others who flocked to see departing emigrés, who seemed to draw some kind of sustenance from them. First among the group, of course, were the refuseniks, who trailed into Alexandr's room with their hangdog smiles and their sad congratulations. Alexandr recalled how he too had automatically taken on that characteristic look that he saw in their faces: wandering Jews going nowhere.

Then there were the so-called "chronics," like Alexandr's friend, Lev. Those were people who had been planning to leave for years, but who were waiting for that one push, one piece of information, one word that would remove all doubts. Misha couldn't help teasing Lev about his family's indecisiveness.

As soon as Lev walked into the room, which was quickly becoming crowded now, Alexandr heard Misha call out, "Lev! Don't tell me! You finally applied!"

And Lev, half smiling, cocked his head to one side and shrugged. "Well, not exactly. I may be getting a new invitation from Israel . . ."

"What are you waiting for, Lev? You've seen off more Odessa Jews than you will ever in your life eat herrings."

In rapid, breathy speech Lev began what was obviously a time-worn recitation. "You see, my mother can't get my father to apply because he's scared to, so we first have to get the invitation from Israel from the relatives, and then, when we already have it, he'll be convinced to try, maybe, but he's scared because his sister's husband is a full professor . . ."

Lev was considered a permanent fixture at these parties. But there were other familiar faces, people who had been hanging around departing emigrés for years to get some last-minute advice or favor. Alexandr tried to maneuver through the crowd, only half aware of who was talking to him, and drifted from person to person, embracing, nodding, smiling. With every step he took, somebody else pulled him by the sleeve and leaned close to his face for a private word.

"Listen, before you leave I'll give you my cousin's name—her first name. She's remarried now, and I don't know her last name, but she lives somewhere in Iowa, or Ohio, or maybe Idaho. In America. If it's too much trouble, never mind, but it means a lot to me, and if you get a chance . . ."

"Sanya! Over here for a second! You got my address? Pass it on to Israel. I'm shopping for an invitation. I know, I got one a few years ago, but . . . well . . ."

"Alexandr, excuse me. Listen, if you could just drop me a line from whatever country you end up in, I need to know the chances for food-processing engineers in the canning industry there . . ."

And as Alexandr moved through the crowd, it occurred to him that there was only one group not represented: his own family. He absentmindedly glanced at his watch, then stiffened.

"The train leaves in thirty-five minutes!"

For a moment, conversation stopped. Then, all at once, everybody ran out the door, thundered down the stairway and onto the street, shouting and waving for private cars for hire.

"To the railway station. Fast!"

"Ten rubles."

"Fine! Get in, Sanya! Here, grab those bags—"

As the station wagon pulled away from the curb, Alexandr saw through the window that Zoya and the others were getting into several small cars they had flagged down. He again experienced that same unreasoning and uncontrollable rush of fear: Who is this driver? How does he suddenly come to be here? Just by chance? When they finally pulled up at the railroad station, Alexandr was almost breathless with relief, his clothes clammy with sweat.

Ten rubles. Zoya had the money! Damn! All he had were the twenty-five rubles hidden in his tie. So the driver stared, uncomprehendingly, as Alexandr nervously removed his tie and started milking ruble notes out of the lining.

"Run . . . hurry . . . here, I'll take the valise . . . only fifteen minutes . . . is that the train?—"

Alexandr and Zoya ran through the station, surrounded by a phalanx of those friends who had accompanied them from the apartment, and who were herding them up to the platform where there were about a hundred people who had come to see the Gorelskys and other emigrés off on the train.

Part of the crowd detached itself from the main body and started shouting, "Where have you been? The others are on the train already! Only fifteen minutes left!"

As Alexandr and Zoya moved through the crowd, people again began whispering into their ears: "Get me an affidavit—call my cousin in Oklahoma. What do you think? I should emigrate?—" Those who couldn't squeeze in close were calling out: ". . . write us everything . . . tell us . . . give regards . . . remember . . . remember . . ."

And just past the outer periphery of the crowd, moving about nonchalantly, was the sprinkling of KGB people, some of their faces by now quite familiar.

Alexandr and Zoya found themselves just outside the train door, facing the crowd, loaded down with last-minute gifts: melting chocolates, marzipan cake, a few silver-plated spoons that someone had just thrust into their hands. Boarding time was a minute or two away; everybody was shouting, laughing, crying, waving (all but the KGB men, who took it all quite calmly), and somebody—was it Misha?—yelled out, "Next year in Jerusalem! *L'shanah haba'a beYerushalayim!*" The same cry began to break out in other parts of the crowd, and others started shouting, "*Do skórovo svidánya!* See you soon, see you soon! Soon! Soon!"

Alexandr glanced over their heads as he waved and grinned, and in the back of the crowd his eye caught one gray, wrinkled face. It belonged to a small, old woman, standing quite still, gazing at him intently, not waving, not weeping, just looking at him and biting her handkerchief. It was his grandmother, Anna's mother, the only one in his family at the station. Alexandr, as a boy, had always resented this old woman. She was constantly watching him, blocking his willfulness whenever he began to act a bit spoiled, making him do things he didn't want to do. She had always been the spirit and the force that kept the family alive and moving, through wars, persecutions, forced evacuations. Within the past month, Alexandr discovered by chance that this grandmother had been his only supporter when his entire family turned against him. She was the one who had always tried to pressure Osip into freeing him to emigrate.

A few minutes earlier, while Alexandr was moving through the crowd toward the train, she passed near him in the press and touched his arm for a moment, but he was afraid to look at her, and she backed away like a small gray mouse. Now, as they climbed into the train and turned around for a last wave good-bye, he caught sight of her, but he kept his eyes moving across the crowd; he couldn't stop to return her gaze. He was pleased to have achieved a certain numbness, within the past few days, an exhausted state that protected him from all those others, even from himself. But that grandmother, in her gray silence, was liable to crack his armor like an eggshell. He waved to the crowd, shouted something incomprehensible, and then he and Zoya turned away and concentrated on maneuvering themselves through the crowded passageway toward their compartment.

Lore. Every aspect of emigration is learned not from official rule books, bulletins, articles, or information bureaus, but through word of mouth, and with conflicting versions and interpretations. Just as there was the lore of application and the lore of shipping crates, for example, so there is also the lore of border crossings, which is passed on from master to disciple among emigrés who must leave the Soviet Union by train. The crucial question is whether a crossing through the city of Brest entails more sadism from the customs agents than a crossing through Chop, or vice versa. The argument can never be resolved, because the answer depends entirely on who happens to be on duty at any given moment.

Alexandr's tickets took him through Chop, and as he and Zoya sat in their compartment on the first leg of the journey, Alexandr nervously reviewed the directions he had assembled from hundreds of letters and conversations. Each of the several stages of the journey has its characteristic problems and its special survival techniques. The first change of trains would be at Lvov, in the western Ukraine, where the train will stop at platform five; the second, at Chop, near the Czech border, where the customs check occurs. Czechoslovakia is outside the U.S.S.R., technically speaking, but the Soviets control it, so there would be no sighs of relief until after they boarded an Austrian train at the other end of Czechoslovakia, in the town of Bratislava. The next stop after that would be Vienna.

Remember: move fast at Lvov. You have to get your ticket to Chop quickly, so you can beat the crowd, or you won't get a seat on the right car of the Chop train. If you're in the right car, you'll be able to make a dash for it at Chop and get toward the front of the lineup at customs. If you're too far toward the back of that line, you'll miss the direct train to Bratislava, and you'll have to try your luck on the indirect train. A mistake could mean being stuck in a Soviet border town overnight, then waking up, still in Soviet territory, with an expired exit visa. Remember you're in competition with the others on the train. Someone will be stuck.

At Lvov, the emigrés were rushing and straining to drag their baggage down the aisle toward the exit, but time was too short. The train for Chop would leave soon, so they started throwing windows open, sweating and trembling as they hoisted boxes, suitcases, baskets and packages almost too heavy for them even to drag along the ground, and heaved everything out the windows onto the platform.

After they somehow managed to find their luggage on the platform, they had to haul it through long tunnels for what seemed like miles to the main station. While Zoya watched the luggage, Alexandr ran around looking for the ticket window. Almost by accident he noticed a long line in front of a window with a tiny square of paper, on which the words "Chop-Uzhgorod Train" were penciled in with small, smudged letters. Alexandr stood on the line for about half an hour, repeatedly checking his watch, calculating how long it would take to get to the platform, how they would get into the correct car, *if* they got to the right train on time. Everyone on the line had the same thought: "One slip now and we may be stuck in Chop overnight, or on the indirect train . . ."

"No, I can't sell you a ticket for your wife unless she comes to the window with you. No tickets for people not here in person."

"Look, I have both visas here. How could I have her visa if she wasn't around?"

"Go back and get your wife and get back on the end of the line."

"I'll miss the damn train! . . ."

After ten minutes of coaxing, yelling, consulting with supervisors, and looking at his watch, Alexandr finally bought the tickets, ran back to get Zoya and the baggage, and then ran for the train. There was no way for the crowd to walk through the entryways of the train with their baggage quickly enough, so again they had to heave their luggage through the train windows—into the windows this time—then push into the passageway and sort everything out. As they dragged their cases to their seats, Alexandr had to stop several times. His throat was burning from the strain of trying to catch his breath. Zoya suddenly stared at him, frightened:

"We had five bags; there are only four here."

"Are you sure? Which one is missing?"

"The one with the vodka bottles for the trainmen."

Alexandr pushed and elbowed his way against the incoming stream of passengers, burst out of the train, and ran back to the waiting room. There it was—the valise that Zoya had been sitting on while she waited for him to get the tickets. He snatched it away from the gaze of two men, who seemed on the point of walking off with it. When he returned to the train, just before it was due to depart, the conductor wouldn't let him on, because he had left his ticket with Zoya, so he started banging on the windows to catch her eye. He could feel his blood pounding in his temples, and waves of heat washing over his body in time to the pounding. Zoya stared at him through the glass for a moment as he pointed with his free hand to the entry and screamed "Ticket! Ticket!" with a barely audible, ragged voice, mouthing the words as clearly as he could. He got back into the car just as they were slamming the doors for departure.

Chop: a three-minute stop.

Through the open windows, swollen, aching hands again hoisted bags and boxes up against the window frames, and tumbled them out onto the platform. The voice of the conductor could be heard from inside the car: "Come on! Get that stuff out! Clear those aisles! Three minutes and the train moves!"

Alexandr squeezed onto the platform, grabbed a few suitcases, and ran to the closed steel gate of the customs office. The line had begun to form, and several families were already ahead of him. He took his place in line and saved it until Zoya came.

He dropped the suitcases and started going through his pockets frantically. For a few minutes he thought he had lost the 100 rubles he had set aside for the porters and customs men. To mislay the money was a potential tragedy. There are awful stories one hears about the delays and harassments directed at those who don't grease the wheels. A person who has chosen to emigrate is a traitor: open game. Here he stands on Soviet soil without a passport, without Soviet citizenship, and with only an exit visa that will expire shortly. Moreover, he is in a border area, a forbidden zone except to those who are legal residents of the town, or have a visitor's pass from the military authorities. If he misses his train, he is violating Soviet law merely by being there.

Fortunately, Alexandr remembered at the last moment that he had put the money in a hidden pocket.

Customs was due to open in two hours. Forty or fifty emigrés were waiting before the metal gate in an uneven row of family clusters. Next to the door there was an elderly couple, perhaps in their seventies, on their way to join their son's family in Canada. The two of them sat on their valises, exhausted, pale, weak from having to grapple with their heavy luggage almost unaided. Next there was a family with several children. The children were crying, upset by the almost palpable fear that hung over the group and affected everybody. In addition to the predictable fear of the strong hand of authority—for these people were slaves to the whims of even the lowliest railroad employee—there was a growing terror of the future. They had chosen to ignore official Soviet reports that claimed that capitalist countries had dog-eat-dog, knife-in-the-back societies in which the strong quickly trample the weak in the stampede for wealth and power. Indeed, the letters from the West had described difficulties, but the letters were often hard to understand; they spoke of things that sounded odd, even incomprehensible to those who knew only Soviet ways.

One thing they all knew about the West: money could buy security. Cash does for Westerners what good connections do for Soviets. You must have money. All the letters say so. It starts as soon as you get to Vienna, and then in Rome. Bring things to sell! And each one was thinking: "What if the Soviet customs agents just on the other side of this door decide to confiscate my stuff? I'll be at the mercy of an unknown breed of bureaucrats."

The people spent the two-hour wait sitting on valises or standing around, some chatting quietly, most silent. Mothers rocked and stroked the crying children absentmindedly. Ten minutes past the time for the door to open, people were standing up, cracking their knuckles, rearranging their suitcases, sitting down again.

Fifteen more minutes passed. Somebody halfway up the line mumbled, "Whatever it is, good or bad, let it happen already!"

The latch clicked and the door began to squeak open slightly, but before anyone had a chance to move, there was a loud rattling and tramping sound from behind, and a porter rushed past the line, pushing a large baggage cart loaded with ten or fifteen suitcases. The door swung open, and he rumbled past the line, shouting, "Watch out! Step aside!" and was hurriedly followed through the doorway by a family of six—two girls, their parents, and two uncles—and before the people on line could even begin to voice their outrage, the door slammed closed. Now the line reshaped itself swiftly as people jumped up and grabbed their belongings, staring at the door and yelling, demanding fair treatment. "That bastard gets ahead, and now the devil knows what'll happen to us . . . We could rot in prison yet, stuck here in Chop without papers, without a train! . . ."

After a while the gate opened for a brief moment, allowing two families through. Alexandr and Zoya were let in with the third group. They found themselves in a large hall with a long row of tables along one wall. Customs inspectors were standing behind the tables, opening baggage, rummaging through everything, and guards were checking documents. The last of the emigrés to enter the hall sat on some benches and waited their turn to open their luggage.

Alexandr glanced toward the end of the hall and saw that the man whose family had run ahead of the line was pacing up and down, clearly upset. He was tall and heavy, a huge bear of a man, and was pacing alongside the table where all his luggage was laid open. The inspectors were picking through every item with great care. Alexandr suddenly realized that he knew that man. He was an engineer whom Alexandr had helped with some application problems many months before. He walked over to where the man was pacing.

"Gittleman! Something wrong?"

"Oh, Gorelsky, I can't talk about it now, I can't . . ." At that moment a door opened, and a uniformed man called out: "Gittelman, in here!" Gittelman went in. A moment later his wife came out the same door, weeping, her puffy face beet-red: "The girls—they took them to another office—a half hour already . . ."

As Alexandr rushed back to his place on line—he had just been summoned to open his luggage—he heard one of the men behind him saying under his breath: "Looks like a bad shift. There's good shifts and there's bad shifts, and you never know which you got 'til you're there . . ."

After a few minutes a uniformed woman stepped up to their luggage, looked at some of Alexandr's books, rechecked his documents, then reached both arms into a suitcase and stirred its contents completely, as though she were kneading bread dough. She did that to all five suitcases, glanced at a few things, tossed the books back into the valise, and handed back the documents.

"Done. Move along."

Alexandr was amazed that it all had happened so quickly. He noticed that one of the other customs inspectors, an angry-looking young woman with large red hands, was casually tearing all the collars off the dress shirts in somebody's valise. She was searching the linings of the shirts, though she hadn't managed to come up with any hidden diamonds.

Alexandr and Zoya hurriedly crammed the suitcases, and tried to snap them closed as they moved toward the exit leading to the train platforms. The valise with the medicines wouldn't close properly so Zoya was holding it flat in front of her chest. It would have to be rearranged before it would close, but the first objective was to get out of that customs area.

As Alexandr approached the exit he was startled by a loud crash and a scream. He spun around and saw Zoya standing there, frozen with fear. The bottle of ether her mother had packed was lying shattered on the floor, and a foul-smelling, rapidly evaporating pool of liquid spread at her feet. For a moment, everyone in the hall stared at the two of them.

The chief inspector, who had been going through Gittelman's baggage earlier, looked up from his work, stared at Alexandr coldly for a second, then pointed to the wall behind him, where there were some brooms leaning in a corner.

As the train hissed into the station, a crowd of nervous, exhausted people clustered protectively around one or two large baggage carts that were piled high with shoddy, old-fashioned luggage. The slowly moving engine passed the cart itself, and a few of the hardier-looking members of the crowd climbed onto the pile of luggage and grasped the nearest valise handles, preparing to toss everything into the windows of the train.

The train was scheduled to leave in exactly four minutes, and would keep its schedule whether the emigrés were ready or not. As usual, it would be impossible to carry the baggage on through the blocked passageways. As soon as the train stopped, a few emigrés squeezed in and opened some of the windows, and a wave of hysteria began to sweep through the crowd surrounding the baggage on the platform. Feverishly angry and terrified by what they had experienced on the journey thus far, fearful for their safety and for these last few belongings that had come to represent the remnants of their lives, a number of people became wild when they saw other emigrés grabbing their luggage to toss it onto the train. One man was ready to leap onto the baggage cart to attack the others.

"Get your thieving hands off my suitcase! I'll smash your face!"

"Please! Friends!" A balding middle-aged man stood in the shoving, milling crowd with both hands raised above his head and tried to make himself heard. "Please! We'll sort out the baggage on the train, but we only have a few minutes to get on!"

They were momentarily distracted by a valise that missed the open train window, struck the window frame, and split open, spilling a dazzling array of merchandise—underwear, cameras, dolls, ballet slippers, opera glasses, bottles of vodka—all over the tracks.

127

Meanwhile, hands reached out to separate the contending parties, others heaved baggage into the windows, and the rest of the people streamed toward the doors of the train.

Less than two minutes before the train was to pull out, those still shoving the last few suitcases through the windows heard a strange noise on the platform passageway leading from the station. It was the Gittelman family running alongside a rumbling baggage cart filled with their belongings. The cart was clattering at top speed, and Gittelman was yelling, "Watch out! Watch out! No time!" The two small girls were there, pale and shaken, and the mother, almost staggering from the unaccustomed exertion and strain, was unable to speak, her face a flushed, rigid mask. The two uncles were helping to push the cart. Before the cart could come to a complete stop, Gittelman started hurling valises into the windows, regardless of who might be in his way, while his wife herded the girls onto the train.

Inside the train, exhausted emigrés were pawing through the almost impassable heaps of luggage that blocked the passageways. Husbands tried to get their wives and children quickly situated in compartments, with their belongings, and then pitched in to help the elderly, the infirm, or those who had simply come too close to collapse to be able to wrestle with the heavy loads of baggage.

As Alexandr bent and strained to haul an old man's half-crushed suitcase from under a stack of bags, another young man, who was helping to clear some valises out of his way, leaned close to Alexandr's ear and whispered, "Smile for the audience." Alexandr glanced up and noticed an amused group of tall, powerfully built Soviet athletes, bound for a competition in Czechoslovakia, sitting back and grinning from their seats in a nearby compartment.

Alexandr heaved his luggage into the compartment that Gittelman had just stepped into. He heard the conductor shouting at the last of the emigrés to get their suitcases out of the passageway: "Move, you idiots! Where are you Jews running away to anyhow, with all that crap! What you need is to be cleared out with a machine-gun, that's what you need!"

The train budged, jarred slightly, and then the station's columns, baggage carts, and mud-stained concrete drifted slowly backward. Without warning, Gittelman flung open the window, and began spitting out onto the receding platform. He spat quickly, repeatedly, thrusting his large flushed face out past the window frame each time he spat. The train was still moving very slowly. Some emigrés standing in the passageway happened to glance into the compartment, and started yelling, "What, are you crazy? This isn't Vienna yet! They'll haul you off the train, you idiot!"

But Gittelman paid no attention to them or to his wife, who was trying to pull him away from the window. He started bellowing in a tremendous voice that echoed off the ever more rapidly receding platform stanchions:

"I spit on you! I fuck you all!"

A few other emigrés rushed into the compartment and forcibly pulled Gittelman back by the shoulders, but he kept yelling, "I fuck you all!" His head thrust farther out as they pulled his shoulders back, his voice cracked from the strain, "Even the girls you wouldn't spare! Even the girls . . ."

They finally pulled him inside and slammed the window. Gittelman sat and stared straight ahead for a while, as his breathing gradually became less ragged, and he began to calm down. The others drifted away to their own compartments. One of the last to leave turned around at the door and asked, "How long before we cross into Czechoslovakia?"

"What the hell's the difference?" Gittelman barked. "They can squeeze your guts out there, too!"

At the other end of Czechoslovakia, in the town of Bratislava, after a day and a half of travel, the group of emigrés dragged themselves exhaustedly through the usual train-changing procedure, to board the train to Vienna. Although there was less rushing this time, their utter fatigue made this change of trains as difficult as those that had come before.

Shortly after the train left the Bratislava station, and before the whistle stop at the Austrian border crossing, the Czech porters came through the train and panicked the emigrés—most of whom had been fast asleep—by demanding loudly that they pay a "baggage-handling" fee, either in dollars or in Czech koruny. Everyone knew that there was no such fee; nonetheless, the porters threatened to have those who didn't pay thrown off the train before they crossed into Austria. The emigrés were muddled by fatigue and fright, but one level-headed fellow quietly opened his valise and handed several small bottles of vodka to the porters. The rest followed suit; they had been warned that the "liquid currency" would be needed somewhere along the line.

After the brief whistle stop at the Austrian border, Alexandr dug some crumpled pieces of memo-book paper out of the bottom of his pocket, laboriously flattened them, and started deciphering and rewriting them. These were the cryptic, coded notes he had taken before leaving Odessa, to record some of the missions his friends and relatives had asked him to perform in the West. Such notes had to be cryptic in case they were confiscated by the inspectors.

The first one read: *Len 2 neph, G.T. Iz.* "Neph" must be "Nephews"; so who has two nephews? "Len"? Wait! There was a woman, a friend of Misha's, who had two nephews. No! Two sons; Elena, of course! Right: Elena has two sons who emigrated a year ago. One is in Galveston, Texas, and the other is in Israel, and she wants to know why she hasn't been getting letters from them. *Dm mirror saucepan.* "Dm"? Deutsche Mark? Something about German money? Doesn't ring a bell. "Mirror." Through the looking glass. Magic mirror. Reflection. Mirror image. Right! "Dm" is Dmitry, Dmitry Kogan. His situation "mirrors" Alexandr's: his parents at first wouldn't sign the forms, and now, even after they've signed, he's been refused a visa. "Saucepan"? Yes, it comes back now. It's the last word of that Russian saying that Dmitry used, "Don't jump in the saucepan," meaning, "Don't make more of a fuss than is necessary." Don't make waves, as the Americans say. So: The refusenik Dmitry Kogan, who is having the same kind of problem Alexandr had, needs help from the West, but nothing too dramatic: no headlines, just some quiet information slipped to the right sources so that subtle pressure can be applied to OVIR from the West.

A few minutes after the train made a quick whistle stop, as it crossed the Czech-Austrian border, Alexandr heard excited voices from the passageway. He leaned out of the compartment and saw that at both ends of the car there were uniformed soldiers with submachine guns. Most of them were blond, Germanic looking, in their early twenties. A jolt of fear shot through him for an instant, but then he realized that these were the Austrian soldiers who guard the emigrés. In September 1973, a small group of Arab terrorists hijacked a train such as this one, and held the emigrés hostage, demanding that the Austrian government close the emigré transfer point at Schönau, near Vienna. Since then, as soon as the train crosses into Austrian territory, soldiers embark to guard against similar incidents.

The soldiers seemed friendly, they smiled easily, and chatted quite freely with those few emigrés who could converse in German. But Alexandr couldn't help picturing to himself this same railroad line thirty-odd years earlier: the handsome, blond young soldiers; the guns; the cargo of Jews . . .

Alexandr and Gittelman were sitting in the compartment, listening to Simkha, a young man who had taken some English lessons from Alexandr back in Odessa. Simkha was reading aloud from a letter he had just written to his uncle in Kharkov, in which he was boasting that, in spite of all the harassment, scare tactics, and searches, he had gotten away with plenty when he crossed into the West: one pair of worn Sabbath candleholders and an old tablecloth that had belonged to his grandmother.

Gittelman suddenly laughed bitterly. Simkha's pride in getting such things across the border was ludicrous enough, but what really struck Gittelman as grotesque was the fact that those candleholders, though shoddy and dented, *were* a triumph. Technically, they could have been declared "antiques" by the customs agent at Chop, and then confiscated. A great deal of the confiscation was purely arbitrary, even vengeful: Why should those deserting Jews get away with anything? Let them be forced to repurchase everything in the West! And how many items were smashed to pieces at the customs counters, as the agents searched for secret compartments with "contraband goods"? And what percentage of the items confiscated were sold off for vodka by the customs men?

Gittelman understood quite well the underlying reason for those stringent, often illegal, applications of the customs agent's power to impound. The parents and grandparents of those emigrés had often had to flee pogroms quickly and resettle immediately in unknown places. Something had to be sold for cash to start life over, something small, light, portable, and easily secreted from bandits. Thus, jewelry had become a traditional hedge against desperation. Even a poor man tried to keep a few paltry bits of semiprecious jewelry so that the next forced march across one border or another wouldn't drive his children into starvation. But the Soviets were determined that these Jewish emigrés of the 1970s would start their new lives with the maximum disadvantage: a hundred dollars or so apiece, and no jewelry to speak of, no antiques. So Simkha was right. He'd brought his dented old candleholders and his tablecloth out without having to bribe anybody to look the other way? A triumph!

Gittleman, in fact, was one of the rare ones with the guts, the good luck, and the determination to succeed in bribing his way past customs. Now that the train was on Austrian territory he was willing to tell the others what had happened to him in Chop.

Gittelman's grandfather was one of those who had been driven from pillar to post by the pogroms, and he had rescued his family from hunger more than once. From this grandfather, Gittelman had inherited a small packet of jewels. He looked upon these jewels not only as objects with a given trade-in value, but as a symbol of his grandfather's real bequest: the ability to survive against all odds, the power to refuse defeat, the skill to protect his children. Gittelman had no intention of leaving this bequest behind in Odessa. That very porter who had taken him into the customs office ahead of the line earned his bribe by doing one other thing for him: the packet of jewels was in the porter's pocket all through Gittelman's customs ordeal, and only after they approached the train platform to leave Chop did the porter hand the jewels back to Gittelman.

Word must have leaked out that Gittelman would try to get the jewels out, because the customs agents put his family through "personal checks." The family was split up, put into separate rooms, and made to strip. Everyone was given thorough rectal examinations, and Mrs. Gittelman and the girls were also examined vaginally. The idea of keeping the Gittelmans until it was almost too late to catch the train was part of the scheme.

Gittelman was interrupted by a stranger stepping into the compartment, a short, heavyset man in a Western-style suit; a rather sad-looking fellow whose eyes slanted downward at their outside corners, and whose slightly stubbly, jowled cheeks gave him the forlorn expression of a basset hound. He seemed bored and disappointed, but intelligent. What's more, he was from that world ahead—their destination—and he knew things! He could dispel some of that frightening mystery. He had probably boarded the train just after it had crossed over into Austria.

"Excuse me, may I see your visas? And could you please let me know which of you are going to Israel?"

"Me." Simkha stood up and handed his visa to the man. "And my mother, in the next compartment."

"Right. I've spoken to her already." The newcomer's Russian was a bit awkward, as though he'd used it as a child, and had brushed up on it recently, but had never had native fluency in it.

"Nobody else going to Israel? Where are you off to? New Zealand? South Pole?" His face just hung there in the doorway.

Gittelman was the first to recover his composure. He started to say, "I'm going to my brother, in America," but before he could finish the sentence, the Israeli had already turned away and stepped out toward the next compartment. He was a representative of *Sokhnut ha-Yehudit*, the Jewish Agency—usually called simply Sokhnut—which had the task of getting the emigrés to Israel. An important part of this assignment was to talk with those who had chosen to go to Western countries and to convince them to go to Israel instead.

Alexandr was puzzled at his own sensations. He had thought that he would be feeling triumphant, optimistic, free. But as he sat in the compartment, smoking cigarette after cigarette, he felt tired, depressed, and, underneath everything else, guilty. That was what most bothered him: that slight but corrosive undercurrent of guilt. Was it because of the man from Sokhnut? Alexandr did find something depressing in that air of foreordained defeat with which the Sokhnut man confirmed his worst suspicions—that not many of those on the train were planning to go to Israel. There was something a bit supercilious in his disappointment, a kind of invisible sneer, as though he were chastising himself for having expected better from such trash as these emigrés.

By this time, in 1975, the percentage of Soviet-Jewish emigrés who planned to go to the West instead of to Israel was growing. Over ninety-five percent of the 31,000 emigrés who left the U.S.S.R. in 1972 chose Israel as their destination. In 1975 only about

12,000 exit visas were issued, and of these emigrés, between one-third and one-half chose to live in the West. The reasons were varied. Despite Soviet insistence on invitations from relatives in Israel, many emigrés actually had their relatives in America; some were frightened of losing their sons in another Middle Eastern war—they had lost too many close relatives in World War II; and others, while still in the Soviet Union, had received letters from emigrés in Israel warning of serious unemployment and massive inflation. One consideration was paramount: once a person risks emigration there is no room for error. A false start might be irreparable. An emigré to the West, who later realizes that he should have gone to Israel, could easily do so. From the letters that eked back to the Soviet Union, people learned that it was extremely difficult for the emigrés to leave Israel once they had gone there. They had to repay the government the money it had spent on their resettlement; they could be admitted into Western countries only under the Israeli immigration quota, not as fugitives from "iron-curtain" countries; and finally, the Jewish agencies in America and Europe would offer no help.

Not long before the train was due in Vienna, Alexandr stepped into the passageway to try to walk off his tension. He and Zoya had been traveling since Wednesday afternoon, and it was now Friday. He had begun to wonder whether part of his malaise wasn't caused by being confined in train compartments for all that time. His progress through the passageway was suddenly blocked by the Sokhnut man, who was arguing with two emigrés, both in their early thirties, who were trying to justify their decisions not to go to Israel. One of the two men was leaning against the metal wall of the passageway, alongside the entrance to a compartment; the other was standing in the doorway itself, his elbow propped against the doorjamb.

Alexandr didn't feel like listening to these arguments again, but he was still curious about the Israeli, and wanted to see how he would answer the emigrés. Alexandr could see that the discussion would be futile. Both young men had close relatives in America; one of them also had an uncle in Haifa, but the uncle had written to urge him to join the American relatives, because the job opportunities in his field would be better in America.

Part One: ENDINGS

The Sokhnut representative dismissed such talk as untrustworthy rumor. He insisted that American Jews were simply trying to cover up their second-class status, and said that they were as isolated and oppressed as Jews in the Soviet Union. He denied that the emigrés would face unemployment or inflation in Israel, and guaranteed that the young men would find work in their fields.

Alexandr was baffled. Could he simply be lying? Just a free-world version of the Party propagandist? Perhaps those letters that Alexandr saw in Odessa were even more fragmentary and distorted than he had realized. The best thing would be to suspend judgment until he and Zoya had been in the West for at least a few days, and had gathered some solid facts.

Several dozen emigrés were crowded around a clutter of open valises, overnight bags and sacks in a dingy corridor on one of the lower floors of the Southern Terminal in Vienna. They had just been informed that they could each take only one piece of luggage to the hotel, and must leave the rest of their belongings in storage at the station until proceeding to Rome, in a week or two. Those who had decided to go to Israel had already been whisked off in a bus to the Sokhnut camp outside Vienna. Here in the station, those who were going to countries other than Israel were hurriedly shifting piles of their belongings from one suitcase to another, trying to figure out what they would need in the hotel. Husbands and wives were stooped over open baggage, shouting to one another.

"No! That's for Rome! It's the *champagne* we need to sell here. Isn't that it? . . ."

". . . We'll need more clothes. Both my shirts are in the black valise. . . ."

Here and there people were standing, numb, shocked, mumbling: "That's it! They're confiscating our luggage! We're finished . . . we've been tricked! . . ."

Gradually, suitcases were snapped closed, and the piles of luggage to be stored at the station were moved off to one side. The crowd began to condense around the area where the agency representatives were waiting.

Some distance beyond the opposite end of the group, a young

man dressed in Western-style clothes, who had been standing off to one side with two rather dour-looking older men, suddenly walked toward the emigrés. As he approached them he became boisterous and put on a broad, almost rakish smile.

"ANYBODY HERE SEEN FRIEDMAN? FRIEDMAN HERE? FRIEDMAN?" He slipped into the crowd, beaming as though anticipating a joyful meeting with his dearest friends from the Soviet Union. "FRIEDMAN? EXCUSE ME, DO YOU HAPPEN TO KNOW FRIEDMAN?" Then, suddenly, in a low voice, but without altering his radiant smile, "*Got champagne to sell? I can buy champagne from you* . . . OH, MADAM, HAVE YOU SEEN A FRIEDMAN HERE? . . . *Sell your champagne . . . no police to worry about* . . . FRIEDMAN? . . ."

The small, neatly dressed Sokhnut woman at the end of the crowd cupped her hands in front of her mouth and tried to shout over the noise of the station and the rumble of the passing baggage carts.

"Attention please! There are some unscrupulous elements among the Russian community here in Vienna who are trying to buy goods from you. This is strictly prohibited, and neither HIAS nor Sokhnut takes responsibility for these people's actions. Please avoid contact with these people and be advised . . ."

"FRIEDMAN HERE? *Champagne to sell? Linens?* MR. FRIEDMAN? . . . ."

The enthusiastic young man with the big smile was moving gradually toward Zoya and Alexandr, who kept looking from him to the officials and back again.

Gittelman, standing just behind the Gorelskys, leaned over and whispered, "Don't deal with those guys; they'll rob you. I've heard all about that crowd. They're emigrés who went to Israel, couldn't make it there, and left somehow. Vienna and Rome are full of them. They're a bunch of hungry animals. Keep away from them."

At that moment the crowd began shuffling toward the exit, where there were cars waiting to take them to their quarters. As they crammed themselves into the rear seat of the car, Alexandr noticed that Zoya looked pale. She had been sluggish and withdrawn, almost as though drugged, for most of the trip, and he was worried about her health. Rumors had reached Odessa that living conditions for the emigrés in Vienna could be awful, and he was beginning to wonder about Zoya's ability to cope with them. A few months earlier Alexandr had received a letter from a friend who had emigrated:

> . . . When the agency assigns you to a hotel, pray to God that you can avoid one of the places owned by a woman called Frau Carlotta. She has a miserable reputation. Even the caseworkers in the agencies hate her, but there's nothing they can do about her. The places she owns are crowded, piled high with garbage in the kitchens. She jams more families than she's supposed to into each room; she demands gifts, and insists on being the sole agent for selling the goods people bring out, and those who don't cooperate with her are threatened with being placed in the worst rooms. Because of the overcrowding, her places have a terrible shortage of cooking space. Carlotta only lets you use the kitchen for about ten minutes per meal. It's a living hell there . . .

Inside the ill-lit hotel lobby, somebody was calling people's names and handing them keys to their rooms. They had already been given envelopes with their living allotment for their first few days, in cash, which would be used for food, carfare, and incidentals. Alexandr wasn't even listening for his name now. He was standing off to one side, trying to steel himself to speak to a thin, sharp-faced, gnomelike little woman with red hair and a canny look in her eyes. She seemed tremendously energetic, bustling about from the sidewalk through the lobby, out through one door and in through another. She seemed able to handle herself in at least three languages—English, German, and Russian—all in the same acrid, aggressive tone. This was Carlotta.

Alexandr stood, waiting for her to pause from the shower of orders, demands, and remarks that she scattered in all directions. At the moment, one extremely nervous, professorial-looking man in his early sixties—who spoke a polite, educated Russian—stood before her shyly, as though before a ruling monarch.

"Madame Carlotta, my wife is resting now, so I thought it best that I relieve her of the task of discussing those, ah, those linen tablecloths . . ."

"I've got rooms full of that junk. Nobody buys it, so I'll give you the price I told your wife yesterday, and not a schilling more. If you had old silver, that would be different. I'm in the market for old silver." And now she let her abrasive voice become just a bit louder. "If you think my prices are too low, run around town and sell the stuff yourself. You're free to. Just don't tangle with the police or you'll be tossed right out of this country."

Without actually pausing to give Alexandr a chance to bring himself to her attention, she suddenly stared at him and said, "What is it?"

"Um, excuse me. I was wondering if my wife and I mightn't be able to stay in some other place. My name is Gorelsky."

"Why? Why not here?"

"My wife isn't well. She can't take the crowding . . ."

"Wh-a-at?" Her voice became shrill, and her thin features drew even tighter in anger. "You're lucky you don't end up in the damn street! I can tell you one thing, you're not staying in any of *my* hotels! No sir!" And she stalked away into another room.

Alexandr and Zoya waited in the lobby. For several hours Zoya dozed, huddled into the corner of an armchair, while Alexandr alternated between sitting and pacing. He imagined that this Carlotta, who was obviously quite important, would now do her best to sabotage his life in the West. She would probably put something in his dossier, or whatever records they kept, and see that his chances were ruined wherever he went.

Suddenly she burst back into the lobby. She was wearing a flapping, black raincoat, and was pulling its hood up over her wiry red hair. Alexandr stepped toward her as she passed near him.

"Excuse me, I'm not sure you remember us, we . . ."

"Don't worry," she said, without slowing down to look at him, "nobody's going to forget *you* around here!" And as he and Zoya followed her into the street, she repeated, "People like you will *not* be forgotten so soon!" She pointed to a cab, and rattled off an address to the driver, while Alexandr helped Zoya in, and pulled their luggage into the back seat. Alexandr peered out of the taxi window as it maneuvered through streets crowded with what

138

looked like a massive number of automobiles. He barely caught a glimpse of one or two handsome streets with graceful old buildings—the kind he had always associated with Vienna—but within a few moments they had entered an industrial section of the city. Here the buildings looked more like warehouses, and the streets were a maze of freshly dug pipe trenches and workmen's excavations. It was raining now, and after splashing through a sludge compounded of mud and pulverized pavement, the taxi stopped in front of a small building. It was flat-fronted and devoid of most of the decorations usually found on old residential structures. The color had worn down to an indefinite brownish-gray that matched the rain-spattered pipe trenches in the roadway.

The rooming-house clerk gave Alexandr a key, and directed him and Zoya to cross the courtyard to the rear wing of the building. The courtyard consisted of a large expanse of heaped rubble that had never been cleared away after some former construction. The slow drizzle was soaking the deep mud ruts that were now dotted with tan pools; it was seeping through piles of old bricks, scattered hunks of cement, half-rotted scraps of lumber, and sprinklings of garbage that tenants had been tossing out the windows. This morass could be crossed only by walking along narrow wooden planks that bobbed and sucked at the mire as Alexandr and Zoya teetered along them.

It was evening: the first day in freedom.

Part Two: DESCENT

Chapter Five:
Vienna

Four or five machines, standing in a row, were flashing multicolor lights in a dizzying pattern, accompanied by a clattering and tinkling whose echoes mingled with the hiss of hundreds of voices and foot-clicks. The machines must be some gambling game, Alexandr thought. People were standing next to them, putting coins in slots, pushing buttons.

It was Friday evening, a few hours after Alexandr and Zoya's arrival. They were standing in the Westbahnhof, the Western Terminal, which they had come across while strolling about the area of their hotel. Rest was out of the question. They had tried to nap for an hour or two but they'd finally given it up as hopeless. Their room was separated by a paper-thin partition from the only working bathroom in the hotel. Zoya had still not relaxed at all, and Alexandr was now even more concerned about her state of mind. She was barely communicating with him. When their attempts to relax had been baffled by the bathroom noises and the booming of the flush box, Alexandr insisted that the two of them go out, get some fresh air, and explore the neighborhood.

The rain had ended, but there was a chilly breeze blowing through the poorly lit street. The buildings here were flat and featureless compared with the ornate baroque and rococo facades they had passed that afternoon in the cab. Judging by the signs on the darkened entryways, most of the buildings housed small manufacturers and wholesale merchants. Now that it was dark there was little sign of life, so they walked southward a few blocks where they could make out the lights of a busy thoroughfare and a center of activity of some sort.

After a few minutes they found themselves at the side entrance of the Western Terminal, one of the two major railroad stations in Vienna, several miles from the Southern Terminal where Alexandr and Zoya had arrived earlier that day. The Southern Terminal serves Southern- and Eastern-European railroads. The Western Terminal connects Vienna with the capitals of Western Europe.

When they first approached the building, then walked around to its front, they seemed to have reached a border between two worlds. The vast, modern, oblong station fronted on a broad avenue that was a bit like some of the wider boulevards of Odessa, but much noisier. It was thick with cars of all colors and styles, and there were narrow, whining trams linked in twos and threes. The pedestrians seemed exceptionally well dressed. Unlike the crowds on the Odessa boulevards, these Viennese all seemed to be rushing home: people weren't standing or strolling about on the sidewalk, gossiping away the evening in leisurely groups.

Alexandr and Zoya wandered through the glass doors of the terminal building and stood there for a few minutes, staring left and right at the rows of neon-lighted storefronts—*Tabak* . . . *Apotheke* . . . *Café* . . . *Würste.* . . . They felt momentarily lost, disoriented in the immense multistoried hollow of the building. After staring at the gambling machines, they drifted over to the arrivals-and-departures announcement board. People were milling around, jabbering at one another, glancing at the board, running to the track entrances. The people looked busy, sometimes harried, and rich. Many of them were dressed in well-tailored outfits, probably the latest styles. Alexandr turned back to the announcement board: Salzburg, Bonn, Paris. It was past mid-May, the tourist season was already beginning, and there was something festive about the crowd.

Alexandr and Zoya drifted through the arcade. It didn't matter that at least half the shops were closed already, since the amount of Austrian schillings they had received after arriving in Vienna—a per-diem allowance to spend on food and carfare—would barely purchase coffee and pastry for the two of them in the station café. They moved from window to window. There were cigarettes—even American Marlboros—and dozens of sizes, colors, and shapes of sausages; there were breads, and unidentifiable items in funny-colored wrappers with labels in Arabic, Turkish, Hungarian.

Finally they moved off toward the exit. Exhaustion was catching up with them now. They'd had little sleep since Tuesday night, before they left Odessa.

Back in their hotel room Alexandr stepped carefully across the grimy linoleum floor and felt around for the switch to the one dim overhead light bulb. The room was cramped and dingy, but even so it seemed to be something one could live with—almost a relief after that swamp-walk through the courtyard. At least he and Zoya didn't have to share a room with another family. In the corridor Alexandr had noticed a small sink and stove, obviously meant to be shared with the people across the hall, but he saw nothing like the conditions he'd heard about in Carlotta's hotels: his two small windows did have glass in them, and the cooking area was not heaped with garbage.

The next morning, Saturday, Alexandr and Zoya followed the advice passed along through the emigré grapevine that for good shopping they should take the streetcar to the center of town, then walk a few blocks to an outdoor market—the *Naschmarkt*—where the goods are plentiful and relatively inexpensive. As the tram moved northward toward the heart of the city, the sidewalks became narrower, more crooked, more crowded, and livelier. Every major street was lined with shops, handsomely decorated, clean, and expensive.

The other Soviet emigrés were easily identifiable among the window shoppers: they stopped, stared, but rarely bought. The native Viennese had a prosperous and satisfied air regardless of their actual financial state, but the emigrés looked hungry and anxious however fat they might be, however well they tried to dress.

As Alexandr and Zoya stared into the store windows, they found themselves echoing the same comments they could hear from the other emigrés who were drifting up the street toward the *Naschmarkt*: "Look—boots! Across the street, you see? Bananas! . . . There must be a thousand kinds of shoes in that window! . . . How these people live! How they live! . . ."

Alexandr felt that same sensation that had struck him the night before, as they'd wandered around the Western Terminal: he'd thought it was just fatigue from the trip, but it was more than that. There was a kind of queasiness, as though his body, or his mind, were trying to pull back from too strong a stimulus, something that swamped his nerves and threatened to upset his equilibrium. The emigrés had named it "window shock." There was something disorienting, almost frightening, about stores full of meat, sausages that anyone could buy—not just people with special privileges—and dozens upon dozens of large, yellow, fat chickens, not the thin, fishy smelling, anemic ones you could sometimes get in Odessa. Zoya recalled how her mother used to walk into their kitchen with a triumphant smile on the rare occasions when she was lucky enough to get one of those scrawny fowl for about two days' pay. "Bluebirds," they used to call those chickens, because of their sickly bluish white cast.

The center of Vienna, the old city, is bordered on the north by the Danube Canal, and on the other three sides by the Ringstrasse, a broad, tree-lined avenue that runs where the medieval city walls once stood. One of the boulevards that radiate from the Ringstrasse, a few blocks from the Opera House, is the Wienzeile. Here Alexandr and Zoya joined the crowds that were streaming into a kind of portal formed by the space between two small store buildings that mark the entrance to the long open-air lane of the market.

It took at least ten minutes to walk from one end of the market to the other. All along the way, both sides were lined with produce and fruits imported from Italy, France, the Middle East. There were stands that specialized in pickles and sauerkrauts, others in preserves, yet others in meats, breads, beverages. And here too there were knots of emigrés. Those who had been in Vienna for as long as four or five days were bargaining and buying: husbands and wives were arguing in Russian, then pointing to various items and flashing hand signals to the vendors—one finger for each schilling's worth of the item. The newer emigrés stood hunched over their oddly colored currency, nervously trying to figure out what it was worth.

Part Two: DESCENT

Alexandr and Zoya walked the length of the market once, just to get some idea of the prices. Past the south end of the *Naschmarkt* they came to the large open area that houses the weekly flea market. They were walking, hesitantly, back again along the sidewalk that parallels the food vendors' lane.

"I'd better try to get rid of this now. If we're going shopping we'll need the money." Alexandr carefully shifted a package from one hand to the other. Inside the brown wrapper were two bottles of Crimean champagne. It was a light, fairly dry champagne, equivalent in quality to one of the moderate French products, but cheaper. Alexandr had left Odessa with six bottles, each of which had cost him a bit over two and a half rubles (about three American dollars).

He and Zoya were standing near a bar-restaurant that had just opened its doors. Alexandr hesitated at the entrance. The first customers of the day hadn't yet arrived, and the manager was standing at the other end of the barroom, near a rear door that seemed to lead to a storage area. He was calling to a deliveryman who had just wheeled a dolly out of the back room and was heading past Alexandr toward the door. The two men had one final laugh at whatever the jest was, and Alexandr found himself alone with the manager. The older man glanced at him, flicked his eyes quickly over Alexandr's clothes and his curly, ginger-colored beard, and paused a fraction of a second. Then, without looking at the package—with its telltale clink of full bottles—which Alexandr was setting down onto the bar, the manager went on talking amiably, pointing at his wristwatch and shrugging. Not yet open for business, obviously. Alexandr held up both hands in front of his chest, as though to say, "Slowly! Slowly!" He tried to shake off the thought of Professor Gorelsky's son peddling black-market wine. He also wrenched his mind away from the image of being taken off to jail as a smuggler.

Alexandr removed one bottle from the package, stroking it as though it were a pedigreed Siamese cat, and began to speak in his half-forgotten Odessa University German. After five minutes he had sold both bottles for about what he and Zoya were allotted for one day's living expenses. Even this small amount made a difference. They could hardly put a schilling in a pay telephone or enter a coin-operated public toilet without worrying that they were about to run through their last groschen. That day, the fare from their hotel to the market and back had taken almost a quarter of their daily cash allotment.

Monday, ten A.M., at Brahmsplatz No. 3, second floor. All family members must be present, including infants and the elderly.

Alexandr folded the appointment slip and placed it back in his wallet, glanced again at the map, and looked down the one short block of Tilgnerstrasse. At the end of the block the street widened into a square with a few trees, a bit of grass, and some benches. Brahmsplatz.

A few people on the benches were laughing and tossing crumbs to the largest, ugliest crows Alexandr had ever seen. The birds—Alexandr thought they might be ravens—were waddling through the grass and foraging among the weeds with their heavy black beaks, which seemed too massive even for their outsize bodies. They certainly made their presence known, and weren't easily pushed around by other birds. Alexandr could see why people considered them ugly, though there was also something beautiful about them. They had a kind of comic grace in flight.

The open plaza was surrounded by heavy, square four- and five-story buildings whose facades and window frames were decorated in neobaroque plasterwork and masonry. Alexandr noticed that these buildings were in slightly better condition than those he had seen so far. The heavy stonework of Vienna was usually gray, or a faded yellow or buff, and often stained and weathered. Through much of the city the florid plaster overlays had peeled and cracked away where they were not refurbished by historical commissions.

Vienna lies at the extreme eastern end of Austria and projects deeply into Eastern Europe. The Czech border, in fact, is only a few score miles away. The city has been a natural focal point for people who are either emigrating or escaping westward, and is therefore a center for agencies that assist such refugees or emigrés.

Part Two: DESCENT

Since it was assumed, until late 1972 or 1973, that practically all these Jews would be going to Israel, they were met at the airport, or at the "eastern tracks" of the Southern Terminal, by representatives of the Israeli organization *Sokhnut ha-Yehudit* (The Jewish Agency). The emigrés were bused immediately to a camp outside Vienna where they were housed for several days of processing, and were then flown directly to Israel.

The years 1973 and 1974 marked a profound change in this emigration. Through 1972, over ninety-nine percent of those arriving in Vienna chose to proceed to Israel. In 1973, almost five percent asked permission to go to other countries; in 1974 this figure jumped to almost twenty percent, and continued to climb. The majority of these people wanted to go to America. Word was spreading through the Jewish grapevine within the Soviet Union that the emigrés were not legally bound to live out the fiction of joining relatives in Israel, which had been forced upon them by Soviet policy.

Crowds of Soviet Jews suddenly began jamming into the cramped office space at Brahmsplatz No. 3, where HIAS (originally called the Hebrew Immigrant Aid Society), Joint (The American Jewish Joint Distribution Committee), and Sokhnut share a small suite of offices.

As Alexandr and Zoya entered Brahmsplatz from Tilgnerstrasse they could see, toward the far left-hand corner of the square, a uniformed policeman pacing up and down in front of No. 3. Some young people were handing out literature just across the narrow street that separates the building from the park area, and one of the men was explaining to the crowd of emigrés that had begun to cluster around him that this literature would be important to them. Some of the older people had difficulty understanding his thick American accent, but word spread quickly, and soon everyone was grabbing up the leaflets and books. "*Dayút! Dayút!*" "They're giving stuff out!"

Dayút: the signal that a store has something in stock to sell. Not *on sale*, merely *to sell*, for in a shortage economy there is never any guarantee that the stores will have any particular item, even staple goods. When the Soviet citizen sees a line forming outside a store, he rushes to get a place on the line, and then asks, "*Shto dayút?*"

"What are they giving?" If a passerby in the street hears someone whisper *dayút* to a companion, he will reach into his pocket to pull out his folded string-bag, and then look around for the line. "What are they giving?" "*Dayút molokó.*" "They're giving milk." He's had a stroke of luck: he happens to be standing near a place where milk is being sold at the moment. If he wants a bit for his children he must run to get on line quickly. Those who were not fast enough will stand for hours, whatever the weather, only to be told that the milk is sold out; they will then wander off in hopes of being closer the next time they see a line forming, or hear someone whisper that magic word: *dayút.*

For the emigrés, the only thing that is as important as their childrens' milk—perhaps even more important—is information. The people streaming toward Brahmsplatz on that Monday morning had been in Vienna for at least three days, some longer, and they had still been given almost no official information. When they arrived at their hotels, a Sokhnut representative handed them their appointment slips and some money supplied by Joint, but they still didn't know what was happening to them. What were they doing in Vienna? Would they really be going to the country they chose or was it all a swindle and a sham? They lived entirely on rumors. According to one rumor, the Sokhnut workers kidnap people who ask to go to America and hustle them off to Israel. Other rumors claimed that the emigré must bribe all the officials in the agencies or he and his family will be sent to some Siberia of the Western world. By the time of the Gorelskys' arrival, in mid-1975, some of the owners of hotels and pensions leased for emigré use had already begun to cash in on these rumors and to perpetuate them. Frau Carlotta was developing a reputation among visa applicants still within the Soviet Union: she was supposedly an influential woman whose word could determine the future of any emigré assigned to her keeping, and the emigré's only influence over this future lay in the value of the gifts he presented to Carlotta and to her assistants.

Alexandr shoved through the crowd and took copies of the two books that were being given out. He walked back across the street to where Zoya was waiting and greedily flipped open a booklet as they entered the building. On the frontispiece, where a Soviet book might have a portrait of Lenin, there was a picture of a slender man, his hand raised in a gesture of teaching. "Jesus Christ Our Lord" was the caption, and under that: "Suffer ye little children to come unto me." It was a Fundamentalist Christian tract in Russian. The other book was a simple, large-letter text for children, with color pictures illustrating the life and teachings of Jesus. The open and unhindered operation of Christian missionaries was baffling enough, but the fact that they were handing out their tracts right in front of the HIAS office seemed just another example of the eerie irrationality of the West.

The hallway was liberally sprinkled with hand-lettered signs in Russian. The two most prominently displayed read: USE OF THIS ELEVATOR IS CATEGORICALLY FORBIDDEN! and IT IS FORBIDDEN TO LOITER ON THE STAIRWAY OR ON THE SIDEWALK—IF YOU ARE LEAVING, LEAVE!

The locked door on the second-floor landing opened from within, and Alexandr and Zoya followed the others into the waiting room while the rest of the newcomers on the stairwell shoved in behind them. Outside on the street and in the hallway it was just beginning to become warm, but the air in this room was already stifling. The room was crowded, noisy, and smelled of the mingled odors of sweat, bags of overripe fruit that mothers were carrying to feed their children, and soiled diapers.

Just to the right of the door as they entered was a desk partially enclosed by a glass partition. The woman at the desk took each person's name and pointed vaguely to some already-filled benches along the side of the room. In the middle of the right-hand wall, beyond the desk, was a closed door with yet another of those hand-lettered signs: HIAS—NO ENTRY.

Alexandr and Zoya leaned against the wall across from the stairwell entrance. The waiting room was not very deep, about fifteen feet, and was only about twenty feet from end to end. At the far left of the room—the opposite end from the HIAS-office entrance—it narrowed into a corridor, which also had a few benches along one wall, and was also jammed with people.

Every once in a while one door or another opened and someone leaned out and called a name, but unless the person summoned was standing close to the door he might easily miss the call, for the sound was muffled by the press of bodies, by the loud talk, and by the pervasive whine of hungry, sometimes feverish children. Those near the door had to shout the name again over their shoulders until the family being called realized it was their turn, hastily assembled themselves—parents, grandparents, children—and thrust through the crowd to squeeze through the mysterious door. Sometimes the caseworker who had called the family had to fight off hysterical people who couldn't understand why they hadn't been called yet. The children were becoming crankier and hungrier as the hours passed, and old people with coronary and lung problems were feeling worse by the moment, unable to breathe the soupy air.

After more than an hour, when one of the HIAS workers had just summoned a family, a coarse-featured man—tall, muscular, his eyes wide with anger—thrust himself before the woman in the doorway and shouted, "How can you leave people stranded here like this!" He was carrying a deformed, one-armed infant, about six months old. The caseworker recoiled for an instant, but let no emotion show on her face. She nervously repeated the name of the family she had called, let them into the room, and closed the door. A few other emigrés tried to calm the enraged father, but even as they led him off to one of the benches he was muttering, "Us they abandon, but they take those bastards who give them the bribes . . ."

After Alexandr managed to find a seat for Zoya he started to squeeze through the crowd, slowly, from one part of the room to another, searching for information. Some of the emigrés here had been in Vienna for almost a week, and had been called in to report to the Transportation Section to be given the date and time of their departure for Rome. These veterans quickly became focal points of tight knots of people within the crowd. They were treated like oracles, though it was clear that their stories often didn't jibe with one another, and that their knowledge was limited by their own individual problems and fortunes. Alexandr was leaning in, straining to overhear some people who had huddled together to talk in a whisper. They seemed to be onto something valuable, secret, too good to be shared. Suddenly he snapped to attention. Someone was calling his name.

Part Two: DESCENT

"Gorelsky! Who's Gorelsky?" One of the doors in the narrow corridor branching off the other end of the waiting room was partway open. It was the Sokhnut office, and a flushed, round-faced woman in her forties was looking out. She caught his eye as he came through the crowd, pulling Zoya by the hand. When they arrived at the door she had already reentered the room, leaving the door ajar for them.

The gist of the waiting-room gossip was that the Sokhnut people were a problem. They were putting pressure on the emigrés because they themselves were under pressure. During the previous year—1974—almost one-fifth of the emigrés had chosen not to go to Israel, and it was already becoming obvious that over one-third would make that choice in 1975. The Sokhnut people were commissioned to reverse this trend, but there was little they could do. Word had begun to drift back from Israel describing severe economic hardship, skyrocketing inflation, and the constant fear of war. What many emigrés found more disturbing than all of this, however, were the stories that Israel was run by a large, Soviet-style bureaucracy. When letters arrived back in the cities of Russia and the Ukraine mentioning that the Israeli Ministry of Absorption had separated young men and women from their elderly parents and had settled them at opposite ends of Israel, Soviet Jews began to suspect the worst. They worried that they were about to give up all their potential gains for the sake of high-sounding slogans, as their fathers had done after the revolution. A "homeland for the Jews" was all very well, but if one couldn't make a life there without knuckling under to bureaucrats, without being subject to the resentment of those who had lived there for years, as other rumors claimed was the case, then the wiser course might be to settle in the West first and then make *aliyah* to Israel if those rumors proved to be exaggerated.

The emigrés' increasing tendency to go everywhere but to Israel created serious problems for the Israelis. First of all, it highlighted the general problem that Israelis—both newcomers from the West and native-born —were drifting away, mostly to America. The drift, in fact, was increasing every year, and was threatening to undercut Israel's support, especially among American Jews, or so certain people feared. One of the major bases for the creation of the state of Israel, and for its continued support, was the belief that Israel is the only real home of the Jews, that those living in other countries are essentially exiles; only in Israel can Jews fulfill their destiny; only the existence of Israel guarantees that Jews need no longer dash from country to country for refuge. The failure of American Jews to move to Israel in large numbers was bad enough, but when Soviet Jews began going to America instead of to Israel, many Israelis felt that their basic historical function was being subverted, and that American and other Western Jews would soon begin to question the need to stand behind Israel.

Then, many Israelis were deeply worried about a serious demographic problem. Some experts were predicting that after another generation the Moslem-Arab population within Israel's borders would outnumber the Jewish population to the extent that the Jewish state would be destroyed from within. This was further related to the problem that Israel needed more educated European Jews from modern industrialized countries to offset the heavy influx of Jews from North Africa and the Arab lands, many of whom had been raised in primitive conditions and would take a generation or two to become modernized and productive. The last great reservoir of such modern Jews was the Soviet Union.

Somebody had to be blamed for the increasing loss of emigrés to America. More and more rumors began to circulate that HIAS and Joint workers were seducing emigrés away from Israel, were promising them better jobs and better conditions in America, and that American-Jewish leaders encouraged this in order to bolster their own followings. But HIAS and Joint were able to point out that no Soviet-Jewish emigré was permitted any contact with HIAS or Joint workers until Sokhnut was satisfied that the emigré could not be convinced to go to Israel.

So the pressure was on Sokhnut.

There was a small desk at the far right-hand corner of the narrow office, but the Sokhnut woman, who introduced herself as Mrs. Tsur, had pulled her chair away from the desk to a point somewhat beyond the middle of the room. When Alexandr and Zoya entered she was seated facing them. She held a clipboard on her lap, and motioned Alexandr and Zoya to be seated.

"Names?"

Part Two: DESCENT

"Gorelsky, Alexandr Osipovitch and Zoya Yosifovna."

"And where are you going?"

"America."

"America. You must feel very grateful to the Americans for all the trouble and expense they've gone to—sending you invitations, making it possible for you to leave the Soviet Union—"

Alexandr could see what Sokhnut's mistake was. Mrs. Tsur—formerly Shtain—was originally from Kiev. Sokhnut was using former Soviet emigrés to persuade the new people, but the ex-emigrés were instinctively falling back on Soviet ways. Here was the familiar type again, that chilly, arch condescension so typical of the Soviet official style. Except for the fact that Mrs. Tsur's face looked Jewish, its expression was very much like what one found in OVIR, and among all those bureaucrats who speak in the name of Soviet power.

Mrs. Tsur did hold power over them. They could not be processed by Joint and HIAS until she signed a release form, which she could delay if she so desired. And just as Mrs. Tsur instinctively presumed upon her authority, so Alexandr and Zoya—equally instinctively—stared, without expression, at an imaginary point in space just above Mrs. Tsur's head, and sat in zombielike silence.

"Well, who *did* get you out of the Soviet Union?"

Silence.

"Alexandr Osipovitch, what was the name of the family in Israel whose invitation got you your exit visa?"

Alexandr looked at Zoya. She shook her head; he had handled all that. Almost two years had passed since he'd received that invitation, and it had been one of several. Since applying at OVIR, a year and a half ago, he hadn't had a moment to think of those people. An invitation was just an invitation; the people were strangers. The whole business was a typical Soviet obstacle course, so who in his right mind would take those names seriously? And yet, there was an actual family who had allowed their identities to be used for that invitation, who'd even taken time and trouble to fill out the forms . . .

"Did it occur to either of you to thank those people for their help in getting you out? No? You just had the favor coming, right? Somebody owed you something, right? Right or wrong?"

155

Pause.

"Your profession?"

"I studied history."

"You want to sell neckties on every street corner?"

"Sell what?"

"I've seen them in New York you know—Soviet Ph.D.s, American Ph.D.s—selling neckties, driving taxis; in Israel you'll have a job in the university. I absolutely guarantee it. My nephew was a high-school history teacher in Kiev, and today he's got a teaching job in Tel Aviv."

The woman's tone had begun to change. It was less cold, and was suddenly developing a glaze of friendliness that reminded Alexandr of Uncle Arkadi's attempts to dissuade him from emigrating: ". . . *for your own good, Sanya, I tell you this for your own good. . . .*" But Arkadi was worried about his own Party status, and Alexandr felt no more trust in this Sokhnut woman's sudden warmth than he had for Arkadi's avuncular concern.

Alexandr hesitantly pointed out to Mrs. Tsur that he'd heard that more and more Israeli university positions were being abolished since the '73 war, because of the economic crisis, and that he felt that a large country like America could offer him a much better chance of survival than the small, constricted, overstrained Israeli economy. Besides, a person could help Israel without living there. Look at the American Jews . . . Mrs. Tsur straightened her back and looked up from her clipboard.

"You people! You complain about anti-Semitism in the Soviet Union, but *you're* the anti-Semites, *you're* the traitors, *you're* the ones who turn your backs on your own people. You're a bunch of shams!"

Alexandr could feel his ears burning, but years of training prevented him from answering back. He was itching to cite the example of Yakov and Raya Shkolnik, but he was afraid he would make life harder for himself as well as for Yakov.

Alexandr had met Yakov and his wife Raya on that first Friday night, just after he and Zoya returned from their walk to the Western Terminal. He had gone out to the stove in the hallway to heat some water for tea. As he was lighting the burner, the door next to the sink opened partway, and a thin, middle-aged man peered out at Alexandr. He spoke in Russian:

"You just moved in?"

"Just this afternoon. Have you been here long?"

"Well, I'd say . . . about six months."

Alexandr stared uncomprehendingly at the shadowy face in the doorway. "Six months? I'm not sure . . . Where are you from?"

"Originally, Moscow."

"Originally?"

"But for the last few years we've lived in Israel."

A bit later, when Alexandr and Zoya stopped in to visit with the Shkolniks, Alexandr could see that Yakov was neither as old nor as thin as he had looked in the dim hallway. He was hardly more than thirty-five, but a tense haggardness had added years to him.

Yakov and Raya Shkolnik were living in a room, about ten by fifteen feet, just slightly larger than Alexandr and Zoya's. They shared a narrow bed, and their ten-year-old son slept on a cot behind a folding screen. The screen was in place when the Gorel-skys entered the room. Raya motioned to them to keep their voices down so as not to disturb the boy, who had been seriously ill and was now sleeping.

At first, Alexandr found Yakov's situation difficult to understand. He had a habit of answering Alexandr's questions with a wry smile, a lift of his eyebrows, and a slight palms-up shrug, as he half chuckled and half sighed, "Nu, where do I begin."

In 1973 the Shkolniks left Moscow, where Yakov had built a successful career as a food-processing engineer. With over twenty patents to his name and long experience as a supervisor in the planning and installation of large-scale food-processing equipment, Yakov was sure he could make a real contribution to Israel.

The absorption center they were sent to frightened them at first, but then they told themselves that they wouldn't always be in this isolated compound. After six months or so, once they knew Hebrew, they would be able to go to the city, to work and live like civilized people. But before anything like that could happen, the Yom Kippur War broke out, and Yakov found himself in the army, where he was put to work as a field cook, the closest thing to a food-processing engineer. After the war ended, and after Yakov recovered from shrapnel wounds from a Syrian mortar shell, he was given a job as a cafeteria cook in one of the new, but isolated, housing areas.

As time went on, both Yakov and Raya joined that growing body of emigrés who were becoming convinced that they had made a mistake, and that Israel was the wrong place for them. There seemed to be no way for Yakov to improve his work situation. Whenever he tried to convince the officials that he had valuable skills and experience to contribute to the Israeli food industry, he was given formulaic bureaucratic responses: your application is being checked, no positions are available at present. It all seemed very familiar to Yakov—very Soviet.

Yakov had been willing to forgive the Israelis for what they couldn't help—the war, the inflation, the chaotic and immovable bureaucracy—but he felt that he was rotting. Moreover, his son was having problems in their tough neighborhood, which had poorly run schools with many delinquent children. Yakov and Raya had left Moscow to improve their son's chances, and worried now that they had actually damaged them.

They began to notice increasing resentment against the Soviet emigrés. Some native-born Israelis were bitter that they had been placed farther back on the long waiting lists for new apartments so that the newly arrived Soviet emigrés could be given priority. On one occasion Yakov arrived home to find the phrase RUSSIANS GO HOME scrawled on the outside wall of his apartment house.

He saw that the majority of young Western Jews who had moved to Israel stayed only for a year or two and then left to go back to America, England, Canada. They all spoke of how enriching an experience life in Israel had been, that they might return for a visit some day, and wouldn't it be wonderful if they could settle here, if conditions were only a bit different. Then they left. But the Soviet emigrés couldn't leave. They had no foreign citizenship, no homes and communities in America. Before a Soviet emigré can move away from Israel he must pay back the money that the Ministry of Absorption has spent on him. He is thus forced to spend his first few years working to repay the debt, then to leave the country with very little money. Moreover, because of the time it takes for a working man to save enough money to repay the Ministry, he has had to stay in Israel for at least one year, and Western countries will therefore no longer consider him a refugee from behind the Iron Curtain.

The Israeli government reserves the right to deny those who live in Israel permission to leave the country, especially if it seems likely that they may not return. People like the Shkolniks, therefore, must pretend to be going abroad as tourists. For this reason, they often are unable to ship their household items out, and even are afraid to sell their belongings. In spite of all these obstacles, the Shkolniks were desperate enough to get to Vienna in order to seek entry into a Western country.

They quickly learned what a mistake that was. Once an emigré is accepted by one of the international refugee-assistance organizations, he is eligible for support and medical assistance, but the Jewish organizations, HIAS and Joint, are unwilling to help "returnees" from Israel. The International Rescue Committee (IRC) and the Tolstoy Foundation also had offices in Vienna, as did the Catholic organization Caritas, somewhat later, but they concentrated on handling ethnic Russians and other non-Jewish refugees. Moreover, the Shkolniks were long unaware of these other organizations' existence, and nobody at Joint or HIAS had bothered to tell them.

Thus the Shkolniks were forced to be self-supporting. Raya earned a bit of money as a cleaning woman in one or two cheap hotels, but she was in fact not permitted to work in Austria, and they could barely afford food and shelter on her income. What's more, the Shkolniks were unable to obtain medical help for their son, though one physician had told them that the boy needed surgery. That very Friday afternoon, as Alexandr and Zoya were teetering across the planking over the muddy courtyard, Yakov was at the Joint office to register an appeal, and to beg one more time for assistance, but he was told that no decision could be reached until the director of the office returned from abroad, in about a week.

As Mrs. Tsur railed against him, Alexandr had a brief and glorious fantasy of magically summoning Raya Shkolnik into the office, and allowing her to answer Mrs. Tsur's arguments.

There was nothing to do. Sooner or later this woman would sign their forms and send them on to the next office. Why tempt her to delay the process out of spite? So he swallowed his anger and looked blankly at the floor.

". . . but in America you'll be a flat zero—a nothing!"

Alexandr just shrugged, and finally Mrs. Tsur signed the forms and dismissed the two of them.

It was already mid-afternoon, and the damp heat of the waiting room was reaching its peak. Now that Sokhnut had released Alexandr and Zoya, they could begin their processing. Sokhnut had actually not held them very long. Sometimes an emigré family was lectured, wheedled, or berated for hours in that office. There had even been a few cases of Sokhnut refusing to release a family for several days, but that only produced more resentment. The families used up their first day's allotment from Joint, and the next allotment could not be approved until after Sokhnut released them. Several years later, in the late 1970s, the system would change. Then the Sokhnut interviews, plus lectures and slide shows, would take place in the hotels while the emigrés were continuing to receive their subsistence allowance. This arrangement would allow Sokhnut to spend an average of three or four days trying to convince each emigré family to go to Israel, and it could all take place without the emigrés having to go near the HIAS and Joint offices. Only after those three or four days would they be released to join the crowd in the waiting room at Brahmsplatz. But this change in procedure was still several years away when the Gorelskys were processed.

From now until Alexandr and Zoya arrived in America they would be dealing with two separate organizations: Joint (the American Jewish Joint Distribution Committee, or JDC) and HIAS (the United HIAS Service, formerly called the Hebrew Immigrant Aid Society). Joint is in charge of maintenance—housing, daily cash allowance, medical care—both in Vienna and in Rome. HIAS takes care of the legal processing that gets the emigrés from one country to another, first from Vienna to Rome, then through the various national consulates and immigration services to one of the Western countries.

Not only did Joint disburse the living allowance, but it also made key decisions, the first of which was to rule on whether a given emigré family could be considered Jewish, and would thus qualify for Joint and HIAS assistance. The criteria were complex. If an emigré's parents were both Jewish, then he or she was considered Jewish, as were his or her spouse and children. But if he was only half Jewish, the family could not be handled by Joint and HIAS, and they were referred to one of the non-Jewish organizations. Like HIAS and Joint, these organizations receive much of their budget for the Soviet emigrés from the United States government, but they have less privately donated money that HIAS or Joint, and emigrés processed by them will not be accepted for support by Jewish community organizations in America or other Western countries. It was the head of the Vienna Joint office who decided who was and who was not Jewish, and thus who could or could not be supported, though his decision could be appealed to the central Joint office in Geneva, which sometimes did reverse his rulings.

The main problem was to determine who were the Jews. The emigrés had no Soviet documents that listed their nationality, and even if they had it would prove nothing. There were many Jews, including some active underground Zionists, and even a few who secretly observed Jewish religious practices, who were listed as non-Jews on their Soviet papers. Other ways of spotting Jews were difficult to establish. Most Soviet Jews, even those who feel strongly committed to their Jewishness, know almost nothing about Jewish history or culture, and, in the 1920s and 1930s, their parents or grandparents usually had taken pains to adopt Russian-sounding names.

But the man at Joint who made the decision was determined to weed out all those who, according to his lights, failed to qualify. He therefore devised tests for those whom he suspected on the basis of names or physiognomy of being non-Jews.

As Alexandr and Zoya stood by the door to the Joint office, a slender, tense, middle-aged man from Lvov, who had come for a decision on his own appeal, was describing how he had been tested for Jewishness. The man behind the desk at Joint—an older man, in his late sixties, but large and broad-shouldered—had informed the emigré from Lvov that his name sounded too Russian, and that he didn't look Jewish, so he would have to be tested. The Joint man then took from his desk drawer an old plastic envelope, which had become yellowed and almost opaque with age, and asked the emigré to identify what it contained. Fortunately the Lvov man, who was in his fifties and had grown up among old-fashioned Polish Jews, was able to make out a telltale fringe through the translucent plastic, and correctly identified the contents as a *tallis*, a fringed prayer shawl.

The Joint man was still unconvinced, so he asked the emigré some questions about Jewish holidays. When correct answers to these questions still left the man behind the desk suspicious, the emigré realized that the decision was being made on instinct. Fortunately he remembered some Yiddish from his youth, and the Joint man finally accepted him as a Jew.

But his troubles were not yet over. His wife, a weary-faced, small woman with grayish-brown hair, was only half Jewish: her late mother had been a Jew, but her father was not. Now that her husband was finally considered a Jew, she and her children had also been accepted by Joint. The problem was her old father, a frail, sickly man in his seventies, who was emigrating with them. Since he was not Jewish he couldn't qualify for assistance unless his Jewish wife were with him, but she had died before they received their exit visas. Joint ruled that the son-in-law, his wife, and their children could proceed to Rome, and thence to America, as clients of HIAS and Joint, but that the non-Jewish father would have to remain in Vienna alone and be processed by one of the non-Jewish groups. When the daughter and son-in-law refused to abandon the old father to face the rigors of emigration on his own, the Joint office told the son-in-law that he and his family would have to forgo HIAS-Joint support, and thus lose all Jewish agency support in America. It was this decision that the family was appealing.

Just after the husband was called by one of the Joint workers, Alexandr and Zoya were also summoned, and were shown into a well-appointed inner office with a large wooden desk. A woman in her late thirties, who seemed to be a secretary, was going through some papers on the desk. She explained to Alexandr and Zoya that the director was away that week, and that everything seemed to be in order. They only needed to answer some routine questions and then go to another clerk's desk. This other clerk, who spoke only

German, copied some information from one sheet to another, had them sign a form, and pointed to the waiting-room door. "You wait," he said. "HIAS."

When they stepped back into the waiting room, Zoya noticed that the family from Lvov had left, but one of the bystanders who had also heard their story said that they had lost their case.

By four o'clock, when Alexandr and Zoya were called into the HIAS office, the crowd was much more sparse. Those who remained were quieter than they had been earlier. Their nervous pacing and milling around had given way to exhaustion and fragments of desultory conversation.

The HIAS door opened onto a large room that had a desk in each corner and several banks of filing cabinets and bookcases against the walls and in the middle of the room. A large wooden door on the left wall led into some administrative offices. There was constant activity and noise: two caseworkers were sitting at the desks, interviewing tired, sometimes sullen, sometimes overly hearty emigrés; other people were dashing about, from filing cabinets to jangling phones and back, calling across the room to one another in several languages.

Alexandr felt relieved as he and Zoya entered the room behind their caseworker, Mr. Weitz, a tall, dark-haired man of about forty. It was brighter here than in that murky waiting room. Several large windows were open, and one could feel the stirring of a late-afternoon breeze. Most of the caseworkers, however, looked as weary as the people they were interviewing. Their job was to obtain information, and honest answers were sometimes hard to get. After a lifetime of doing battle with the Soviet bureaucracy, and after days or more of feeling intimidated, herded about, and fleeced, the emigrés were quite beyond trusting, or even perceiving, a friendly overture from that adversary behind the desk. The fear of being unable to survive some unknown and incomprehensible new threat in this baffling environment led some of the people to seize every possible advantage. Word had gotten out, for example, that allotments would add up to a bit more if one family of six could pass as two unrelated groups of three people each, or else that the chances of getting two separate apartments in America were better, instead of having to cram all together into one apartment. Therefore, a married sister, here with her husband and child, might claim to be unrelated to the brother and the old parents with whom she and her husband had left the Soviet Union. It was the HIAS interviewer's job to pry the truth out of the family, and the family's personal duty to hide it, stubbornly, even arrogantly, no matter how transparent the lie.

Leo Weitz wrote rapidly as he questioned the Gorelskys. He asked them the standard questions: names, education, degrees, professions, job histories, destination, whether they had any family in America. He could see that the Gorelskys were a relatively simple case. He didn't see any of the commoner sorts of lies or special demands; both of them were healthy, the wife was not about to give birth, nor were they burdened with ailing parents or children, so they weren't asking to defer their trip to Rome. There were some emigrés who tried in every way to get permission to stay in Vienna instead of proceeding to Rome. Officially, the Austrian government allowed HIAS to keep the emigrés in Vienna for only forty-eight hours, though the regime was willing to overlook the fact that most of the emigrés took ten days to two weeks to be processed out. But there were cases that had to remain in Vienna for legitimate medical reasons. The trip to Rome was long and grueling. It could take up to twenty hours in jammed, sealed trains and buses traveling under guard, and the seriously ill simply could not risk it.

But those who received permission to stay behind for months in Vienna posed an economic problem. Joint's money was limited and could not support too many people in Vienna, one of the more expensive capitals of Europe. Rome had the combined advantages of being much cheaper, and of being able to absorb thousands of homeless emigrés. Only the Italian government was willing to permit hordes of stateless people to remain on her soil for months at a time. But the emigrés dreaded the added agony of another move, this time to a city they had heard was chaotic and crime ridden, so there were those who tried to claim illness. Joint demanded that a professional medical opinion back these claims.

Of course, this was Joint's responsibility more than HIAS', and technically Leo Weitz had no need to become involved in disputes over maintenance and health care. Nonetheless, he took his title of caseworker seriously, and sometimes found himself acting as an emigré family's representative. He knew too well that serious illness was not uncommon among the emigrés. The stresses of the last year in the Soviet Union and the traumas of the emigration itself often ruined people's health, especially that of the elderly. Weitz had begun to keep a file of needed reforms, and he had noted, more than once, Joint's ways of keeping the number of holdovers in Vienna to a minimum. He began to suspect that there was a problem when clients with sickness in their families volunteered to move on to Rome with the others. Someone in Joint had hinted to them that the Jewish hospital in Rome was better than the medical facilities available in Vienna. But Mr. Weitz had worked in Rome's HIAS office, and knew that the hospital, which was not a "Jewish" hospital, was sometimes more of a problem because, unlike Vienna, there were no employees who spoke Russian.

Those patients who insisted that they needed medical care in Vienna were referred to one particular doctor who handled Joint's cases. There were rumors that this doctor, who owed much of his practice to Joint, showed his gratitude by allowing some cases to proceed to Rome that should have been kept in Vienna. Several HIAS workers, including Weitz, privately suspected that the doctor's medical judgment was influenced by his patron's interests, but there was no proof. Emigrés who knew the ropes, however, and could speak some German, preferred to call the ambulance themselves in cases of medical emergencies. This bypassed Joint's doctor and set the case directly into the hospital's hands.

Alexandr had noticed that Mr. Weitz, for all his politeness, seemed a bit distracted, as though his dark, intense eyes were focused someplace else. Weitz was indeed distracted. He had just seen a photocopy of a letter that demonstrated an even more extreme method of avoiding the expense and administrative bother of keeping emigrés in Vienna. One woman, who had been a doctor in the Soviet Union, had written bitterly to her caseworker explaining that several days before she and her mother were scheduled to depart for Rome, her mother had had a heart attack. As a trained physician, the woman was able to diagnose the mother's condition. She called Joint immediately, but they refused to contact the doctor or a hospital, and instead told her to be sure to be at the railroad station on time, with her mother. By departure time, a day or so later, the mother was dead.

Weitz had urged the caseworker to show the letter to their superiors, but the Joint office denied having had any such conversation with the emigré woman, and the whole thing was shrugged off as a tough break. To the higher-ups, the important thing was that the emigrés were being moved and processed quickly and efficiently.

When Leo Weitz saw that the Gorelsky couple would pose no problems, he was relieved. It was the end of the day, he was tired and depressed, and he still had a pile of case reports to type. It was already five o'clock, and the HIAS director had just sent word around: No more today. Finish your reports.

Weitz stood up from the desk, excused himself for a moment while Alexandr signed some forms, and stepped into the waiting room. There were two or three families left. He called them over and told them that there would be no further interviewing that day, that they should return at nine the next morning.

"Please! I have a family here. Babies, an old aunt! How can we sweat through this again—"

Weitz moved off toward the bathroom, where he splashed cold water on his face, lit a cigarette, and glanced into the mirror at the fatigue lines forming around his eyes.

As Weitz stepped back into the HIAS office, he politely begged forgiveness for having kept the Gorelskys waiting, and went on with the final recheck of their papers. But Alexandr and Zoya hadn't felt bored during his absence. While he was out they had been absorbed in eavesdropping on the interview at the neighboring desk. The caseworker, a thin, intelligent-looking woman, had asked what hotel her interviewees had been placed in. While the husband was giving the address, the wife sent the children off to look out of the window at the scenery. As soon as they were out of earshot, she said to the caseworker:

"It's the whorehouse."

"The what?"

The emigré woman rummaged through her handbag and pulled something out of it.

Part Two: DESCENT

"It's a whorehouse. The whores share a bathroom with us. Here. This is what one of them gave my thirteen-year-old girl."

It was a bright red calling card, three and a half or four inches long. On the front, in German, was written: INTIMATE DIVERSION FOR THE BUSY MAN, and under that, in large italics, *MILADY'S LADIES*—DAILY UNTIL FOUR A.M. The stub end of the card was decorated with a sexy side-view silhouette of a naked woman.

"And no one will change us to another hotel. Go ahead, keep the card. The ladies gave my daughter a whole stack of them."

Late that Wednesday afternoon, Alexandr and Zoya approached the side entrance of a hotel building in one of the pleasanter neighborhoods on the outskirts of Vienna. When they tried to enter the hotel they were stopped by a man at the door who gruffly demanded to know who they were and what they wanted. They explained that they had come to pick up a friend of theirs, Lyudmilla, who was staying there. But the man at the door had his orders from the hotel owner, Frau Carlotta: no one may pass until properly identified. He was one of a surly, tough-looking bunch whom the emigrés called "Carlotta's Mafia," people whose job, theoretically, was to prevent the criminal element from preying on the helpless emigrés, though there were those emigrés who claimed that it was a case of the wolves guarding the sheep, and that these men frightened the emigrés into selling them their goods at a much lower price than they would later fetch in the market. Whoever he was, he wouldn't let Alexandr and Zoya into the hotel until Lyudmilla came to the door to vouch that they were her guests.

Lyudmilla, a tall, sophisticated-looking woman in her late thirties, had spotted Alexandr and Zoya as fellow emigrés the previous day, while they were touring St. Stephan's Cathedral. She had been a foreign-language teacher in a Moscow high school, and loved to distinguish herself by peppering her speech with French and English phrases. Somehow, this seemed to insulate her from those humiliations that tattered everyone else's nerves, and the Gorelskys found her amusing to be with.

As she led Alexandr and Zoya through the grimy, poorly lit hallway toward her room, she chattered on about the similarity between the Vienna State Opera House and the one in Odessa, which she had seen once during a vacation trip to the Black Sea. Alexandr noticed an odd smell in the hotel hallway. As they walked, the smell seemed to intensify, as did several distant angry voices.

Farther along the hallway they passed a door leading to an alcove where two women were raging and cursing at each other in Russian. For the past few seconds the noise had prevented Alexandr from hearing Lyudmilla's words, or even her voice, though judging from a certain archness in her gestures, she seemed to have gone on talking about matters of high culture without interruption. By the time Alexandr came abreast of the alcove his eyes had grown accustomed to the dim light, and he held back to glance into the dark entryway from which the shouts were coming. It was a cooking area. He could see at least one sink and one small stove, though there might have been more hidden in the shadows. Three large waste cans without covers stood in a lighter-colored space in the middle of the floor. Rancid food garbage was heaped above the rims of the cans and was trickling down along their sides and onto the floorboards. After an instant Alexandr realized that the lighter-colored area surrounding the cans was a carpet of trampled refuse.

He slowed his pace just enough to glance into this room, but the smell and the shouting discouraged him from stopping. As he walked off after Zoya and Lyudmilla he could hear that the women in the kitchen were arguing about whose turn it was to use the stove. Because of the overcrowding in this hotel, each family was limited to about ten minutes' use of the kitchen per meal.

Lyudmilla's room was darker and smaller than those in Alexandr and Zoya's hotel. Moreover, Lyudmilla and her husband had to share the room with an elderly couple from Latvia. There were two beds, separated by a folding screen, and a small table. The room had a stale, mildewed smell. One window pane was broken so the dampness had fouled the cushions and even the wooden fixtures.

Lyudmilla's husband was waiting for them at the opera house, and the two couples got on line for their ten-schilling standing-room tickets for *I Pagliacci*. Lyudmilla's cultivation fell away for only one moment, when the standees were turned loose to run, thundering full tilt along the orante imperial corridors and up the sweeping marble stairway, to grab for the best standing-room places behind a railing. However, once they had all followed the Viennese custom of marking their places by tying a handkerchief onto the rail, composure reigned again.

It seemed the local custom to avoid mentioning that rather undignified cattle run. Lyudmilla also avoided mentioning that her husband had to meet them downtown because he was delayed by business: like Alexandr, he paid his way by peddling Russian wine and trinkets. This was Lyudmilla's way of living with conditions. There were others like her, who seemed to stand above it all. Then there were those who fought and scratched, or sat for hours at a time on benches in the squares, tossing crumbs to the crows.

At 7:00 P.M. the following Monday, at the Southern Terminal, Alexandr and Zoya found seats in the glassed-in waiting room for southbound passengers already crowded with emigrés, and quickly rechecked their belongings to be sure they had remembered to take bread, sausages, fruit, and bottles of juice. They had been warned that there would be no food available on the train, and perhaps not even any water to drink. Outside the glass walls the HIAS people could be seen running alongside porters and baggage tenders, rounding up the extra luggage that had been kept in storage while the emigrés were in Vienna.

Alexandr felt restless. He left the handbags with Zoya and stepped out of the waiting room into a large concourse on the upper level of the echoing terminal. Along the left-hand wall were food counters and a bar. About twenty feet from the wall, small clusters of people were standing at waist-high, oblong metal tables, sipping wine or beer, and eating. A drunken, tattered Austrian with red, blotchy features, his nose swollen with a thick tracery of capillaries, was staring menacingly at a beer glass that had slipped from his hand and shattered on the floor. One or two of the drunk's buddies had noticed that there were more police around than usual, and were trying to lead him away peacefully.

There were not only several policemen, but also four or five green-clad soldiers, who were there to guard against terrorist attacks. They wore sharply tilted berets, and had automatic weapons slung over their shoulders. They were drifting through the crowds, keeping an eye on this part of the station, and especially on the emigrés in and near the waiting room. One soldier in particular, his submachine gun dwarfed by his large hands, stared at each face as though memorizing its features. The emigrés kept their distance from him. He had a flat, bulldog face, watery gray eyes, and his green combat shirt was squeezed out by a beer belly. His short legs looked bowed, even through the loose trousers bloused into the tops of his combat boots, and gave him an ungainly appearance, but he could move quickly. When a few civilians unwittingly wandered onto the platform where the Rome train was waiting, he leaped through the crowd, barking commands, and scattered them.

After about an hour, the HIAS people called out a gate number, which only a few people could hear, and Alexandr and Zoya followed the baggage tenders and the rest of the emigré crowd out to the platform. They all clustered anxiously alongside the train while a man from the transportation section of HIAS called out each family's name in a thick German accent and assigned them a compartment number. The front cars of the train, just behind the engine, were reserved for the emigrés, and had to be loaded before any other passengers could be permitted near the platform. Each compartment held its maximum of six people, three on each of the two hard benches that faced each other. There was no way out of these guarded cars until their arrival. As soon as everybody was checked off and squeezed into his compartment, one or two soldiers climbed into each car, and the doors were bolted and sealed for the duration of the journey. Only now were the ordinary passengers allowed onto the platform to board the rest of the train.

As Alexandr inched through the passageway toward his compartment with Zoya, he recognized a few faces from the journey across the Ukraine almost two weeks before. They looked different, and he felt the same alteration in himself. Something had hardened, had taken on clearer lines. Perhaps it was his resolve to take possession of his life and to impose upon it some kind of shape; perhaps it was simply a recognition that some of the hidden menace had revealed itself during the past ten days, and had lost in mystery as it had gained in concreteness: failure was real, and despair and apathy as well. Not that this was new to anybody, but the clarity of

Part Two: DESCENT

it was new, and quieted people down a bit. That was the most obvious difference: people were quieter now than ten days before on that Eastern-Track platform, quieter and more watchful, while tourists and commuters scurried past the windows of the sealed cars toward their smokers and *couchettes.*

Chapter Six:
Rome

Early morning. People were stretching and groaning, trying to work the aches of a cold and restless night out of their joints. Someone was striding up and down the passageway, knocking on all the compartment doors and calling, "Out . . . we get out here—" Alexandr pulled down the window and peered out. Emigrés were already handing luggage out through the open windows and crowding out the doors onto a deserted platform.

"Where are we?"

"Near Venice," someone called back. "They're taking us the rest of the way on buses."

Within a few minutes the crowd was herded off the platform and onto a side road to wait. The sun was still not far over the horizon, but the air was beginning to feel warm. People were trying to get the most out of these few minutes' reprieve by stretching out on the grass alongside the road and eating some of the fruit or bread they had taken along. Alexandr walked off to pick some golden-orange wildflowers growing in a nearby field, but when he returned to where Zoya was waiting, she was angry at him for walking away without warning her. Nobody was sure what was happening. It was rumored that transferring the emigrés onto buses for the last part of the trip was a way of discouraging would-be terrorists. The buses supposedly took a different route each time, and the escorts and

173

drivers carried sealed route orders that were opened only when they were under way.

By eight o'clock in the morning they were moving again, and they bounced and sweated southward for ten more hours. The emigrés tried to admire the dramatically beautiful scenery on the road crossing the Apennines and the lush green countryside of their valley rest stops, but they were dulled by fatigue and aching muscles, by worry, and by the ovenlike heat inside the bus.

As the afternoon wore on, Alexandr's seat was pooled with sweat, but he was not about to try opening his window. A bit earlier, a few rows ahead of him, a heavyset man, whose shirt was darkened by large, patchy sweat marks, pulled open his window to let some fresh air into the bus. Someone sitting behind him jumped into the aisle and shouted, "My wife and kids are sick, and you're letting the wind in? You open the window and I'll close your teeth!" Shouting broke out in different sections of the bus almost simultaneously; people were moving into the aisle, yelling and scuffling, reaching over to pull each others' hands away from the window latches. The outburst passed quickly, before anyone was hurt, and the windows remained closed.

Toward evening, as the bus approached Rome, a few of the emigrés began to recite the passing road markers aloud, calling out the diminishing number of kilometers remaining. Alexandr felt empty. One small part of his mind kept nudging at his consciousness: "You're in Rome. This is it! Rome!" But the rest of him was utterly apathetic. To the extent that he could think about it at all he was disturbed and confused by this numbness. It was as though the process of moving, of being herded from one unlivable place to another and being told to figure out a way to survive had become the only life left to him. Perhaps the actual goals he had tried to imagine when he first applied for a visa would recede further and further as he plodded toward them, and only the plodding itself would exist. Now, as the streets of Rome passed by the windows, they seemed empty of meaning and association.

The rest of Alexandr's mind, the part not blurred and disoriented by that sense of apathy, was taken up with a frantic sorting of data, of tips, warnings, rumors, questions.

As the bus pulled up to the curb, the shouts of a small crowd on

174

the sidewalk mingled with the noise, laughter, and excitement on the bus. A young woman stepped in through the front door of the bus and waited for the racket to subside a bit, then she read seven or eight family names off a list, one of which was Gorelsky. After she stepped out the door, people started pushing into the aisles. Zoya was anxious to get out of the bus; she had a headache. But when she and Alexandr finally squeezed through the door and climbed down onto the sidewalk, they had to work their way through a thick crowd milling around the luggage that was being heaped alongside the bus and dragged into the pensione. Somehow, through all the noise and confusion, everyone was accounted for and given a room assignment.

Alexandr and Zoya began to pull their five heavy suitcases into the elevator to take them up to their room, but a dark, squat, middle-aged woman with a furious expression on her face—the manager of the pensione—came barreling after them and grabbed the elevator doors to hold them open. She yelled something in Italian in an ear-splitting, hoarse voice, and screamed even louder when Alexandr and Zoya failed to respond. The woman repeatedly thrust her thumb toward the stairway, and seemed to be trying to chase them off the elevator, but they simply stood there and looked at her blankly. Then she shoved her face up to Alexandr's and began shouting over and over the first genuine bit of Italian that he had understood since arriving: *"Russi porci . . . !"*—"Russian pigs! Russian pigs!"—and she grabbed a valise and tossed it over toward the stairway. Alexandr and Zoya dragged the remaining bags out of the elevator and hauled them up the three flights to their room.

At eight o'clock the next morning breakfast was served in the small dining room of the pensione. Alexandr and Zoya took their seats and waited in silence for their food. Everybody was sitting quietly, behaving as refined and as Western European as they could, as though they were ready now to enter into a more dignified estate. Alexandr had some doubts about this sudden onset of sophistication. Just an hour before, he had stepped into the bathroom only to discover one of the women scrubbing her family's underclothing in the bidet.

After each of the diners had finished a small cup of luke warm coffee and two pieces of toast, a thin, neatly dressed woman entered

175

the dining room—clearly from one of the agencies. She bore that fixed smile and that gaze of distant benignity that were becoming so familiar. Her speech was brief. She told them that they could stay in the pensione for a maximum of ten days, after which they would have to leave, and that they should begin looking for apartments immediately. She described what buses would get them to the HIAS and Joint offices, and then gave each family an appointment card and an envelope with money for carfare and incidentals. The Gorelskys received 2,500 lire.

As the caseworker smiled her way daintily toward the door, a big-busted woman with a large, heavily made-up face who had been shushing and fuming at her three whining children for the past quarter of an hour—since the last of the toast had vanished into their mouths—called out in a heavy Odessa drawl:

"And eating? What about eating?"

"While you're living in the pensione you'll be given your meals here."

She left, and the people stared glumly at their empty plates. A moment later the kitchen door opened and a woman with a blue smock came out and started to clear the dishes away from the tables. The Odessa woman grabbed her plate as the cook tried to lift it, but the cook snatched it away with a practiced motion and strode quickly over to the next table to add their dishes to her tray, as she spoke her one phrase of Russian: "Is all; meal finish." She enunciated it with the ease of one who has already given the words plenty of use.

The emigrés filed out of the dining room and ran to get some advice from those who had arrived earlier.

By the end of the 1970s the agencies would start giving out booklets on life in America, and information sheets that detailed the responsibilities of the various agencies, rules for emigrés, and so on. Still, the basic truth was that there was only one way to get the information needed for survival here: buy a pile of *gettone*—telephone tokens, fifty lire each at the newsstand—then start trying to reach any emigré you know who has been in Rome for more than a few days.

Alexandr and Zoya were lucky. When they first arrived, the evening before, some friends had already left messages for them.

Shortly after breakfast the couple came to meet them at the pensione, and the four of them stood outside on the street, throwing
their arms around each other, kissing, laughing, trading gossip. The
first bit of advice these friends gave the Gorelskys was a warning:
"Watch out—people are stealing here. Everybody's got something
up his sleeve. Everyone's out for himself. Trust nobody . . ."

Back in their room, Alexandr began to make plans to explore
Rome and to visit Ostia, a seaside town about three-quarters of an
hour from Rome by commuter train, where most of the emigrés
were living. Zoya lay on the bed reading. She seemed to have no
desire to leave the room at all, and resisted all of Alexandr's sugges-
tions that they go out and look around. When it was plain that she
simply was not going to change her mind, at least for this first day,
he decided to give her more time to relax, what with all the changes
she'd been through, and he went out for a walk on his own.

The streets were crowded, noisy, blindingly sunny, and hot.
Around the corner Alexandr came to a piazza in which several wide
streets converged. There were no traffic lights or markers visible,
and there seemed to be no way to get across the five lanes of one-
way traffic that poured across the intersection before him in a
dense, rapid, and unceasing stream. Could it be illegal to cross at this
point? Alexandr was ready to walk off along the sidewalk to find
another place to cross, but his attention was caught by an old Italian
woman who had been waiting alongside him. She suddenly stepped
into the stream of traffic, seemingly heedless of the consequences.
Alexandr froze to the spot. He felt that he should help pull her out
of the noisy, honking torrent, but it was too late. She had already
stepped across the nearest lane, which had once again become a
fast-moving, unbroken stream of cars. In fact, the old woman had
already moved gingerly through a not-very-wide space between
cars in the second lane, and was now halfway across the street. As
though crossing a swift river from rock to rock, she stepped carefully, never hurried, and made no sudden or unexpected moves as
she glanced upstream at the oncoming traffic. She needed no help
from Alexandr, or from any of the others who had gathered at the
corner during the past few minutes.

A small group, made up mostly of American and English tourists, plus a few of Alexandr's fellow emigrés, stood and watched

other Italians cross the street just as the old woman had done. Finally, Alexandr decided to try it. He emulated the Italians' nonchalant upstream gaze, and stepped into what seemed like a moderate gap in the closest lane. A horn blared and sent him leaping back onto the curb as a red Fiat swerved into the lane to pass a slower vehicle. As Alexandr gained the curb, the driver of the Fiat leaned out and howled some elaborate Italian imprecation that seemed to echo on down the street even after the car had vanished. After a few tries Alexandr was able to get across by following closely behind one of the natives. The man glanced around suspiciously a few times at this bearded foreigner who was practically walking on his heels, but Alexandr pretended not to notice, and kept his eyes turned toward the oncoming vehicles.

Alexandr did far better than some of the other emigrés on that corner. One of them periodically tried to step out into a gap in the stream of traffic, only to be pulled back forcibly by his wife, who remained rooted to the sidewalk, in tears.

After Alexandr and Zoya climbed down from the streetcar near the HIAS and Joint offices the next morning, they stood on the safety island next to the tracks and looked around for a few moments before crossing to the sidewalk. They paused not so much because they didn't know where to go—a quick glance to the right revealed a crowd of emigrés clustered in front of one of the buildings—but because their experience in Vienna hadn't quite prepared them for the streets of Rome. Thirteen days before, when they arrived in Vienna, it had seemed immensely busy, colorful, confusing, and as overly rich as the elaborate pastries in the window displays of those *Konditorei* near Stefansplatz and on the Graben. Then, after a few days in Vienna, they felt that their nervous systems had begun to adjust. They could walk a straight line without being dizzied by the sensual overload. Now, in Rome, Zoya again held back for a moment or two, waiting for that same vertigo to subside before she was able to join the rushing, chattering swarms milling about on the sidewalk.

The security in this building was much stricter than in Vienna. Alexandr and Zoya's names were checked by a guard, and they were directed to an elevator. Unlike the building on Brahmsplatz or their pensione, using the elevator here was compulsory, and going up the stairs was forbidden.

The elevator door opened onto a room even more crowded, hotter, and noisier than the waiting room at Brahmsplatz. Those lucky people who had found seats on the jammed benches lining the walls were shouting to one another across the packed room. The rest stood and tried to converse over the din. But Alexandr sensed a difference between these people and those waiting at Brahmsplatz. The crowd in Vienna had been baffled, frustrated, and angry; these people showed something more: shame. Many of them had developed a curious mannerism of subtly avoiding one another's eyes as they spoke. Alexandr felt it himself, not so much the shame that arises from guilt as the shame that arises from degradation. Here he was, begging for help again, one indistinguishable beast in a cattle drive. For the first time, in that room, Alexandr felt what it was to be a refugee. He was no longer an emigré—one who has chosen to leave. He was now a runaway; faceless, one of a herd, all his individual qualities—his accomplishments, desires, his sense of humor—all lost in the mass face of that herd: contemptible and scared stupid.

The one calm emigré in the room was the man whom HIAS had hired as the receptionist. He categorically refused to look at those who were waiting or to answer their questions. When pestered for information he simply mumbled, "Wait your turn, *gospodin* . . ."

That word *gospodin*—"sir" or "mister"—took some getting used to. It had been banished from Soviet speech after the revolution of 1917, and has since been used only to address foreigners, whom one obviously cannot call "comrade." Since arriving in Vienna the emigrés were regularly addressed as *gospodin*, but some of those receptionists, and others who had been given a bit of power, drawled out the word sarcastically, so that its touch of archaic politesse was distorted into acid mockery.

The walls of the waiting room were covered with posters and announcements: YOU ARE URGED TO AVOID LIVING IN THE FOLLOWING AREAS, AND ON THE FOLLOWING STREETS, BECAUSE OF THE HIGH RATE OF VIOLENT CRIMES . . . YOU MUST NOTIFY THIS OFFICE OF ALL

CHANGES OF ADDRESS . . . YOU ARE FORBIDDEN TO OWN OR DRIVE
MOTOR VEHICLES OF ANY KIND . . . YOU ARE FORBIDDEN
TO . . . YOU ARE FORBIDDEN . . .

After more than an hour in the waiting room, Alexandr and
Zoya heard their names called. They followed fifteen or twenty
other people into a room a bit like a classroom, with a few rows of
folding chairs, and waited there for about twenty minutes until a
middle-aged woman entered followed by her interpreter. Obviously this was going to be some kind of briefing. The emigrés perked
up at the hope that now they would be given some solid information, some direction, some excuse for yet further hope. The HIAS
representative spoke in English, and after every few sentences her
interpreter translated into Russian.

"You're all starting over again," she began. "Nobody knows you,
or what you were back in Russia . . ." Alexandr wondered again
why so few of these agency workers knew the difference between
Russia and the Soviet Union, but he shook it off and tried to concentrate on the briefing. "There's been lots of complaining about
you people. Apartments have been wrecked, the fixtures stolen and
sold, and the Italians are getting fed up." Here she began to stress
each accented word with a slight forward nod of her head. "Don't
steal, you understand? No stealing, no vandalism. Nothing is yours
unless you pay for it." The room was absolutely silent now except
for the woman's kindergarten-teacher chant and her translator's of-
ficious Soviet-announcer voice.

"You're here illegally. According to Italian law you don't exist,
but the government of Italy is allowing us to keep you here anyway. You have no legal right to be in Italy, and therefore no legal
rights in Italy except the right to go to prison if you break the law.
So. No stealing or fighting, no driving cars, no working at any jobs
unless you tell us about it. We must be informed of every single lira
you earn. Women should avoid strange men. Stay away from the
high-crime areas we've listed for you. . . ."

Some of the emigrés were leaning forward and staring at this
woman with blank incomprehension, as though she were speaking
in sibylline riddles; others were looking down at their laps and
blushing; still others tried to maintain expressions of blank neutral-
ity.

180

Part Two: DESCENT

Although the woman had not tried to offend anyone—if anything, she thought she was simply being forthright—all this talk of stealing and whatnot could only mean one thing to her audience: they all stood condemned of the crimes of the worst few. They had never been public charges before, had no idea how to deal with a social agency, what the nature of the relationship would be, and suddenly they were being called thieves and vandals. In their very anxiety to hear and understand every nuance of the briefing, they heard, perhaps, more than they were intended to hear, and they were shocked, embarrassed.

After the briefing ended, two men entered the room carrying stacks of plastic vanity cases—black for the men, brown for the women. Each of the bags was inscribed, A GIFT FROM THE PEOPLE OF AMERICA. Inside each case was a bar of soap, a toothbrush, toothpaste, and a packet of tissue paper. A few of the people in the room considered this the final insult. "Do they think we've never heard of *toothpaste*?! They really think we're scum . . ." One or two others politely refused to accept theirs. Some were asking for extras for their sick old mothers, who hadn't been able to come that day. Alexandr and Zoya were among those who simply accepted the bags, nodded their thanks, and left.

They had a bit over a week left to find an apartment. Practically everybody was settling in Ostia. In the economic boom of the 1960s Ostia had expanded a good deal, and had become a popular working-class and lower-middle-class watering place. After the boom passed, Ostia was left with a rather large area of shoddily built and quickly decaying apartment complexes. In the local parlance, the older, somewhat better part of Ostia was known as the "fascist" section; the poorest part, which had the highest rate of violent crime, was called the "communist" section; between them lay the "neutral" section.

Apartments in Rome itself were almost impossible to find, or were available only at luxury prices, and the emigrés' mutual support system did not exist there. It functioned primarily in Ostia, where there was a fairly dense emigré population. That support system was necessary even to find an apartment which, as in most cities, is done largely by word of mouth. In addition, no emigré

181

could afford to rent an entire apartment for his own family. He had to share it with as many other families as could fit, which made the presence of other emigrés a necessity. Even with apartment-sharing, half or more of an emigré's allotment might have to be spent for housing.

On Friday, the day after their HIAS briefing, Alexandr walked to the underground station just outside the Termini railroad station and took the rickety commuter train to Ostia. He had to make this first trip without Zoya. He was finding it harder and harder to get her to leave the pensione at all now. She preferred to sit by the window and stare out, lost in thought, or to lie on the bed, reading and dozing. She insisted that she was just as happy staying alone, but Alexandr suspected that she was really too frightened to leave, that all her defenses had been torn away, and that she had to isolate herself to survive, like a burn victim whose blistered skin is agonized even by the lightest touch.

Alexandr's friends had told him that his first stop in Ostia must be the post office, which was a ten-minute walk from the station. "You'll know when you get close to the Piazzale della Posta," they told him, and indeed, as he turned onto the Viale della Marina he could see a crowd a few blocks ahead.

The post office itself was a modern building that formed a concave arc set back from the intersection. The curve of the building contained a small open area in which there was a fountain basin rimmed with a low parapet, and this fountain area was set off from the street by a colonnade, an open semicircle of modernistic light-brown pillars.

Hundreds of emigrés were swarming the steps of the post office and the area around the fountain. They were sitting on the fountain parapet, leaning against the pillars, and spilling out onto the sidewalk and even into the streets. As Alexandr approached, the mass of people resolved itself into many clusters, with streams of emigrés drifting from one cluster to another.

Alexandr had been told only that the place to find an apartment was the *Posta*, though he didn't know what he was supposed to do when he got there. As he approached that mass of people it seemed

Part Two: DESCENT

to him there was some kind of sale going on. It looked a bit like the
flea-market crowd in Odessa, but there was no merchandise here,
just mobs of people, talking, scurrying from group to group. As he
entered the crowd he heard a familiar voice: "Alek! What are *you*
doing here!" Alexandr immediately recognized this young man, the
broad smile, that wispy red hair plastered down to the brow by
sweat. It was one of his former English students from the old refusenik days in Odessa.

"Never mind explaining, Alek. You're looking for an apartment,
right? *I'll* find you an apartment. Wait here, I'll be back."

He didn't return that afternoon, and Alexandr was quite willing
to forget, for a little while, about looking for an apartment. At that
moment he wanted only to find faces he knew in that alien crowd.
He bumped and drifted through the press, shoving his way toward
features he recognized.

"It's Sanya Gorelsky! How's your wife? Did you marry that
Zoya girl after all? . . . They let you go finally? . . . Is Misha
still in Odessa? . . . I heard your Uncle Arkadi is still a Party
mouthpiece, even with his demotion. . . ."

They were up on all the latest gossip, and they wanted to hear
more. For the first time in weeks Alexandr stopped to think about
many of those people he had left back in that other world.

"You heard about Vitali Leonov, the writer? They say he's trying to get an invitation from Israel—wasn't he a friend of Arkadi's?
A good writer like Leonov, and the KGB bans him from publishing! He'll be lost in the West . . . a writer . . ."

Vitali. The man was a fiction writer, a real talent. He'd struggled
for years, and no sooner did his career begin to blossom than the
KGB accused him of being an underground Zionist, and the career
ended. Odd to think about it now, but it was Vitali who had told
Alexandr a story about Uncle Arkadi's one glorious moment, as a
university student in the 1940s, when Arkadi refused to go along
with the political intimidation of a fellow student. Hard to imagine
that Arkadi had done that. Perhaps he then spent the rest of his life
cringing in the wake of the fear left by that passing moment of
principle.

"Remember Borya and Galya? They went to Israel last Au-

183

gust . . . Borya's at the university, in mathematics . . . They're all right now . . . Remember when Borya started his craziness all of a sudden? . . ."

Borya and Galya had held up well, even under some particularly vicious official harassment while they were refuseniks. It was after they received permission to leave that Borya began to change. He was suddenly staying out for nights at a time, and didn't even hide his new girl friends from Galya.

As Alexandr wandered on through this chattering mob, greeting and embracing other old acquaintances, he suddenly understood something about Borya. After all, Borya wasn't the only one who'd acted erratically in those days. Borya had been an extreme case of something that had affected all of them: there was something appalling about the impending departure. It was like the approach of death. It was a passage through an opaque barrier, translucent at best, through which one could distinguish only an incomprehensible play of shadows. And who could tell how any man would face his death? Some people, like Borya, hugged the earth to themselves in a last angry, euphoric, bitter embrace. Others tried to shrug the whole thing off as being nothing more than a passage from one level of hell to another.

One or two people in the crowd were anxious to hear about Osip, Anna and Arkadi, and were curious to know whether their careers had recovered from the anger of the Party. As he talked, Alexandr wondered whether his parents and his uncle ever reminisced and gossipped about these former friends who had vanished into Vienna, Rome, Ostia, Tel Aviv, God knows where. Perhaps, Alexandr thought, they feel that we're best left buried, unexhumed, lest we become a defilement.

Suddenly it was evening. The daylight was disappearing rapidly, and those hundreds of people who had turned the Piazzale della Posta into a carnival of stories and faces were gone. Only about twenty people remained, scattered about the colonnade and the sidewalk, and they too were disappearing down different streets. Alexandr walked up the darkening sidewalk toward the avenue, then turned right toward the station. He felt confused. The entire afternoon had been a shock. He had not been prepared for the crowds, the noise, the sudden reappearance of those old ghosts, the recognitions and embraces; nobody had cautioned him about that swarm of recollections, nor warned him that the light gives way to darkness so suddenly at this latitude.

He walked onward toward the station and the train to Rome. Tomorrow Zoya would have to come with him to Ostia, and they would start the apartment hunting in earnest.

"Watch out for the *meklers*, the commission-grabbers. They're a bunch of veterans, and you're a green recruit. They'll walk all over you." Alexandr's friends didn't have to warn him twice. He was determined to find his own apartment without the help of those "brokers" who were always hanging around the post-office crowd in Ostia, offering to find apartments for a fee. Zoya felt more confident about leaving their room the next day, and when she and Alexandr approached the *Posta*, the go-betweens seemed to smell fresh meat. A young emigré, in an Italian jacket with a sharper cut than any self-respecting Italian would wear, tapped Alexandr's arm.

"Looking for a place to live?"

"No."

"You'll be back, you'll be back . . ."

A few feet farther on there was another one: "You want to trade dollars for lire? What do you have, dollars? Schillings? . . ."

But the most prevalent were those offering apartments. Alexandr and Zoya decided to walk through the town and stop at every likely looking building until they found a vacancy. After several hours of trudging through the dusty heat they still had found nothing. Some friends suggested that they speak only English and pretend to be American tourists, because the Italians hated to deal with the Soviet emigrés. Rumors of emigrés stealing furniture, or calling Moscow on the house phone and running away without paying the bill, were rife among the Italians. Though such things did happen, the local people were ready to hold all the emigrés guilty.

After a few days, Alexandr was ready to try anything. Early one afternoon, while he and Zoya were standing at the *Posta*, a tall, slender, exquisitely dressed man stepped up to them. He had neatly trimmed black hair, with a bit of gray at the temples, and a thin mustache. He bowed slightly and said, with a tinge of Soviet Georgia in his speech:

"You're experiencing some difficulties, am I correct?"

Alexandr mumbled something about not being too familiar with the surroundings.

"It's a pity. I probably can't be of too much help. Nonetheless, it is painful to see how people who have fallen into difficult circumstances are preyed upon by unscrupulous individuals. Your problem is that of finding quarters?"

Alexandr and Zoya were momentarily overwhelmed by this smooth Caucasian prince. He didn't wave his hands around as he spoke, he didn't wheedle, shout, or cajole.

"Perhaps I can be of some assistance, after all. Please step over to my car for a moment." He led them past the usual array of dented Fiats and spattered, peeling Volkswagens, and stepped up to a new-looking, polished white Mercedes with leather upholstery. Maintaining an air of careless elegance, he flicked open the doors, nodded Alexandr and Zoya into the car, and settled himself behind the wheel.

They cruised through the different sections of the town, as the Georgian, who introduced himself as Mikhail, prattled on amiably. The streets were becoming shoddier, the buildings more run-down and neglected looking. Mikhail pulled up in front of an apartment house; the paint was peeling, windows were broken, and patched linens were hanging from clotheslines strung across the little terraces. He gracefully stepped out of the car. "I'll be back in a moment, I just want a quick word with the managerial personnel."

As soon as he left the car, Alexandr and Zoya began to whisper hurriedly: "What's his game? Do you think he'll try to rob us? This place looks like hell! . . ."

After almost ten minutes Mikhail was back. As they drove off he smiled and reassured Alexandr and Zoya:

"Not that I thought you'd want to live there, but the woman who owns that place also has some lovely apartments. Unfortunately she was out, but we can try somebody on this block . . ."

Another broken-down slum building, and another ten-minute

wait until Mikhail returned to announce that the manager wasn't in. After the same thing happened a third time, Alexandr asked Mikhail to take them back to the *Posta*. The Georgian's tone suddenly changed. He spoke quickly and angrily, clenching his teeth, "Listen, I've been good enough to help you, and now you're spitting in my face!" But then, after they had driven for a few minutes, he tried to resume some of his earlier suavity. "Well, I guess it's my responsibility to get you back to the *Posta*, where I first had the pleasure of offering you my assistance. My God! Look at the time! We've been at this for three whole hours! You know"—and here he nodded philosophically—"one thing I like about the West is that people really understand the value of a man's time. Of course, I wouldn't expect you to offer what you would if we'd found a place for you, but I'm sure you'll have the simple courtesy to reimburse me for the time I've spent . . ."

That was too much. Alexandr's voice became steely and uncompromising. "No apartment, no money." Nothing further was said. At the *Posta*, Alexandr and Zoya climbed out of the Mercedes, and Mikhail drove off without a word.

Later, they met Yasha, the former student of Alexandr's who had recognized him on his first afternoon in Ostia. Alexandr was even more overcome by the warmth of his greeting and his smile than he had been the week before. He and Zoya felt wrung out from that ride with the Georgian, they were tired, hungry—they'd had to miss lunch at the pensione, and couldn't afford to eat out—and were utterly disheartened. Yasha was all sympathy. He'd heard a lot of unpleasant talk about that Georgian, who supposedly had left his wife and children in Israel, and had come to Rome to make enough money to take his family to some other country.

Yasha was effusive. He reminisced about how Alexandr had worked to help him improve his English, back in Odessa, and as they walked toward the curb he assured Alexandr and Zoya that he would do everything in his power to help him find an apartment, and to bring some order out of this chaos. What's more, he would do so at much better terms than anybody else around.

When Alexandr heard Yasha mention "terms," he knew that there was no way back, that this was the new life, and he'd better learn to accept it. For that matter he had not given those English

187

lessons for nothing in Odessa. It was understood that he was supporting himself that way.

Yasha led them to an old Volkswagen van, colorless, dusty, and rusted through in several places, which looked as though it had just been taken from the scrap heap. In a few minutes they were bouncing along the road, Alexandr and Zoya crouched painfully on the steel bands that had formerly supported the seat upholstery, and once again passed the better part of town, watching the villas give way to slums, and slums give way to sparsely developed, run-down suburbs. After a drive of about fifteen minutes, they stopped where the last houses looked out over scrubby sand dunes.

"Take a look at that palace!"

Alexandr and Zoya looked from Yasha to the small apartment house, and again at Yasha. From the outside, the house did not appear to be occupied. There was almost no paint left on the trim, and most of the windows were boarded up with plywood. When they stepped inside it took a moment to adjust to the dim light. The apartment, which smelled of mildew, had the appearance of an old furniture warehouse. There were three sofas in the room, and several damaged chairs, a table, suitcases, and scattered clothing. Yasha was stumbling through the half light, explaining that three families were in the apartment at the moment, but that one of them was expected to leave for the States pretty soon—maybe in a few weeks, maybe less. And the place wasn't really as inconvenient as it seemed. The bus to downtown Ostia was supposed to come every half hour during rush periods—although, this being Italy, it might be a lot less frequent, of course—and there was a market of sorts only ten blocks away. Naturally, another bed would have to be moved into place . . . well, not actually a bed, but a beach chair that unfolds so that you could lie down in it, and there was a mattress around someplace. The whole thing, including cold water, would be only sixty-thousand lire per month, a bit under half their monthly allotment.

As Yasha stepped through a doorway to show them the kitchen, Zoya whispered, "I'd rather die!"

On the way back to the van, Alexandr explained to Yasha that he was deeply grateful to him for his help, and that they would let him know their decision in a day or two.

Part Two: DESCENT

"Remember, Alek, I can't hold the place for you. There are hundreds of new people pouring in every week . . ."

Trust.

All through the dense emigré colony in Ostia, thousands were intoning that same warning that Alexandr and Zoya had heard from their friends almost a week and a half earlier: "You can't trust anybody here; everybody's hustling, grabbing . . ." And back in their former home cities, from Odessa to Leningrad, the rumormongers were reechoing their old refrain: something happens to those people when they emigrate; they become sharks, predators fit only for life in the capitalist jungle. In this way the emigrés had been well prepared to believe the worst about one another, that is, about themselves. Like Dante's fallen souls, they knew by heart the litany of their own and their neighbors' transgressions, and retold to each newcomer their inglorious history.

Yet that vulnerability, that moral flimsiness ought not to have come as a surprise. The instinct to be wary of one's neighbor is as automatic to Soviets as that careful scan of oncoming traffic is to a native Italian pedestrian halfway across the piazza.

In fact, there were those in the emigré scramble in Rome who understood quite well the source of this pervasive mistrust, and were not permitted to forget it. In late 1974, seven or eight months before the Gorelskys arrived, Mikhail and Natalya Markov and their teenaged daughter Irina were sharing their cramped quarters in Rome with a fellow named Kleinman, an acquaintance from Moscow. They had first met Kleinman two months earlier, in the crowd at OVIR, where he offered to help them with some of their paperwork problems. Short and hunched by a congenitally malformed back, Kleinman seemed to have that openhearted ability to offer himself that is sometimes so well developed in people toughened by lesser opportunity and by greater affliction. Perhaps it was the contrast between himself and the Markovs that attracted him to them, the contrast between his seeming lack of complexity and Natalya's thin, high-strung intellectuality, or between his misshapen torso and Mikhail's stocky, firmly planted body, that physical strength that seemed to express Mikhail's faith in his own talents and accomplishments. On the other hand, when Kleinman first met the Markovs, Mikhail was standing, baffled and disoriented, among the distressed mobs at OVIR.

Whatever the reason, Kleinman had attached himself to the Markovs, and he didn't abandon them, even when his visa came through a week earlier than theirs. He still managed to brighten the loneliness and bewilderment of their arrival in the Vienna airport by meeting their plane, smiling, with three carnations held out to them in his right hand. Later he shared quarters with them in Rome, and it was here that they discovered that Kleinman was keeping elaborately detailed logs of their every move.

Why? For whom did he write these reports? Mikhail and Natalya were particularly sensitive to this question. Technically Mikhail was an emigré; in fact, his position was more delicate than usual: he had been ordered to emigrate, forced into exile, by the KGB.

They stood in silence for several minutes, bent over the lamp table, and peered at that sheet of paper written in Kleinman's script. Would a real KGB man be so sloppy as to leave part of his report where it could be found? Perhaps that was part of the strategy: a warning: a small sortie into that psychological war between the regime and its less cooperative citizens—just a reminder to Mikhail that it was too soon to relax.

Alexandr and Zoya's luck improved the day after Yasha took them out in his van. They were standing in the shadows of the colonnade at the *Posta*, wondering whether to accept a room offered a few moments before by a large woman in her mid-forties, when another woman interrupted their conversation and asked Alexandr whether he was planning to rent a place from that disreputable person in the flouncy black dress.

"She's a whore, she's running a brothel. She just wants you to be there to baby-sit for her ten-year-old boy, a neglected kid, poor thing. . . ."

While she rattled on, sighing and shaking her head over that shameless woman, she was looking Alexandr and Zoya over carefully. She seemed to like what she saw, for she leaned toward them and whispered conspiratorially:

Part Two: DESCENT

"You look like nicely brought-up kids. I've got a room in my apartment—"

In a rather well-kept apartment house not far from the post office, Sonya Nikolayeva and her husband Petya had a three-room apartment. They kept one room for themselves and rented out the other two, a room next to theirs—which they showed to Alexandr and Zoya—and one down the hall, rented to some man from Leningrad whom they hardly ever saw.

The Nikolayevs seemed a pleasant enough couple. Petya, a Russian, was Sonya's fourth husband, and he let her handle all the business arrangements. Since they were applying to join her children in Canada, which normally takes six or eight months to accept applicants, they were relatively long-term tenants, and had been able to make a deal with the building manager to be responsible for the entire rent for the apartment, and for collecting the rent from the sublessees. This left them free to charge whatever they could get, and thus to cover their own third of the rent with the receipts from the other two rooms.

Alexandr and Zoya sat in the little shared kitchen with Sonya and listened patiently as she prattled on about how important it is to find honest people. Then she made her offer. She would let them have the room for only a hundred thousand lire per month, almost two-thirds of their monthly allotment from Joint. When the bargaining was over, Alexandr had talked her down to sixty-five thousand lire.

Now that the vacation season was at its height, the streets in this part of Ostia came to life after dark. Ice cream parlors and cafés set out their lights and their tables across the sidewalk, sometimes across the entire width of the street. There was something exciting about walking among the vacationers seated at the tables, looking into their faces, meeting their eyes, pretending to be one of the blessed. Alexandr liked to imagine that someday he and Zoya would come back as tourists, and order a cappuccino with some sweet pastry or a dish of Italian ice cream. But now it was all a dream. Even a little snack at one of those places would exhaust their food budget for several days.

Before Alexandr and Zoya could get their allotment they had to clear out of the pensione and give HIAS and Joint their new address. They were given an appointment with their HIAS case-worker for the day after they moved.

Again they found themselves in a crowded, stifling waiting room at HIAS. Every once in a while the receptionist summoned a family to pass through the door and up a flight of steps into some mysterious inner sanctum to speak with one of the caseworkers, but it was impossible to understand what the fellow at the desk was mumbling. Every time he opened his mouth, the head-splitting din in the room was redoubled as people started shouting: "Who? Us? Smolyensky? Obolyensky? Who?—"

"Gorelsky to see Simon . . ." With this formula the receptionist motioned Alexandr and Zoya through the door and up the steps. They rang a bell alongside a metal security door on the next landing. The peephole in the door opened for a moment, and an Italian guard peered out at them. Alexandr repeated the ritual formula, "Gorelsky to see Simon." A moment later the guard pulled open the door and a young emigré woman led them back along a corridor, past a number of interviewing rooms, then into a small office.

Alexandr's first impression of Mr. Simon was of a large mouth full of oversized teeth set in a stereotypical American grin. That propensity to pull the corners of the lips back, on occasions when other nationalities, notably the Russians, would preserve a grim deadpan, had become an essential part of the American image.

Alexandr was acutely conscious of the desire to distinguish himself from the mob of emigrés. He wanted this Mr. Simon to like him, to appreciate that he was not a slob, not a thief, a *mekler*, a boor, a *shnorrer*. It wasn't that Alexandr wanted to butter Simon up or to get special treatment. Alexandr had no respect for people who did things like that. He wanted only to be spotted for his true worth, hauled out of the quicksand of the mass, resurrected, redeemed. But that in fact would be favored treatment, Alexandr realized, as he gripped Mr. Simon's hand in a firm shake and cracked some sort of joke, mimicking the American manner he had read about.

Zoya spoke hardly a word. Alexandr seemed to understand intuitively that the best way of making an impression on Mr. Simon was to speak English, which Zoya hadn't yet learned. Except for the few questions that Mr. Simon addressed to her directly, in Russian, she was left out of the conversation. Alexandr handled everything.

There were two ways for Alexandr to earn extra money: one was to sell the items he had brought from Odessa, the other was to give English lessons. A few of his former students were in Ostia and were beginning to recommend him to other emigrés as a teacher.

The easiest way to sell his goods would be to use one of the many *perekúptchiks*, the go-betweens. This would bring him only half of what he could make by selling the items himself, at the flea market, but it would save him the trouble and embarrassment of hawking goods, as well as the danger of being arrested. He decided to go to the Porta Portese market, which the emigrés call the "Americana," to sell his goods himself.

By midmorning on any Sunday, from all parts of Rome, crowds stream westward across the Ponte Sublicio bridge toward the partly open area near the ancient Portese gate. Hundreds of stands are set up at which almost anything can be bought, new or used, from plumbing fixtures to leather goods, clothes, cameras, toys, all as cheap as the customer's bargaining abilities can make them. Even on a wet day the crowd is so dense that the shopper has to struggle to move from one side of the lane to the other. In addition to vendors at stalls and stands there are people who wander through the crowd selling small hand-carried items. There are also Gypsies, beggars, and pickpockets.

By mid-1975 the Italians had become used to the idea of these *Russi* setting up stands of their own in the Americana. The police had never quite made peace with it, however, and sometimes raided the emigré section of the market, confiscating the goods and even arresting the emigrés who were selling. Usually one of the emigré vendors set himself the task of watching out for the police and warning the others, who would then throw all their merchandise into bags and boxes and drift away for a few minutes.

Alexandr arrived at seven in the morning to get a good spot in the "Russian section," one small row of stalls used by the emigrés. Several times during the course of the morning a man who was strolling up and down the row, selling small toys, started to whistle a well-known Russian folk song that begins with the words, "The wind is driving the clouds along. Let's all go home." His loud, rapid, and repeated whistling of this melody threw the more nervous among the emigrés into a panic—as well as those who had already had their goods confiscated once by the police, or had even spent a few hours in the lockup—and they hurriedly tossed their goods into bags or cartons each time they heard the warning. After three false alarms people began to grumble that the self-appointed lookout was either overanxious or a practical joker. The fourth time he gave the alarm, one of the emigrés, in rushing to hide his goods, broke a handsome crystal vase that might have brought him enough money to support himself for a month. After a moment of silence, when it became clear that there were no police around, he grabbed the strolling lookout by the shoulder, spun him around, and punched him in the face. The others waited a few moments before pulling the two men apart.

Relatives and friends in the Soviet Union were constantly receiving lists of items that were selling well in the Americana: linen, porcelain figurines, folk art, phonograph records, scissors, and *matryoshkas*—jug-shaped dolls painted to resemble squat peasant women, each with a smaller doll inside it, and a still smaller one inside that, and so on. The favored items were spools of thread, buttons, scissors, all kinds of optical instruments, cameras and lacquered boxes.

Periodically, word flashed through the rumor mill that one particular item was a hit, a sure seller, and for months afterward the market was glutted with this item. Usually the rumors were exaggerated, if not completely wrong. One day somebody managed to sell a packet of Soviet condoms, famous for their toughness and unreliability. The amazed emigrés spread the story, probably exaggerated it in the retelling, and within a month vast quantities of these unsalable items were flooding the Roman birth-control market. Another time it was ballet shoes. A Kiev man informed his clumsy daughter that he had no intention of continuing her expensive ballet lessons in America, and he sold her shoes to a German tourist at a good price. For several months afterward the Russian section of the Americana was thick with satin footwear, leotards, and fluffy tutus.

Part Two: DESCENT

Alexandr went to the Americana a few times to sell some cameras, on which he made over one hundred thousand lire, and some linens that Zoya's mother sent through the mail, but he usually tried to avoid selling. He felt degraded by it, as though it were a minor form of prostitution. At the same time, however, he felt pleased with himself for having been able to take home some much-needed extra money. It meant that he was a man, someone who could take charge of his life, who could survive by his own strength, wits, or talent, not merely a beast in a barn, ready at the trough when feeding time came.

As Alexandr's expertise in teaching English became known, he began to develop a following. He spent hours each day preparing lessons and vocabulary lists, and walking miles from lesson to lesson through the baking, deserted midday streets in order to save bus fare. Although he and Zoya tried to save some of the money he made, a sightseeing trip or the price of a pair of shoes was usually enough to set them back again.

Alexandr found that he could save quite a bit of money by shopping at the "round market" in Rome. As he walked south from the Termini station he could tell when he was getting close to the market, even before he saw the crowds. The numbers of street vendors selling leather goods, umbrellas, or trinkets, from large wooden stands, suddenly increased. When he turned the corner opening into the Piazza Vittorio Emanuele II—a large rectangular plaza several blocks long—there was a sudden rush of sounds and smells. The wide street bordering the piazza was lined on both sides with wooden stalls surrounded by crowds. The throng ringed the piazza and moved between the double row of stalls, gawking and haggling.

The round market sold just about everything: fresh fruits and vegetables, fish, meat, poultry, clothing, luggage, even some hardware. Not only was the merchandise cheap here, but Alexandr discovered that if he waited till just before closing time and then bought in large quantities he could bargain the prices even lower. He used to bring three or four large-sized elastic string-bags, and drag home over a hundred pounds of merchandise at a time, everything he and Zoya would need for at least a few weeks, plus orders from one or two of their friends. Usually he was lucky enough to find somebody with a car who could give him a lift back to Ostia for a reasonable fee.

The weather was beginning to cool, the beach crowds were heading back to Rome, and now the question of which American community would accept the Gorelskys became more pressing. They had asked to be sent to San Francisco, as some of Alexandr's former students were already there, and were trying to arrange it with the San Francisco branch of the Jewish Family Service. By law, all these emigrés to America must be sponsored by some person or organization within the country. With few exceptions the emigrés are sponsored by the Jewish Welfare Federation and its affiliated organizations. Most cities with sizable Jewish populations have branches of these organizations, and it is up to the local chapters to decide how many and which emigrés it can take. The New York HIAS office sends the emigrés' dossiers to the local Jewish agencies in the cities they have requested, and the agencies are free to accept or reject, theoretically on the basis of whether the emigré will fit in well with the community, the local job market, and so on.

Certain cities quickly became popular among the emigrés, usually because they developed a reputation for being easy to adjust to and for having a good job market. In later years, the Jewish agencies in these cities, swamped with more requests than they could handle, began to create blanket requirements to reduce the number of eligible requests, such as insisting that the applicant already have a first-degree relative living in the area: a parent, sibling, or child. Those rejected were usually sent to New York. NYANA, the New York Association for New Americans, was pledged to accept up to half of the incoming emigrés.

By September it had become apparent that there would be a problem. Alexandr and Zoya's friends in San Francisco wrote to say that the local Jewish Family Service claimed that its quota of emigrés for that year had already been filled, so they were making inquiries into neighboring communities.

A few weeks later, Alexandr stepped into his apartment and found a message that he should call Mr. Simon at HIAS. Simon's first words threw Alexandr into despair:

Part Two: DESCENT

"You'll have to forget Seattle . . ."

When the San Francisco agency notified HIAS that they were full, the Gorelskys had been assigned to Seattle. For weeks they had been searching out magazine articles about the Northwest, reading, looking at photographs: Alexandr had sent letters to Washington State University and other colleges in the area, and now that was also falling through. This might mean being sent to New York.

The emigrés' image of New York was based on a combination of Soviet propaganda descriptions of the city and of fragmentary reports from those who had been sent there. It was said to be immense and confusing, the people aloof at best, when not overtly hostile, and the streets and subways dangerous, dirty, frightening.

"Don't tell me New York."

"What's wrong with it? You'd love New York. It's fast-moving, full of Odessans . . ."

"Please. Don't tell me New York!"

"All right, I won't. In fact, you're being sent to San Francisco, after all. Another family that was supposed to go there made a fuss, wanted the Northeast, so they're going to New York and you'll take their places in California. Come to the office tomorrow afternoon. You'll probably be leaving in a few weeks—maybe early October."

Alexandr and Zoya now moved into the final phase of their stay in Italy. Once again the tempo of official business picked up. They had to have medical examinations to satisfy the health standards of the United States Immigration and Naturalization Service, and they had to appear at the American Consulate to sign various forms and pledges, including a statement that they would not be dependent upon public assistance in the United States.

Alexandr began to bring his teaching practice to an end. He was glad that he'd done that teaching, not only because of the money— in fact, he had charged much less than he might have—but because it had given him an opportunity to move out of that narrow circle of people whom he had known back in Odessa and who had then surfaced here in Italy. It also allowed him to appreciate the level on which he had managed to live here in Ostia, compared with some of his students whose apartments he'd visited. Many apartments had

197

perpetually malfunctioning plumbing, broken windows, vermin-infested hallways, and, as late autumn approached, cold, dampness, and mildew.

Alexandr was unaware that in one such apartment, though by no means the worst, Tatyana and Grigory Levin were now trying to make themselves comfortable. They had been out of touch with Alexandr since that going-away party at the Goffs' apartment in Moscow the previous February. Fortunately they did have some friends here from Leningrad who had already been in Ostia for a while, and who were able to secure an apartment for the Levins in the "fascist" section. But even though this part of Ostia was cleaner and safer than the "communist" section, they and their daughter, Lyuba, were jammed into an uncomfortable four-room apartment with three other families.

Winter was approaching, the weather was getting cold and damp, and the lack of hot water was becoming a major problem for the Levins. Nobody could bathe, or even warm themselves, without spending hours heating large pots of water over the stove in the small kitchen that all four families shared, then hauling the hot water to a clammy, freezing bathroom, in which some sort of mildew scum had to be scraped off every surface.

Early one morning, during the second week of October, Zoya and Alexandr were picked up by a minibus and driven to Fiumicino Airport, where they and about ten other families waited for three hours for a plane to New York. The bus had picked them up at dawn; they were sleepy and felt a bit muddled from the past few days of rushing around, packing, and signing forms. Zoya had gradually come out of her shell after a few weeks in Ostia, but as their departure for America approached she began to show the same symptoms she'd had in Vienna and during their first weeks in Rome: an almost total withdrawal.

Alexandr—in fact, most of the emigrés who sat at the gate, dozing, waiting for the plane—felt an unpleasant, queasy numbness compounded of anxiety and an immense weariness: not the weariness caused merely by a few sleepless nights separated by days of exertion and worry, but the larger weariness brought on by a grinding, exhausting sense of constant motion, motion with no promise of rest, going and again going. Even the recollection of peace became stained with this going, until it was hard for them to tell whether their own childhood memories weren't perhaps wishful dreams congealed out of that numb, chilled half-sleep in stations and departure gates.

Tatyana Levin usually tried to avoid the *Posta*. Now that the weather was getting cold the crowd had diminished, and the few people there seemed shabbier, more depressed than they had in the warm days. The fountain basin inside the post-office colonnade had been emptied, and one morning a message in large, black, spray-painted letters appeared on the inside of the fountain rim: PER EBREI NÈ SCUOLE NÈ OSPEDALI MA CAMPI DI INFERNO, "For Jews, no schools or hospitals, only the fields of Hell."

At about the time of the Gorelskys' departure, Tatyana Levin was informed that she could begin work as a translator in the Joint office in Rome. The caseworkers, mostly Italian women, spoke a bit of English, but few of them knew any Russian.

Every evening Tatyana left the Joint office in a state of exhaustion. She couldn't shake off those angry voices or the atmosphere of frustration, grief, and fear. The office was always filled with emergency cases, people with sick or senile parents, feverish children, parents whose youngsters had been hit by cars or who had accidentally hurled their own illegally driven and ill-repaired Volkswagens into stanchions or over embankments. An old man became hysterical and doubled over with a heart attack, his face a pasty bluish white, contorted. Women wept with stories of running out of money before the end of the month, their children left without food, because they'd had to pay two-thirds of their allotments for rent. They were not given extra money. Men pleaded for more cash because they had been mugged and robbed outside of the one bank that would cash their checks. Their requests were also denied.

Some of their stories may have been true, some were probably lies, some exaggerations. Old people really did die, perhaps for lack of proper care. Other elderly men and women sat in the office, not understanding where they were, alone, on their way to join children in America, some without any children anywhere—lost, like plants pulled out of the ground and tossed aside to wither.

Every evening after work, Tatyana shuffled out and took the bus to the Termini to get the metro to Ostia. Once in November she tried to cleanse her heart of the day's toxins before boarding that crowded, rickety, badly lit train. She wanted to calm down before walking into that one very unprivate room and that kitchen seething with the accumulated noise and anger of four troubled families. She knew Grigory would be depressed because he'd had to shop and cook while she was working, a rare thing for Soviet men to do. He would be sullen in spite of his attempts to convince himself that he was doing what had to be done. Lyuba would chatter on and on, and finally begin whining after she failed to capture anyone's full attention.

No; let the train go. In another twenty minutes Tatyana could catch another. Right now she would relax on one of the benches off the Piazza del Cinquecento, a block from the Termini. She sat with her back to the large open square that fronted on the station, an area thick with buses, cabs, cars, masses of pedestrians, all trying to move at once, all honking, threatening, running; all outshouted by the black-market cigarette pushers, toy sellers, and lottery-ticket vendors whose voices were ragged from yelling.

Tatyana leaned back on the bench and stared up over the twin groves of trees that stretched northward for one long block past the piazza. Although she tried to shut out the Termini bedlam behind her, all the surrounding avenues were jammed with the infernal chaos of day's end. Only above the trees was there any peace for the eyes. It was just that time between sunset and dark, when great flocks of birds converge above these trees, in which they would later roost for the night. The lane between the two groves was white with the birds' droppings, and its air was heavy with their stench.

They had already gathered into flocks, like twisting gray clouds against the dusk. One group wheeled off to the side while another tilted, then narrowed to a funneling, tumbling stream. Again—suddenly swirling—the mass banked and soared.

A few birds landed for a moment, and Tatyana thought they

looked like starlings. She wondered if they weren't those same win-ter-driven migrants that Dante had described; and again she felt a twinge of annoyance that all her good books, including her Russian version of Dante, had been sold at that outdoor book market in Leningrad, when she and Grigory were raising money to apply for a visa. Anyway, she doubted that she could concentrate on a good book now.

She stood up to walk across the piazza toward the underground stairway to the Ostia trains. As she glanced up one last time, the flocks were pouring through one another like some magic fluid, suddenly thick and black as all wings thrust flat out together to block the last light, then transparent again as they pulled in for the slow dive.

Tatyana allowed herself to be carried along by the crowd across the square and down the steps to the train. The wind had borne a slight odor of bird droppings right through the entrance to the underground.

That night a heavy throbbing pain encircled Tatyana's back and stomach. She collapsed, and was unable to move. She lay curled in pain, washed over by waves of panic, and unable to catch her breath, as though she had been placed in an atmosphere devoid of oxygen. Sometimes, especially in the middle of the night, she could catch her breath only by screaming herself awake. For three weeks Tatyana was almost immobile, unable to take any solid food except thin, unsalted kasha. Although she had never felt the seizure quite so severely, she recognized it as related to those attacks she'd had while teaching at the military school in Leningrad. She wondered whether this was some kind of nervous breakdown. Her suspicions were supported by a local Italian doctor, who came to the apart-ment to examine her, and who prescribed a strong tranquilizer.

By the end of November Tatyana was able to eat some solid food, but even after she got back on her feet she did not return to her job. By then, however, Grigory had been hired as an elevator operator at HIAS, and later as a doorman in one of the offices.

Since Grigory's brother, Volodya, who had emigrated the year before, was settled near San Francisco, Grigory and Tatyana had none of the Gorelskys' worries about where they would be accepted. Those with first-degree relatives would be taken. When their last days came, in mid-January, Tatyana and Grigory were stricken with that same malaise that Alexandr and Zoya had felt over three months before. Something within resisted that next move, even though it was a step closer to the goal they had long dreamed of. Something held back, wanting to burrow down here, in a place where they knew at least one or two tricks of survival.

But when the day came, they and the others rushed through the predawn drizzle to get on the minibus to the airport, squeezing through the door as though the last one might be left out. And when the airline attendants opened the departure gate, the emigrés were not content to allow other passengers to crowd ahead of them, though everyone had reserved seats. Perhaps they were simply reliving those train rides from Odessa, Lvov, Kiev, or the more subdued terrors of the Moscow and Leningrad airports.

So they pushed themselves onto yet another joyless flight, as they had already shoved and wept their way through questionnaires, bureaucracies, officials, and would even have broken past that ferryman on the Styx if he'd dared to block their path to God knows where.

Part Three: BEGINNINGS

Chapter Seven:
International Arrivals

Kennedy Airport, International Arrivals Building, 5:00 P.M. Two young men and a middle-aged woman, Americans, pressed themselves against one wall of the jammed corridor to avoid being swept away in the rush, as periodic waves of arriving passengers poured by. Another young woman in her early twenties was trying to shout something to them from the end of the corridor, but one of the men simply shrugged and pointed to his ear. They couldn't hear her over the noise of the shuffling, clattering throng and the voices of uniformed guides who kept chanting, "Passengers with American passports, please turn to the left at the end of the hall, all others go to the right. Passengers with American passports . . ."

The young woman forced her way closer against the current of the crowd, stood on her toes, and called out, "Immigration's holding the last two booths open for us. First take care of those making connections out tonight, then those being bused to the motels. Those staying in New York can wait till last. . . ."

A few minutes later a small crowd of about thirty people began to move out of a stairwell that led from an upper-level deplaning ramp. The three workers, who spoke no Russian, were calling out, "HIAS! HIAS!" and motioned the emigrés to line up along the wall of the corridor so that they wouldn't be swept off in the passing crowd.

They were then led away to a long open area that was divided down its length by a row of gates, like small toll booths. In each of the booths sat an officer of the United States Immigration and Naturalization Service. The emigrés had their records of acceptance from the American Consulate in Rome, but the officers in the booths had to fill out a new set of forms, and issued the emigrés their status documents attesting that they had permission to live and work in the United States.

"You can believe me, this is a high-technology country. I can tell—" A tall, heavy-faced man from Lvov, walking behind Grigory and Tatyana Levin, was holding forth to a smaller, sad-looking fellow next to him. "I can tell. Did you see those telescoping ramps that come right out to the airplane door? An advanced nation."

The smaller one, without altering his hangdog look, spoke in a sort of whining drone. "When I was in Armenia I saw the same thing in the airport at Yerevan."

The larger man scowled down at him. "So if it's so wonderful back home in Yerevan you should have stayed!" he snapped.

"Who says I'm from Yerevan? I'm from Odessa."

The other man glared straight ahead for a moment as they shuffled into the Immigration Service area, then turned to the hefty woman at his other side, and hissed loudly: *"Puskay takikh v Ameriku!"* "Go let such people into America! . . ."

"Kogan—" Kogan jumped forward, leaving his wife and his elderly mother where they were, leaning against a column, trying to get some rest after nearly twenty-four hours without sleep. The HIAS man called out again, "Kogan!"

"*Da! Da!* Kogan—" The man pointed to himself and nodded.

"With your whole family," the young man from HIAS enunciated carefully, in English. "Family. Understand? *Familia. Familia.*" The two Russian-speaking HIAS people were away at the moment, so there was nobody to remind the young worker that the Russian word *familia* means "family name," not "family." In fact, he had been told this before, but he tended to forget in the stress of the moment. So he repeated, *"Familia! Familia!"* and the emigré, nodding rapidly, and with repressed but mounting hysteria, babbled, "Kogan, Kogan! . . ."

An emigré who understood some English finally cleared up the misunderstanding. It took about two hours for the Immigration Service officers to pass the group through the two booths. As soon as a family passed through, one of the HIAS people led them along a corridor and into a vast, echoing area where throngs of people were milling about. As they entered this customs area, one of the Russian-speaking HIAS workers handed them an envelope with some cash and directed them to follow another HIAS worker to collect their baggage and take it through the customs check.

Grigory and Tatyana pulled their valises together out of the luggage heap and dragged it over to a customs agent at a row of counters across the room. The HIAS worker who accompanied them was surprisingly helpful. She smiled at little Lyuba, tried to amuse her, and even helped Tatyana lift a valise onto the customs counter. The customs agent glanced briefly into one suitcase and mumbled a question as he looked at their papers. The HIAS woman said, "No, no fruits or produce."

"Ga 'head," he nodded, and the Levins found themselves being led through a broad guarded doorway, then through a large waiting room. They passed a roped-off area where crowds of people were jammed together, waiting to meet incoming passengers. A short, hefty man with curly black hair and an old Navy pea jacket leaned out of the crowd and bellowed, with a thick Russian accent:

"Missis Hayaas! Missis Hayaas! More Rahshians to come?"

"Plenty more, plenty more."

Tatyana stumbled along, staring ahead like a sleepwalker, clutching Lyuba by the hand. But Grigory was wide awake. From the moment he got off the plane he tried to absorb every impression, to look into every face. In Rome he had read anything he could find about America, especially about the experiences of those who had been immigrants in the early 1900s—those first glimpses of the Statue of Liberty from the ship, Ellis Island—but that stately pilotage up New York Harbor, past the tall Lady with the torch, happened only in those books, which Grigory had left behind for other emigrés still in Rome. Instead there was an Alitalia jet, which he and Tatyana dubbed "Noah's Ark" because of the loud, jabbering mélange of ethnic and national types that made up the passenger list.

Wet snowflakes spattered against the minibus they had been led to, which was now picking its way through a maze of headlights and out of Kennedy Airport. Grigory wiped clear a patch of the fogged window and peered out at the snow-blown streams of lights. Now it was the cars that looked strange—too big. Wherever he glanced something else seemed peculiar. In Italy, the inefficiency and the general sense of institutional decay had seemed familiar, a link with Grigory's Soviet past. But now a nagging sense of strangeness leaped forth at the oddest moments. He had sensed it suddenly among all those scribbling immigration and customs officers. Wherever he looked, at least one of them was gripping his pen in his left hand and scratching across the page in a wierd, crablike manner, with the *left* hand, like a Martian imperfectly posing as a human being, in some science-fiction story. In the Soviet Union children were simply not permitted to develop that habit.

Strange is frightening. The Levins were standing in the open door to their hotel room. Lyuba was holding on to Tatyana's dress, rubbing her eyes sleepily. Grigory's shoulders were stooped from the weight of the luggage. After a few seconds he moved across the carpet—shyly, as though suddenly finding himself in someone else's flower patch—and set their bags down on the large expanse of the double bed, while Tatyana leaned against the door frame. Her face showed a touch of shock—not merely of surprise, but also a bit of vertigo, of disorientation—through her fatigue.

Not Europe, not Russia: the smells were different, the furniture, the lights; a *carpet*, of all things, not just an area rug next to the bed, but a carpet over the entire floor. Yes, perhaps it was partly from fatigue and emotional exhaustion, but there was something unnerving about this; it was a bit like being hurled back into infancy by the unfamiliarity of everything, by the sense that the simplest things here are strange, ill-understood.

And a toilet, with a shower and a sink, just for them . . .

Grigory suddenly called out to Tatyana from the bathroom, "Water in the toilet bowl . . . it must be clogged . . . don't flush it!"

Tatyana hesitantly lifted the phone and told the desk clerk that the toilet was broken, then she started to undress for bed. Who knew when the toilet might get fixed—probably not until the next day. They'd have to ask the people across the hall if they could use their toilet. She barely had time to step out of her dress and her slip when there was a knock at the door.

"Grisha! Who can that be! HIAS?"

Grigory opened the door and stepped back for an instant, speechless. An immensely tall black man was standing in the corridor.

"Trouble wit y' baffroom?"

Grigory glanced over his shoulder at Tatyana, wide-eyed, helpless. The man smiled, white-toothed, and looked Tatyana up and down once as she stood there in her pantyhose and bra, then he turned to Grigory and spoke again, slowly, one word at a time.

"Y'got . . . trouble . . . with . . . y'baff . . . room?"

"Ah! Ah! Yes! Bassroom . . ." The black man nodded politely and stepped across the rug and through the bathroom door. He stared down at the toilet for a moment. Grigory decided to give his English a try, while Tatyana fumbled around for something to wear.

"Is water. Look? Water in bottom. So, is breaken."

The man suddenly laughed. "These people," he thought, "if it wasn't one thing it was another. This one had only seen those foreign toilets, the kind with almost no water in the bottom." He pushed the flush handle to show Grigory that the toilet worked.

"It's not like the toilets in Europe. American style, y'see? That's America, man—lotsa water in the bowl—that's America."

They hardly knew what the word "California" was supposed to mean to them. What they longed for was a bit of minimal comfort and privacy; not luxury, merely a place where they could rest and live without being harassed, crowded out, or chased from their beds at 5:30 A.M.—which was when they were awakened, after a restless night in the hotel, to catch a midmorning flight out of Kennedy.

If the flight from Rome to New York had been a Noah's Ark, then the one from New York to Oakland was precisely the opposite, as sterile as a hospital. In one way, Tatyana and Grigory felt more like immigrants now than ever before, because they were the single odd element in this silent, clean, smooth planeload. On the Alitalia flight nobody knew what language he would hear next, whether from the stewardesses, the captain's microphone, or the neighboring seat. But now *only* English was heard, and that *only* out of the loudspeaker or from the stewardesses. The other passengers seemed either to be asleep or voiceless.

The immaculate marmoreal—or rather, plastic—purity of this flight was particularly surprising because there was nothing about Kennedy Airport to prepare them for it. Quite the contrary, Kennedy was a living catalogue of human types. Shortly before they boarded their flight that morning they were approached by two young men in the black coats, black hats, and untrimmed beards of the Chassidim. The two men had noticed the blue and white HIAS badge worn by the worker who was helping Grigory and Tatyana check their luggage, and thus spotted them as Soviet-Jewish emigrés. The Levins, in their turn, immediately saw the resemblance between these two young men and the Chassidim described in Potok's novels, which they had read in Rome. The young men were surprisingly diffident, and addressed all their remarks to Grigory, even though Tatyana acted as translator. She could barely understand their English, which combined a noticeable Yiddish lilt with a peculiarly elided, lisping, and rapid New Yorkese.

They passionately urged Tatyana and Grigory to abandon their plans to go to California. "Stay in New York, in Brooklyn. It's the only place you can live a *real* Jewish life. Once you leave here you'll be lost to it."

Of course, the whole thing was ridiculous, impossible! Right in the middle of a major international airport, where any Soviet would expect maximum security precautions, which is to say, maximum conformity to the norm, these relics were trying to convince emigrés to turn their backs on the rest of America because the "real" Jewish life exists only in Brooklyn, not even in Israel: in Brooklyn, wherever that might be.

After the immense maze, the vast self-enclosed city that is Kennedy Airport, Oakland Airport seemed like a toy. As they went through the now familiar motions of waiting for their luggage, Grigory was engrossed in talking to his brother, Volodya, whom he hadn't seen for over a year. At first Volodya seemed to have changed since Leningrad. This natty young man in his thirties, now sporting a neatly trimmed, curly brown beard, and dressed in a buff-colored sports jacket with large brown checks, pranced snappily and confidently among the baggage carousels, the porters, and the entire noisy airport kaleidoscope. At first it seemed to Tatyana that the most familiar thing about Volodya were those gleaming silver-capped teeth he flashed at them, but after a few minutes the old familiar Volodya revealed himself through that sharp-cut American veneer: tense, awkward, and proudly in love with his own exaggerations as he fired his words in machine-gun bursts separated by tight, tooth-sucking pauses.

Grigory found it hard to imagine his younger brother actually driving a car, especially among all those other immensely long vehicles crowding the roads. After they climbed into the ten-year-old Chevy, which Volodya had bought for a few hundred dollars a month earlier, he could see that Volodya was new to the craft of driving, but that hardly diminished Grigory's admiration.

The building in which the Levins were to live was obviously some sort of apartment house, but it looked surprisingly flat, a featureless plaster wall with rectangular glazed window openings, unrelieved by window sills, cornices, or other decorations. The wall was not that soft aged color of some of the buildings in Vienna, but a harsh, grimy yellow, with the hardness of cheap paint that had once been garish.

Volodya used a key to open the street door and led them into a courtyard. Tatyana and Grigory looked around with as much puzzlement as their weary, dulled nerves could sustain. Two sides of the courtyard were enclosed by the inside wall of the apartment house, along which ran four tiers or walkways connected by outside staircases of cement or concrete. The apartment doors were placed along the outside walkways. There was no inside corridor. The whole thing had a flimsy look, as though it could barely withstand the force of the elements, but Volodya waved their worries away and assured them that in this area there were no elements to withstand. Nonetheless, Grigory and Tatyana felt strangely exposed as they walked along that third-floor ramp which vibrated and thrummed with every step they took, with other people's living-room windows at waist height on one side, and a two-story drop past the slender railing on the other.

Still, it was an apartment, and it was their own. They could lock the door and spread out a bit without fetching up against some other family in the kitchen or the bathroom. The plumbing worked, there was hot water, a small refrigerator, a working gas stove, a bedroom, an alcove where Lyuba could sleep, some chairs, tables, and beds. The furniture was ugly and rickety, but usable.

Tatyana often thought of herself as someone who had partaken in a miracle. Before she and Grigory married, she had worked briefly as an English-speaking tour guide, showing groups of visiting Western businessmen and professionals the Leningrad sights. But whenever a tour ended, and her charges returned to the West, she felt an odd sensation, almost as though she were in the presence of death, as though those people had ceased to exist. Friends who moved far away to Siberia or Kazakhstan still existed in the world; she could have gotten on a plane to visit them. But those Swedes, Englishmen, Americans—like the dead, once they left they were utterly beyond reach.

When she and Grigory actually took off in that plane to Vienna she was overwhelmed by the sense of a present miracle, as though she were some mythic hero who had performed an impossible labor. It was Orpheus who came most clearly to her mind, who crossed the uncrossable border and descended alive to the Kingdom of the Dead.

During those first months in Oakland, Tatyana became as disturbed by being a kind of Orpheus as she had at first been thrilled by it. Orpheus had crossed the boundaries of death to reclaim his lost Eurydice, but, though he returned alive, he returned alone. He had failed. Tatyana tried to shrug the thought away. After all, any metaphor could be extended too far, she thought. She had simply meant that Orpheus had benefited from a miracle and so had she, and there was no good in analyzing it any further during those anxious, wakeful nights.

Yet miracles do bring devastation, even as they offer renewal. They thrust the blessed into sudden and profound change, into a world altered beyond understanding, and thus into a kind of infantile helplessness. Back in Leningrad Grigory had understood quite well that as soon as he applied for an exit visa he would cease to exist as a respectable, contributing member of Soviet society, and would be instantly transformed into a traitor, at best a nonentity. He recognized, in Vienna and in Rome, that he was just another shabby, shuffling figure in the mob. But now he was in America; he was as adult, as able, as professional as he had always been. He knew he hadn't lost his talent, his knowledge, his research experience on the flight over the Atlantic, and he was sure that American technology could use his experience at least as well as the Soviets could. But suddenly his experience and ability seemed not to count. They were hidden behind his inarticulateness and his foreignness.

Nobody at the Jewish Family Service office in Oakland taught him the rudiments of survival in the American job market. How was he to know, for example, that in America letters of inquiry about jobs must be neatly typed on decent paper if they are to be taken seriously? In the Soviet Union, such letters are always handwritten because the applicant is not expected to own a typewriter. This was only one among many discoveries that Grigory had to make through time-wasting trial and error. For example, it wouldn't to save his precious little allotment money by having a cheap typist do his résumés on the cheapest paper. Professionals in America must have professional-looking résumés. Above all, Grigory discovered that he must avoid telephone contacts. In a personal interview he could figure out what the boss was talking about even though he couldn't understand all the words. Body language communicated a great deal. On the telephone he was simply inarticulate—stuttering, grunting, sweating, like a shy little boy in the school play, his speech forgotten.

His American cousins, the Gellmans, as well as other friends he had made, began to introduce him to chemists, and on each occasion Grigory repeated his litany: education, experience, job titles, responsibilities. And time and again people shrugged or shook their heads: if only he had some American work experience . . . his job description doesn't quite fit the American categories, perhaps his field doesn't exist here . . . maybe on the East Coast . . .

Over the months, Grigory developed a routine: look up job listings, compose letters, follow through on contacts, go to the Jewish Family Service every few weeks with a record of his applications and rejections; talk with more technologists, repeat the litany, watch them shake their heads; show his rejection letters to the caseworker at the Family Service . . .

Every few weeks Grigory had to sit patiently while this chubby functionary frowned, looked through Grigory's stack of rejection letters, and seemed to ponder with slow, deliberate skepticism whether he was worthy of another few weeks' assistance. It took a while for Grigory to realize that the $180 per month he was given for rent and the $270 for food and maintenance had already been allocated, and that there was no real question of his eligibility. Every local Jewish agency that sponsors the emigrés is autonomous, makes its own commitments, and determines its own budget. The emigrés in each locality must follow the rules peculiar to the local agency. In Oakland, when the Levins arrived, the Jewish Family Service allocated money to give each family under their jurisdiction support for six months, after which the support was cut off. By the end of the 1970s this support period had been reduced to three months. Grigory dutifully rendered an account of himself each month, like a child who is being put to the question.

Tatyana helped Grigory prepare his application letters and sometimes translated for him at interviews and during especially difficult telephone conversations, but there was little else she could do to relieve him of that knot of anguish that he carried home with their support checks. She had learned her way around the neighborhood, she could shop, take the bus, visit some of the friends they had begun to make among the other emigrés, but she was wearied as though from carrying a constant weight, fatigued by the unremitting burden of strangeness. They lived in a low-rent district, a borderline slum, not in the most violent part of Oakland, but in an area that was unsafe to walk through, especially at night. There were frequent newspaper reports of assaults on elderly people, who were robbed and sometimes beaten. Women never went out alone at night; even during the day there were muggings. Bands of arrogantly strutting young blacks, often only in their teens, stared at Tatyana insolently and sometimes called out snickering remarks, which she couldn't understand, but which seemed intended to cow her. On the other hand, Tatyana noticed that those boys seemed to be talking to one another in the same tone.

The few remaining whites in the neighborhood blamed the blacks for the crime, the blacks blamed the whites and the police, and the Levins couldn't make much sense out of either side of the debate. Tatyana had some questions concerning those easy clichés about the violence and criminality of the blacks, for she had heard the same anti-black slurs among Russians in Leningrad, where the only blacks were the highly educated upper-class exchange students from Africa. Most of them were cultured, polished, rich, and yet many Russians considered them dirty, simian, violent. But these Oakland blacks weren't rich African exchange students. They were ghetto kids, and some of them loved to play the part of street toughs, whether or not they all actually fit the role. What the Levins knew was that whoever was at fault, there was no debating that the place was dangerous.

Even the campuses of the neighboring colleges and universities left Tatyana feeling lost and confused. She visited several of the campuses with Grigory when he went to meet members of the science departments. Tatyana was making inquiries to see if she could work as an assistant to a Russian professor, and perhaps even to be admitted as a graduate student herself.

In a conference with the chairman of one of the local departments, Tatyana had difficulty in responding to the friendliness and cordiality with which he treated her. In all her experience with Soviet university life, she had never seen the difference in rank between faculty and students breached. As in Soviet life generally, the man in authority is treated with the formal reverence due his position, and he treats his subordinates, or his students, with the coolness appropriate to his own superior rank. For a new arrival to sit and chat with a department chairman would be unthinkable. Though Tatyana knew better, she found herself sitting at the edge of her chair, her back straight, every muscle strained, her face flushed, her hands shaking. And she could see that the professor was beginning to wonder what could be the matter with her.

Strangeness, worry, anxiety over Grigory and his career—all these left Tatyana increasingly fatigued during the day and restless during the nights, when dream images of Leningrad, of her father and brother, of suddenly finding herself back at OVIR, wove in and around the frequent nocturnal sorties of police and fire sirens past the Levins' bedroom windows. One night, at the end of February, Tatyana snapped awake in terror, gasping for air, strangling. She felt that same band of pain around her stomach that had heralded her many weeks of sickness in Italy. Grigory had her rushed to the hospital emergency room. After a young Chinese doctor gave her a shot to calm her nerves and to allay her muscle spasms, she started to cry uncontrollably. The doctor tried to talk to her, slowly and clearly, so that she could understand his Chinese accent, while the nurse, who was also Chinese, busied herself taking Tatyana's blood pressure and temperature.

Tatyana lay on the bed, sobbing without letup. After several minutes the doctor turned away from his charts, looked at her, and tried again to get her to speak. He asked why she was crying, but she was wracked and shaking, unable to speak. Then the nurse called across the room to the doctor:

"Don't you remember? We're both immigrants, Doctor Liu. Don't you remember how it was? Of course she's crying! . . ."

Just a few years before the Levins arrived in Oakland, a former fraternity house near the Berkeley campus of the University of California was acquired by Chabad, the outreach organization of the Lyubavitcher Chassidim in New York. They sent two young rabbis to Berkeley, who proceeded to transform the large house into an outpost of Chassidism. On an evening in March, a bit over two months after the Levins arrived in Oakland, The Chabad House on fraternity row was packed with Jews from all over the area, who had come for the Purim party. By now the house had become a gathering place for all kinds of Jews, from the most pious to the least, who shared a taste for the old-fashioned singing, dancing, and *davvening*. The room was packed with people, groups of men were circling about in traditional Chassidic dances; others watched, clapped their hands, and sang in Yiddish or Hebrew. Many stood around and gossiped. Everyone was in motion, mouths wide with food or talk; some people were gesticulating with their hands, others shouting to be heard by their friends.

Near one edge of the crowd, a strong-looking dark-haired man, whose sensitive features slipped naturally into a slight but warm smile, was talking quietly to a shorter, heavy woman with a chubby Russian-Jewish face. Ella and Leonid Novogradsky had arrived about a year earlier, from Odessa. At this moment their expressions were veiled as they glanced around, trying not to stare too obviously, and exchanged swift comments in Russian.

"Look over there," Leonid mumbled, "a real Soviet face on that girl—a cold fish!"

Ella intoned, with a slightly nasal voice, in that Odessan sing-song, "What do you expect, Lyonya. They only came a month or two ago. They're the Levins."

"She's wearing her official Soviet face, Ella. I know the type."

"Quiet, Lyonya. The mask won't last. We learned, they'll learn too."

"Hm. The husband, too. Stiff, like wood."

Not that Leonid Novogradsky categorically disliked or even avoided newly arrived emigrés. In fact, when help and advice were needed he and Ella were usually glad to extend themselves. The previous October, five months before this Chabad party, they had driven to San Francisco International Airport to meet their old friends, Alexandr and Zoya Gorelsky, and had spent days helping them and showing them around the area. But then, the Gorelskys were special. Alexandr had been not only the Novogradskys' English tutor back in Odessa, but also their all-around advisor and helper, and that was while Alexandr was undergoing the first agonies of his refusenik days.

As the Novogradskys watched Alexandr and Zoya Gorelsky stumbling along the deplaning ramp at San Francisco Airport on that mild October afternoon in 1975, they were a bit shocked at how wrung out Zoya looked. Just before the Novogradskys left Odessa, more than a year ago, Alexandr had seemed half starved and near collapse, but Zoya was healthy, if a bit shy. Now Alexandr looked thin but basically healthy, while Zoya seemed ill. Her skin was pale and a bit puffy, and her eyes were red.

Zoya's extreme exhaustion was at least partly Alexandr's fault. As soon as they reached the motel in New York, rather than allowing themselves some desperately needed sleep, Alexandr insisted that they telephone an American acquaintance, a rabbi who had once helped Alexandr and some other refuseniks while a tourist in Odessa. The rabbi and his family drove straight to the motel to take the Gorelskys out for dinner and a drive around New York, and that was the end of their night's sleep.

As they all sat in the motel room and chatted, before going out to eat, the Gorelskys were treated to their first taste of the peculiarities of American behavior. The rabbi's two teenaged sons plumped themselves down on the floor and sat there, leaning back on their elbows, their legs thrust out before them, as though they were at a beach picnic. The sight of people sitting on the floor was new to the Gorelskys. It wasn't merely that such behavior would be considered gauche in the Soviet Union, it was simply unheard of. At gatherings where there weren't enough seats, people stood.

Alexandr had seen and heard of restaurants with specialized menus in the Soviet Union, as well as in Vienna and in Rome, so he was not surprised that there were kosher restaurants in New York. It made perfect sense in a city with one or two million Jews. But a kosher Chinese restaurant? It had to be a joke, yet there it was. As they walked to their table the humor of the situation was replaced by distaste. The Chinese waiters were wearing *yarmulkas*, Jewish skullcaps. Alexandr had a momentary recollection of Grandpa Naum wearing a hat like that as he prayed or studied those tomes of his, and to see them on those Chinese waiters seemed a mockery, a maniacal joke, a perversion. And yet there were scores of Jewish customers at these tables—some of them also wearing *yarmulkas*— eating, talking, accepting all this as quite natural.

After the meal, the rabbi asked the waiter for a "doggy bag," a phrase Alexandr had never heard before, and the waiter started to pack the leftover food in cardboard containers. Alexandr's heart sank in horror. When the rabbi had insisted that they be his guests for dinner Alexandr and Zoya had naturally assumed that he could afford it. Now it seemed that the rabbi couldn't even afford to feed his own family. Alexandr was embarrassed, baffled as to what he could do to help. The little bit of cash he'd received from the HIAS people at Kennedy Airport that afternoon was nowhere enough to pay for this meal, and it would have been impossibly awkward for Alexandr even to broach the subject of lending his hosts a hand with the expenses.

Alexandr and Zoya looked at each other, then stared at the rabbi, who seemed utterly nonchalant, as though nothing were out of place. Alexandr leaned over to the rabbi's ear.

"You're all right? I mean, everything is OK?"

"What? Yes, of course."

Part Three: BEGINNINGS

"You're . . . you're still employed?"

With a reassuring if slightly puzzled look the rabbi led them all out of the restaurant and into his car. Alexandr tried to tell himself that it would be interesting, perhaps even fun, to observe all these weird habits of the Americans; but, of course, he would also have to adjust to these new ways, to absorb them, even to embrace them. He was here for life.

As Leonid Novogradsky drove north on the Freeway there seemed to be a constant babble of talk in the car, though Alexandr couldn't quite remember, afterward, who had done all the talking. Zoya was curled in the corner of the back seat next to Alexandr, half asleep, and Leonid wasn't saying very much as he drove. Alexandr himself must have been answering Ella's questions and comments automatically. Later on he could remember clearly only two things about the drive: one was that he was very impressed that Leonid was actually driving, and especially that he was driving his own car; the other was a moment when he suddenly felt his eyes filling with tears. They had been driving through rather barren territory; the highway was bordered by treeless dunes covered with dry brown grass, and a large hillside loomed up ahead. Scored into the side of the hill were immense, ugly, yellowish letters: SOUTH SAN FRANCISCO, THE INDUSTRIAL CITY. As Alexandr saw those words on that barren hillside he was suddenly overcome by a memory of the dreamlike joy that the name San Francisco used to touch off in him when he was a schoolboy. At home they used to sing a song with a funny line about pirates drinking "bitter rum in Jamaica, whisky in San Francisco," and that line came back to him now. Buccaneers; rum in tropical Jamaica; San Francisco: something ethereal, intoxicating, wanton—Shangri-la or Xanadu—and suddenly, for just an instant there on the highway surrounded by dry and broken dunes, he had that feeling: *I'm here, I'm here—San Francisco!* A few sweet tears of relief rolled out of his eyes, unnoticed by the others, and the moment passed.

They left the Freeway before it cut through the San Francisco one always saw in pictures, and entered Daly City. The light here was strangely flat. There were long, unbroken rows of identical houses, and very few trees. Ella explained that Daly City was a

219

fairly new town, built largely on dunes, and Alexandr could see that the atmosphere hadn't lost that glaring, desiccated quality of salt-encrusted coast.

They entered the apartment-house courtyard, and Alexandr and Zoya were amazed to see a swimming pool for the use of the tenants. Alexandr was delighted. Ella explained that rents in Daly City were lower than in San Francisco itself. That was why some people in the Jewish Family Service had been thinking of settling the new emigrés here. "But don't worry about it," she went on, "as soon as you get set up you can look for a decent place."

Alexandr's slightly giddy mood evaporated. He was prepared to fall in love with the apartment, swimming pool and all, and here was Ella telling him that it was somehow undesirable. What was wrong with it he didn't know, but simply being told that he should have more sense than to like it cooled his enthusiasm.

They sat in the small living room, and Ella warned Alexandr and Zoya about the difficulties that emigrés were having with some of the workers in the San Francisco Jewish Family and Children's Service. "They don't like the emigrés there, I can tell you, Alex. They don't like us there. . . ."

Alexandr's mind flashed back over the people he'd known in Vienna, Rome, Ostia, on lines at HIAS and Joint, in the marketplaces, running the gouging rackets that thrived in Ostia.

"Who likes the emigrés, Ella? Do you?"

Ella smiled wryly and turned from the bitchiness of the agency workers to the treachery of many of their old friends from Odessa. She told about how some of them had begun to turn against one another, how people change when they emigrate, abandon old values, and begin to drift into strange, new, sometimes not very admirable directions.

Leonid sat quietly while Ella did most of the talking. It was only after Alexandr asked Leonid directly how things were for him, and whether he was able to practice medicine here, that Leonid began to talk about himself. Life had not been easy here for the Novograd-skys. Leonid had so far not been able to pass the medical licensing examination that all foreign doctors had to pass before they could practice in the United States. Most of them, no matter how competent, had to study constantly for months, even for years, before they could pass the tests.

But Ella was determined that Leonid would pass them, even if he took them ten times. Thus, she had to support the family if he were to have the opportunity to study. She therefore labored nine hours a day at a cheap women's-clothing factory in San Francisco. The place was almost reminiscent of the New York garment district of the 1920s. Rows of women sat at long tables and sewed dresses, blouses, jackets, and those tables were increasingly occupied by Soviet emigrés, many of whom had once been teachers, musicians, librarians. Their six months' support from the agency had run out, and they, or their husbands, had not yet found their way into something better. Some never would.

Friends of the Novogradskys suggested that Leonid get a job as a lab technician, or the like, but Ella wouldn't hear of it. Although she was driven almost to nervous exhaustion by trying to run a household, shop, take care of the two children, and earn enough to support the family, she insisted that if Leonid once stopped studying intensively and spent that time working for money he would never be able to get back into his profession. Ella had seen too many others give up halfway through. Ella would do everything, but Leonid must work his way through a wall of medical books in English until he finally passed the exams.

The major problem with Daly City was its isolation. Although solidly built up, it was essentially a suburb, a bedroom community. Except for a few emigrés, every family that lived there owned at least one car, so a decent bus service had never really developed. The buses ran to and from the Gorelskys' area only during weekdays, from the morning to the evening rush hours. After six P.M. on weekdays, and all day on weekends or holidays, their neighborhood was cut off.

Alexandr and Zoya were periodically invited to the large, luxurious homes of a few wealthy San Franciscans, benefactors of the local Jewish community, some of whom helped in the emigré resettlement programs. At first, Alexandr and Zoya were excited by these invitations, which seemed to indicate that people of position and influence were taking an interest in their fates. After a few such gatherings, however, Alexandr began to notice that the Americans preferred to stand around and talk with one another rather than with the emigrés. Ultimately they did introduce themselves to the emigré guests, and always asked the same general questions about life in "Russia" (they never spoke of it as the Soviet Union), what the emigré's profession had been, or how it felt to be in America. For the most part, those people wanted simple answers. If the emigrés attempted to tell them anything too complex the American guests lost interest. They had wanted to be polite, not to become involved, and soon found ways to drift back to more diverting conversations with their old San Francisco friends.

How unlike Russian parties these affairs were! They were more like small-scale academic or diplomatic receptions minus the wit and polish. Emigrés like Alexandr knew what a party should be like: everybody sits around one big table, talking and eating. If there's noplace to sit, they stand, but they talk, they laugh, and they eat. Food and warmth, that's what a party should center around. It seemed strange to nibble peanuts and remain cold sober. The Jews in the Soviet Union don't drink like the Russians do, of course, but actual sobriety is out of place at a party, which is an occasion for laughter, and then for song: political parodies, love songs, songs of departure. Most Russian songs, especially Russian-Jewish songs, are about longing and departure. And from all this talking, laughing, tipsiness and singing, the scattered crowd of guests becomes close, hot, unforgettable.

No freshly arrived emigré could recognize this scattering of motionless, quiet, dégagé, soft-spoken Californians as a roomful of Jews.

But it was their lack of interest that left Alexandr most frustrated, for he had long held to the dream that he and others like him would broach the wall of lies with which the Soviet Union surrounds itself, and would bring the true word to America. He had expected Americans to be hungry for the real story of Soviet life, just as he and others in Odessa had taken every risk to nuzzle up greedily to any source of information about the West.

At first Alexandr was baffled to discover that these educated, successful Americans knew little about the Soviet Union. They'd been told something about anti-Semitism there, but vaguely had the impression that such things had mostly vanished with the fall of the Tsar in 1917. What was most baffling was that some of these people were surprised that the emigrés were so "un-Jewish," for there were those among the Americans at these parties who expected the emigrés to be charmingly old-fashioned Sholem Aleichem characters, full of ghetto shrugs and Yiddish-sounding folk wisdom.

Alexandr and the other emigré guests at these gatherings had not had a chance to absorb the fact that American Jews, over the years, had simply become less East European and more Anglo-Saxon in their cultural habits, and that Americans were not "hungry" for information for the simple reason that they were surrounded by it, that, in general, it was available for the asking. The realization that Americans, and even American Jews, were less interested in information than Europeans, would take a bit more getting used to.

One never quite knew what to expect from these American Jews, at least not at first. There were indeed those who had worked tirelessly to promote emigration, and who had developed considerable understanding of Soviet Jews and of Soviet problems generally. Even while Alexandr was still in Odessa he'd heard about the Union of Councils on Soviet Jewry, as well as similar organizations, and he had assumed that these people were representative of a good percentage of educated American Jews. But now it seemed that many of the people at these parties, who, Alexandr assumed, were supposed to be representing the local American-Jewish community, were cut from different cloth. In fact, Alexandr occasionally caught a glimmer of something worse than mere boredom at the emigrés' failure to be amusing, something more frustrating than raised eyebrows at the emigrés' apocalyptic pronouncements on world politics, and more than simple surprise at their lack of Yiddishness. He sometimes detected a flash of resentment in his hosts' eyes, an edge of impatience not only at the extent to which Alexandr and other emigrés had lost any resemblance to these American Jews' dimly remembered grandfathers, but also a trace of politely concealed dismay that these "Russians" even had pretentions to modernity, to sophistications of their own, and even to strengths and superiorities of their own.

Alexandr had a tremendous advantage over practically all the other recent emigrés vis-à-vis their American hosts at these parties:

his English was fluent, and he quickly caught on to the American style of light banter, so the Americans found him interesting and amusing to talk to. At one of these parties he was fortunate enough to meet a professor from a college in a nearby city, and was actually given an appointment to come to the campus to meet people who might be helpful in finding him a job. After several weeks of interviewing, it was arranged that Alexandr would teach a single course, to graduate students in history, from January through May, for a few hundred dollars per month. Alexandr had already come to realize that jobs in American universities, especially in the humanities, were hard to get. Even American Ph.D.s, with all the help of their professors, were having difficulty finding positions. If Alexandr were a native-born American, he might have looked upon this job as at best a chance to make some contacts in the academic world, as a foot in the door; but Alexandr thought that he'd made it, that his American career had now begun in earnest. True, it was only a one-semester course on Soviet approaches to historical studies; true, it would be an economic disaster for Alexandr and Zoya, since they would now be earning even less than the Family Service had been giving them, and they would probably have difficulty paying their rent. Moreover, Zoya couldn't go to work because she was planning to go back to college to finish her B.A. But Alexandr either could not or would not evaluate just how small a step this job was. To him at this point, there was no distinction between a foot in the door and a major victory. Any step at all was a quantum leap. Although a certain innate caution, an intuitive wariness, forced him to repress any outward expression of it, something in him leaped with joy and triumph when he was offered the course to teach. He had made it! He couldn't live on the salary, but that was an irrelevant matter.

This triumph came not a moment too soon. Alexandr had been finding it harder and harder to face the caseworker in the agency. Every few weeks he was cross-examined about his job search, and all but accused of trying to defraud the community, or so it seemed to him. What was more frightening, his caseworker was unpredictable. This small, volatile woman would at one time urge the Gorelskys to relax, not to try to solve all their problems at once; then, on the next interview, she would be furious that they hadn't yet found work, and threaten that this was to be their last check. They never knew what to believe, and thus believed nothing the bureaucrats told them. Alexandr found it beyond his endurance to be beholden to these people, and was only too happy to abandon his last few months of benefits, and to accept that part-time lectureship.

The problem of transportation to and from Daly City now became crucial. The only way for somebody without a car to travel the thirty miles or so to the campus at which Alexandr was teaching was to take a local bus to downtown San Francisco, and then an intercity bus. The process took hours and was expensive. What was worse, there was no way to get back to the Gorelskys' neighborhood after six P.M., and Alexandr's class ended too late for that. The only alternative was to hitchhike. Every Thursday, as he walked backward along the Freeway entrance with a hitchhiking sign in his right hand, Alexandr's tall, wiry figure could be seen wearing a spotless three-piece suit, his reddish-brown hair looping down toward the collar of his dress shirt, and a necktie carefully knotted just below his curly ginger-colored beard.

Although winters are relatively mild in that part of California, they can be rainy, damp, chilly, and unpredictable. On more than one occasion Alexandr left his apartment in sunny, springlike warmth and came dragging back along the road, soaked and shivering, through a chill and blustery Pacific squall.

His worst night occurred early in the semester. He had left home wearing only an extra sweater under his lightweight suit jacket, but by the time he was ready to hitch homeward the temperature had dropped fifteen degrees and a snowstorm had swept in across the entire north-central California coast. Alexandr left his class at about four-thirty, and at nine-thirty he was still trudging down the road, holding out his sign. His head and his beard were caked white, and he was numb and shivering with cold. Two highway patrolmen pulled up alongside him to find out what he was up to. He told them his story, showed them his papers, and they kindly decided to leave him alone, waved him out of their warm patrol car, and drove off leaving him in the blizzard, without prejudice.

About a half hour later, the driver of a sports car that was zipping past decided to give Alexandr a lift, so he slammed on his brakes, practically putting the car into a spin on the snowy road. As Alexandr leaned into the window he could make out just enough to tell that the driver was one of those California golden boys, deeply tanned even in January, with large, perfect teeth and eyes glowing ruby-red from pot. Alexandr was beyond caring, and they drove off together. The car was unheated, the wind was whistling through the leaky canvas convertible top, but the golden boy was in magnificent humor and babbled on loudly and incoherently.

After fifteen or twenty minutes the driver wondered out loud whether he had remembered to turn off the stove in his cabin. Finally he became so obsessed with the worry that his place would burn down that he turned the car around, and Alexandr found himself heading in the wrong direction. After another hour and a half, as they were again nearing the San Francisco area, the driver decided that he had to speak to his girl friend, so they headed westward over the hills to a beach area. They never did succeed in locating the girl friend.

Some time between midnight and one A.M., Alexandr stumbled through the doorway of the apartment. Zoya was frantic. She was sure he had been killed on the highway, or had frozen to death. Alexandr staggered past her without a word, dropped onto the living-room rug in a dead faint, and slept there for the next sixteen hours.

The Gorelskys' biggest problem at this time was the depression and anxiety into which Zoya had been slipping since they'd arrived. It began as an intensification of that general sense of fear that most emigrés feel at the strangeness of what confronts them in the streets. For one thing, there were those groups of young men, their presence announced by the blare of portable radios as though in warning to all others to step aside or be shoved aside. Their aim seemed to be to humiliate and dominate all who were not of their own group, and this aim was achieved without the slightest demur from other passersby. Zoya could remember that Soviet streets were sometimes cluttered with drunks—far more than in America—drunks who occasionally became insolent and even violent. But *groups*, swaggering about noisily, frightening people, tossing garbage out of waste cans, defacing everything with spray-painted slogans—any group like that would quickly be attended to by the Soviet police.

Even if a pedestrian in Moscow or Odessa were to witness a violent crime, the sense of threat was not resonated and amplified by the news media, for crime reports are rarely published in the Soviet press. But in San Francisco the terror inflicted by street gangs was multiplied a thousandfold by the constant reports of assault, rape, and street killings detailed in the newspapers and on television. Every leather-jacketed tough Zoya saw had two daily papers and three major television stations behind him, endlessly advertising his power, so he didn't have to do very much growling or shoving to instill fear.

There were other grotesque sights here in America. Wherever Zoya walked she came across nightmarishly twisted cripples haunting the sidewalks in motorized wheelchairs, their skeletal limbs or unmuscled flesh moving about jerkily as they directed their electric wheelchairs with a single barely functioning palsied limb, or by means of a control stick gripped in skewed jaws. Back in the Soviet Union Zoya had never seen such things. People who suffered such mutilation either perished or were kept out of sight in hospitals or homes. But here there were groups that trained such people to maneuver their little vehicles about, that agitated to get them jobs, and even brought political pressure on bus companies and on architects to build ramps and other devices to accommodate them. Thus, the streets here were dotted with this human wreckage. The Americans seemed quite used to all this, but Zoya felt her heart pound whenever she heard that characteristic soft whine of a motorized wheelchair coming up behind her, with its erratic clicking as it lurched about among the pedestrians.

Most emigrés experienced similar fears and misgivings, but then adjusted. The initial shock wore off after a while, and they came to understand that America is neither a nation of gangs nor of paralytics. Many of those leather-jacketed kids turned out to be harmless, and the virtues of making it possible for people in wheelchairs to move about freely was too obvious even to think about. Zoya, however, could tell that her fears were growing rather than subsiding. As Alexandr had noticed in Rome, she became increasingly reluctant to leave the apartment. Then she was unable to sleep, and lay in bed most of the night trembling. An emigré acquaintance who worked in a local hospital brought her a small bottle of Valium pills, and assured her that what she was going through was not so unusual, that practically every emigré goes through some kind of breakdown, though hers was perhaps a bit more acute, a bit more obvious. In fact, the more people the Gorelskys met, the more truth there seemed in that statement. Practically everyone, even those who'd had little trouble finding jobs, remembered periods of waking up in blind predawn panic, night after night, of hours and days lost in a kind of paralyzing grief, of sudden disorientation, rage, weeping, and a hundred varieties of despair. But Zoya's anxieties seemed more crippling and more tenacious.

Alexandr began to take her to a local mental-health clinic once a week, though the therapy made little sense to Zoya . She was most interested in the doses of Valium they prescribed for her, and on which she had now become dependent.

As December passed the worst of Zoya's attack seemed to be waning, and when she received word that she was being awarded a scholarship for her first semester's tuition at college, she felt a surge of optimism. The start of classes, in January, represented to Zoya the beginning of her successful entrance into her new life, just as that part-time teaching job represented to Alexandr the beginning of his new career. Zoya had picked up enough English to talk with her fellow students and to absorb much of what her professors said in their lectures. By the time the semester was well under way she had returned to some semblance of health, though the social life of the college often left her feeling lost.

In the Soviet Union, undergraduates have little choice of courses, especially when they are new students. They usually travel together, from class to class, and thus form tightly knit, mutually supportive groups. But here, every class Zoya went to was made up of a totally different cluster of strangers. At the end of the class the students simply dispersed. They didn't huddle together to share their impressions of the professors or of the course material, to study together, to talk, share books, or even simply to enjoy one another's company. They simply stood up, walked out the classroom door without a word, and vanished.

After her second or third day, Zoya found herself walking toward the exit alongside one of the other young women in her last class. They exchanged a few comments, and Zoya assumed, quite automatically, that they would spend at least a few minutes together, perhaps go for some coffee, and that a closer acquaintance would arise. But then the other girl stepped into a car, slammed the door, and drove off with hardly a nod of good-bye, while Zoya stood alone in the parking lot.

Zoya heard the other students' voices only when she least expected to: during the lectures. Until now she had been used to students who sat absolutely still while the professor spoke. In the Soviet Union students did not interrupt the professor to ask questions, and to submit one's own opinion was almost unthinkable. But now Zoya watched in amazement as students took up half the hour and more to "share" their "ideas." They droned on in dull, soft, flat voices. Although Zoya understood most of the words, she found it hard to follow the gist of what was being said. It was months before she realized that there usually was no gist. What was most amazing to her was that the professors seemed to encourage these interruptions.

At first Zoya tried desperately to think of a question to ask, but the whole process was simply too foreign for her. Besides, the lectures usually parroted the textbook, which was quite simple to understand. Questions were only rarely needed. Even going to see the professor during his office hours was a new and strange thing to her, and she was simply unable to see the need for it.

And yet, in spite of the fact that the other students were talking gibberish and were asking for explanations of the obvious and the irrelevant, there was something attractive to her about that lack of authoritarian domination. Though she was bored with her classmates' endless effusions, she still felt that she herself somehow lacked creativity, that her mind must really be too dull, too sluggish to frame questions and comments. It took months for Zoya to realize that the students were talking only to save themselves the trouble of listening, and that the professors encouraged it only to save themselves the trouble of teaching.

By the time Alexandr and Zoya had been living in Daly City for a few months they realized that Ella Novogradsky had been right on that first day, when she said that they would ultimately want to find a different place to live. The Novogradskys had an apartment on the other side of the bay, near Oakland. The Gorelskys used to visit them there on weekends, occasionally, but the intimacy between the two families was limited by the fact that the Novogradskys were well over ten years older, and therefore had a somewhat different life style; they seemed almost of a different generation.

They had enrolled their children in an afternoon religious-school program at a local synagogue, and occasionally attended social activities at the temples or the Jewish Community Center. Neither Ella nor Leonid could become believers, not after being indoctrinated in Soviet public schools, but they were Jews, after all, and they were anxious to give their children a knowledge and an understanding of that heritage. It was some such desire to engage that part of themselves that drew numbers of emigrés to the party at Chabad House on that evening in March, that, and a desire to get close to others who were comfortable to be with, certain other emigrés, even American Jews of a somewhat old-world stamp. It was important. Back in Odessa, the Russians and Ukrainians had effectively prevented the Jews from forgetting that they were Jews, and from dissolving into the Slavic population. In places like California the Jews had to remind *themselves* who they were.

Tatyana and Grigory Levin hung back at the edge of the noisy crowd, which was pressing close to the walls of a large room in Chabad House, thus leaving an open space in the middle of the room. Within the space about thirty men of all ages and types, from college students to Chassidic rabbis, were dancing in a ring and singing out the same Hebrew refrain over and over again. The Levins just watched, while all around them people were clapping in cadence and singing along with the dancers. Though Grigory and Tatyana were utterly unaware of Leonid Novogradsky and of his flash of annoyance at their "Soviet" look, they were very much aware that they had that look. They knew that they hadn't yet lost that public rigidity, and felt a touch of envy toward some of those who had been in America longer and who seemed able to blend in.

Later that evening, several long tables were set up for a *farbrengen*. The Levins were curious about a certain rabbi who was to speak that night, and who was said to be a Soviet emigré. How could there be an emigré rabbi? The whole thing seemed strange.

Part Three: BEGINNINGS

Four or five of the men at the front table were dressed in black suits with peculiarly cut jackets, a bit longer than usual. After the Levins had sat through several *l'chaims* with ice-cold vodka, some group singing, and a few speeches, one of the rabbinical-looking men stood up to introduce the "Russian" rabbi, Izak Mendelyevitch. According to this introduction, before leaving the Soviet Union, Izak had studied and then taught in the underground yeshivas there.

Some of the emigrés in the room began to whisper to one another at the mention of underground yeshivas in the Soviet Union. None of them had heard of this phenomenon, nor could they conceive of anybody getting away with that under the noses of the KGB. Grigory could only think of all that trouble that his co-worker Rubenshtain had put up with, back in Leningrad, over owning one measly Hebrew grammar book. No doubt, one learned all sorts of things about the Soviet Union here in the West, facts unavailable to people over there, but underground yeshivas?

A diminutive, energetic-looking young man with slightly oversized ears was getting up now. His thin face looked mischievous, in a boyish way, and he had a vitality that was undamped by his black garb and beard. His nose seemed to pull up the midpoint of his upper lip slightly, so that his top front teeth showed even at the merest hint of a smile. This lent his face a quick, unpredictable glee, though that was countered by a slight, dark hollowness below the cheekbones, a shadow accented by his beard.

Even Tatyana had some difficulty understanding Rabbi Mendelyevitch's broken English, and she could tell that it wasn't the usual Russian accent that was making him so difficult to understand. He used a thick, guttural *gh* sound for the *r*, as is done by old-fashioned Yiddish speakers, and his intonation rose and fell in a typical shtetl singsong. He stood silent for a few seconds, seemingly lost in thought as he looked out over the crowd, then smiled.

"Nu—first we should make a little *l'chaim*, and then I can talk."

Several of the emigrés present glanced at one another out of the corners of their eyes in silent comment at the provinciality of the man.

Izak pointed to some flakes of ice clinging to the outside of a vodka bottle that had just been taken from the freezer. "You see?

231

That's why vodka is a symbol for the Chassid: no matter how cold, it never freezes . . ."

He told some stories about his childhood in the underground, about moving from classroom to classroom across the Soviet Union; he told about his arrival in Vienna, in 1969, and about how he and his family had refused to trust the religious authority of the rabbi in charge at Schönau Castle, which had been converted to a dormitory and processing center for those emigrés going to Israel, how those crazy Mendelyevitches and the other underground Chassidim were so used to trusting only their own religious authorities that they wouldn't touch the meat for fear it was unkosher. Izak set the room laughing with his description of that official rabbi, a fearsomely dignified man with an immense beard who was so furious with the Mendelyevitches for not trusting his food that he even refused to lend Izak his *tfillin*.

"He said to me, 'Eat by me the food, so I'll lend you the *tfillin*. No eating, so no *tfillin!*' But I was a little bit a *vilder*, you know, a hooligan. I used to sneak in his room when he wasn't there, steal the *tfillin* out from his desk, put on quick the *tfillin*, pray, put back in the desk, run away quick—"

As the laughter subsided he explained that his own *tfillin* had been left behind in the Soviet Union for other underground students who would still have to wear them while hidden away in basements for months, years, lifetimes—some of whom would inevitably be caught.

That chief rabbi in the Schönau transfer center, Kalman Solotviner, was bothered by more than the refusal of those crazy Chassidim to trust that his meat was kosher. It was the Mendelyevitches' son, Izak, who really got to him. The boy was far too frisky for his own good. He never stopped nagging, in that high, husky, teasing voice, complaining that everything was taking too long, insisting that he had to fly right to Israel so that he could then get permission to visit the Rebbe in New York over the High Holidays, which were now just a few weeks off.

Several days after landing in Vienna Izak went too far. He made some grinning wisecrack about running to the American Consulate to demand that he be sent straight to Brooklyn, to the Rebbe. Kalman Solotviner saw no humor in such talk. He refused to take Izak along on the sightseeing tour of Vienna that afternoon just in case the crazy kid was planning some disgrace, but this restriction only seemed to tickle Izak even more. A lot those Chassidim cared about Vienna, anyway! The only trip Izak wanted to make was to the ritual bath, the *mikveh.*

At this period, in 1969, it could take a week or more to be processed to Israel through Vienna, though later this was shortened to about two days. In fact, Izak was desperate to get going. He was not impressed by Vienna's wealth, by the cars, by the goods in the stores or the clothes on people's backs. His mind was filled with two long-time dreams: Israel, and the Rebbe. Israel, of course, was the earthly, actual, touchable vehicle not only of liberation for the Jews but of redemption for the world. To Izak it was not only the Promised Land but the Land of the Promise, a promise built into the fabric and the fate of Creation.

As for the Rebbe, in Izak's mind, and to all the Rebbe's followers, he was the living heart of Jewry, the tactical center of the movement, the spiritual root of survival. For most of his life Izak had been hearing about this elderly man who daily saved him from extinction, and about how all the thousands upon thousands of Lyubavitcher Chassidim went to see him, sooner or later, to be blessed by his hands. Now that Izak had passed the one great obstacle that had long prevented him from approaching the Rebbe, he saw no reason to delay. The first order of business was to get to Israel so he could settle in. Then he would rush off to New York for the Rebbe's blessing sometime before the High Holiday season was past. Rosh ha-Shanah, the Jewish New Year, was almost upon them, then—a week later—Yom Kippur, the Day of Atonement. There could be no better time for the Rebbe's blessing.

Until their landing approach over Lod Airport the following week, the Mendelyevitches had felt no very strong reaction toward the West except relief at being beyond the reach of the Soviets. But now, as they stepped out onto holy soil, they felt something they had never known before: this was a country of their own. Nissen was embracing everybody, weeping, laughing, practically capering despite his limp, while Izak literally bent down to kiss the ancient sun-pocked stones.

Izak had never met most of these relatives who came to greet them at the airport, though some he had seen when he was a small child. His maternal grandmother had been one of a handful of elderly Jews who had been allowed to emigrate to Israel during the late 1950s; there she had located one of her sons, who had been smuggled out of the Soviet Union shortly after World War II. Izak's parents and brothers stayed with the relatives, not far from Tel Aviv, but the next morning he himself was sent straight to the Lyubavitcher Yeshiva in Kfar Chabad, a village founded by Chassidim who had survived the Holocaust or had gotten out of the Soviet Union in the late 1940s.

This was like no yeshiva in Izak's experience. Hundreds of men and boys studied and debated right out in the open, talking Yiddish or Hebrew in loud voices as though there were nothing to hide. Their books lay open on the tables as they studied and chanted the traditional questions, analogies, and syllogisms of the Talmud to one another, rocking back and forth to the quick rhythm of their minds. And at night they studied and prayed with the lights on and the window shades open.

While Izak's fellow students listened to the stories he told about his life, his questions to them centered about one topic: the Rebbe. "You went to see him? How often? What happens there? What did he tell you?" Izak's plans to go right to the Rebbe in New York were now absorbing much of his energy, and were causing even more shouting and fuming in Israel than they had in Vienna.

A deputy minister whose office handled passport questions was in no mood to bypass the regulations for this young malingerer, who might only be trying to avoid military service, after all. "What does he think? He just got to Israel, now he wants to go off to America!" The deputy minister insisted that Izak not be exempt from the regulation that he wait for at least a month before receiving a passport. Even then he wasn't supposed to leave until he'd done his military training.

Izak tried to explain that he was a Chassid, that he had to see his Rebbe before the High Holidays passed. He promised to spend no more than a month abroad. The rabbi who had accompanied Izak to the Ministry even offered his own guarantee, but the deputy minister was adamant. He was furious that Izak even had the temerity to make such a request.

Later that day they managed to get in to see the head of the Ministry himself. He was an older Ashkenazic Jew, originally from Russia, and seemed a bit more mellowed by age and experience than his deputy. After listening to Izak's explanations he called the deputy in and told him to rush Izak's passport application through.

"But he just got here! Who does he think he is!?"

"I'll tell you who he is," the minister said wearily, the traces of Yiddish phrasing and intonation in his Hebrew contrasting oddly with the deputy's crisp North-African Sephardic.

"Who is he? He's one of those Chassidim, and he wants to see his Rebbe, and if a Chassid says he's going to see his Rebbe, and if we don't give him the papers, he'll sneak across God knows what border, and bring on our heads God knows what complications, and disasters, and plagues, and I want you to do it, so please do it."

Fortunately, the military authorities were willing to accept the guarantee of the heads of Kfar Chabad that Izak would indeed return to do his military service after one month. With the help of Izak's relatives, who raised the money for the fare, he soon found himself on board an El Al jet bound for New York.

By late 1969 only the first few thousand Jews had left the Soviet Union. This small advance party—small compared to what was to become a wave of more than 200,000 within the next decade—still contained just a few people from the Chassidic underground. Izak, therefore, was a rare representative of a group upon which the previous and the present Rebbes had expended so much care, and as such Izak was welcomed with special attention.

From Kennedy Airport Izak ran straight to the ritual bath, then joined the crowd for *Maariv*, the afternoon prayer service. By the time the Rebbe entered the synagogue there were hundreds of men packed tightly into the room, though the crowd stopped abruptly several feet from the alcove in which the Rebbe stood to pray. Izak, who was short and bone-thin (he weighed only about ninety pounds), was swallowed up in the press. He caught a brief glimpse of the Rebbe's large gray-white beard and his elderly face. Then he could see nothing but the long black coats of the men crowded around him. Suddenly a hand fastened on his shoulder and began to propel him forward through the crowd as a whisper preceded him: "The Russian boy—the Russian—put him in front . . ."

Izak was frightened of being too conspicuous. That was the *Rebbe* up there in front. He had just returned from visiting the grave of his father-in-law, the previous Rebbe, where, as people said, he communed directly with the former Rebbe's spirit. One of the older Chassidim had told Izak that someone once asked the Rebbe why he spent so much time meditating at his father-in-law's grave. "You need a Rebbe," he answered, "so I also need a Rebbe."

And now these people were pushing Izak right in front of that man. Izak tried to concentrate on his *davvening*. When *Maariv* was concluded the Rebbe took a long look around the room, at each face. This was a hard moment for Izak, for he had heard that when the Rebbe looks at a person's eyes, he sees that person's whole life as though on a screen, acts and words and thoughts.

A few moments later, as the crowd was shuffling out the door, the principal of the yeshiva collared Izak and rushed him off to eat. Some of the others who had been on Izak's flight from Israel had mentioned that Izak had refused to eat any airline food on the day-long flight to New York, because he didn't trust El Al's observance of the kosher laws. But now Izak was too excited to eat. He tried to explain that he wasn't hungry, that he wanted to talk with the other students, but the older man shoved him into a library room, ordered someone to bring food from the kitchen, and scolded Izak.

"Eat, you hear? A day and a half, two days, no food, how can you study? You have to have a healthy body, so eat—*ich heiss dir!* I'm ordering you to!"

He closed the door on Izak and called from the other side that he wouldn't open it again until Izak calmed down and had some nourishment.

That entire first week in Brooklyn was a time of near ecstasy for Izak. For one thing, he was staying with his uncle, a younger brother of Nissen's, who had escaped from the Soviet Union into Sweden at the end of World War II. This uncle was a family legend. In the late 1930s he and a group of other boys had escaped after their whole yeshiva class had been captured in a raid by the secret police. Now, seated at his crowded dining-room table in Brooklyn, he and Izak discussed the latest news of the underground, and the emigration of the Mendelyevitches to Israel.

But, of course, the most important event for Izak was meeting the Rebbe, who, in fact, singularly honored Izak. During a *farbrengen* the Rebbe beckoned Izak over to him, handed him a bottle of vodka, and said, "Pour out a *l'chaim* for everybody, and don't forget yourself." Izak stood there with the bottle, baffled, embarrassed, until someone reached over and tilted the bottle to fill a little cup, thrust the cup into Izak's hand, and laughed, "Come on! Make *l'chaim!*" Izak mumbled the prayer and the toast, drank the vodka, and suddenly found himself the center of outstretched hands with empty cups.

The high point of Izak's stay in New York was his *yekhiddes*, his personal interview with the Rebbe. They talked for a while about the latest news of the underground; then, just as the session was about to end the Rebbe said, "You just came from Russia, now eat, build yourself up, you're too skinny. You'll need health. And one other thing . . ." He smiled . . . "You gave your word you'd go back to Israel, you gave a handshake, right? Don't forget."

Izak did return to Israel in November, but he was now determined that as soon as he had done his military training there he would go back to study at the main Lyubavitch yeshiva in Brooklyn. Traveling from one Lyubavitch community to another hardly seemed like a real move. The life styles and the people were almost the same. Whether the surrounding population spoke Russian, English, or French, these Chassidim got along quite well among themselves with Yiddish, plus a smattering of words and phrases of whatever language was spoken outside the group. Even the children, who usually did pick up the dominant surrounding language, could move to any city where there were Lyubavitcher Chassidim and feel quite at home, as most Yiddish-speaking Jews had once been able to do all over Europe and the West. Now that Izak was living in the Crown Heights section of Brooklyn, the old and rather dingy apartment houses and the streets lined with stone and brick private houses and duplexes were quite peripheral to Izak's experience of the place. The particulars of architecture and local culture

237

were incidental and unimportant details, to be dealt with only when absolutely necessary.

Izak spent two years in New York after he completed his army service in Israel. By late 1972 the percentage of emigrés from the Soviet Union who were settling in America rather than in Israel was still minuscule, and amounted to only a few hundred people. Nonetheless, the Rebbe told his Chassidim that many more would be coming, and he worried that most of them would simply "go native." They would assimilate, forget their identity as Jews, and would then have lost everything that made freedom worthwhile. Jewish organizations were all joining the chorus to "save Soviet Jewry," but what, the Rebbe asked, would these philanthropists do once they'd "saved" Soviet Jews? Would they also be prepared to help them? Perhaps, God forbid, they would only hand out some money, point the newcomers toward some possible jobs, and then forget them.

Not long after Izak returned to New York, the Rebbe instructed him to prepare help for those new emigrés who would be coming over. They would need personal support in dozens of ways that the philanthropic organizations and the fancy synagogues wouldn't even think of, but mostly they would need help being Jews. The emigrés themselves thought that they were leaving the Soviet Union for better jobs or better living conditions, but they were ignorant of the deeper meaning of the emigration: in fact, the Rebbe said, they are coming to find the Torah, though many have never even heard of it.

Izak spent a good part of his time, during those two years in New York, working with one or two others who had come here from the underground, and together they built an organization called Friends of Refugees from Eastern Europe (FREE), which provided a liaison between the new arrivals to America and the world of the Chassidim. This began with arranging for emigré children to be admitted into the Lyubavitch schools in New York, publishing Russian translations of liturgical texts such as the Passover *Haggadah*, and arranging for meetings, classes, and holiday celebrations for the emigrés.

During this period, Izak was married to a girl who had grown up in the Chassidic community in Brooklyn, and by late 1972 the two of them had made plans to leave New York. During a *farbrengen* at which the Rebbe had again spoken of the need to help the Soviet emigrés, Izak had gotten into a conversation with a heavyset young rabbi, a proud and intensely enthusiastic man, who worked at the Chabad-Lyubavitch branch in Los Angeles. He and Izak agreed that it would be a good thing for Izak to work with the emigrés who were only now beginning to come to southern California. New York had plenty of new arrivals from the underground to take Izak's place in FREE, so Izak could be spared. Izak now felt that his real work was about to begin.

Chapter Eight:
The City

In the late Autumn of 1976, about one year after the Gorelskys arrived in California, Alexandr heard that some old acquaintances from Odessa, the Leonovs, had just arrived in New York. He hadn't thought of Vitali Leonov since his own first visit to the post office square in Ostia almost a year and a half before, in June of 1975, when Vitali's name surfaced in that tidal wrack of gossip. Someone in the crowd had mentioned that the writer Leonov was in trouble and was trying to obtain a visa, which Alexandr already knew. But now, in 1976, Alexandr heard from a friend in New York that Vitali and Galina had arrived with their seven-year-old son, Sergei, and Alexandr asked himself the same question those gossipers in the Ostia crowd had asked: "A writer? An author from Odessa—what will he do in America?"

Vitali Leonov had been thrust into the decision to emigrate much more cruelly than Alexandr, for Vitali had achieved success in his career, and the Soviet government had then snatched it away from him. From the mid-1960s through the early 1970s a number of books by Vitali had appeared and had become popular, while still others were being published in various magazines. He was then earning ten times the pay of the average skilled worker, for the Soviet government values its writers and pays them well.

But success had come to Vitali only after a long and debilitating struggle. Not until he was nearing the end of his thirties did he begin to make real headway in his career as a writér. At that time, in the mid-1960s, his stories came to the attention of some of the leading editors in Moscow, who helped to get his work into print. However, this only gave the regime a new arena for their harassment of Vitali, whom they had long looked upon as an overly independent sort.

His first serious trouble began just after World War II, when he was a university student, barely out of his teens. A professor of Marxism had just read to the class Joseph Stalin's praise of the Russian people's victory over the Nazis, in which he vaunted the Russians as the bravest and best of nations. Vitali spoke up to suggest that Stalin's singling out one national group as superior to all others was contrary to Marxian doctrine. A few weeks later word leaked out that the boy's records were being passed on to the MGB, forerunner to the KGB, and Vitali saved himself by moving away to a provincial Ukrainian city. There he finished his education and went to work as a teacher, but his record caught up with him just under a decade later, and in the mid-1950s he found himself out of work again. He taught in various Ukrainian and Moldavian cities, but was constantly harassed by official suspicion.

In 1967, just about one year after Vitali had begun to enjoy real literary success, and had been able to give up teaching to devote full time to his writing, a Party official summoned him and promised him any favors he might want—a new apartment, a car, a country datcha—if he would turn his talents toward expounding the "general line of the Party." Vitali tried to explain that the effectiveness of his style was the result of more than technical gimmicks. It arose from his use of writing as a means of exploring people, of probing the truth about their lives, their feelings. To try to mimic the sinew of truth while relaxing into the old clichés was by definition impossible.

The matter was dropped for a while, but a few years later Vitali was again summoned to Party headquarters, and that same official now accused him of organizing Zionist clubs, and cautioned him to toe the line. The fact that the people behind these accusations were both powerful and serious became apparent later on when Vitali again received an invitation, this time from a ranking general in the

KGB. The general began by making it plain that he was an admirer of Vitali's talents.

"I'll tell you straight off, Leonov, that you're the one man I can respect in the entire Odessa branch of the Writers' Union." The general's tone was relaxed, and he spoke in a crisp, open manner, as though analyzing some professional operation with a fellow officer, an equal. "And I'm not ashamed to say it, even though you *are* our enemy."

In a way, Vitali did seem the general's equal as they sat across the desk from one another. The general was a few years older than Vitali, and looked commanding and trim in his uniform, but Vitali was of that strong, redheaded Russian-Jewish stock, and carried his more than six-foot height proudly. He looked nothing like the archetypical slope-shouldered Jewish intellectual. Though the general's phrase "our enemy" caused Vitali to thrust his face forward a fraction of an inch, he didn't give the impression of being either awed or cowed.

"Your enemy, General?"

"Well," the general went on, "a resident agent of the international Zionist conspiracy, which is saying quite enough. Your anti-Soviet attitudes are clear in your stories, and, what's more, your stories perpetuate these attitudes among readers. Your writing, you see, is absolutely Jewish. I don't say that your stories are *about* Jews. Certainly not. But let's not be naive, Leonov; they *are* Jewish."

Vitali was less and less able to match the general's casual air.

"And yet—Konstantin Simonov himself has spoken highly of my work, and he's anything but a Jew. And what about the editors of *The Soviet Writer* . . ."

"Please, please—" The general dismissed Vitali's point with a broad, loose wave of both hands. "Of course those people aren't Jews, though the truth is they've been *infected* by Jews. Anyway, they're completely beside the point. Let's look at your work. Obviously you ignore the general line of the Party, but that's not all. Your attitude to people, to the characters in your stories, and, I imagine, to people generally, is Jewish. You're fascinated by those little men and women, their little lives and feelings. This is a very Jewish trait, Leonov, absolutely a characteristic of Jewish writing."

The general leaned forward, satisfied, and propped his folded arms on the desk top. If Vitali hadn't been too nervous to be amused he might have laughed at the irony, for he considered the general's analysis to be fairly astute except in one detail: he was not a "resident agent" of any "Zionist conspiracy." On the other hand, Vitali knew that his actual guilt or innocence was of no importance to the general.

The general did not wait for Vitali's comments on his speech. He went on to explain that he could have Vitali arrested, if it came down to that, and suggested that Vitali place his talents at the service of the Party.

But he had called Vitali in at a bad time. Vitali's little boy, Sergei, was seriously ill, and his old mother was dying. Vitali himself, though he looked strong, was seriously undermined by ulcers and a bad heart, thanks to years of tension, and had almost died in the hospital on two occasions. He was overburdened and he was again becoming ill—and now this.

"But General, what can I say?" Vitali's words came out in quick, distinct bursts. "What can I say?—I don't care, General. Even dying, General—I just don't care about it—"

A few months later, in mid-1973, Vitali's literary career ended. While he lay seriously ill with bleeding ulcers in a hospital in Moscow, he received word that he was henceforth to be banned from publishing in the Soviet Union.

The death of Vitali's mother, just before his works were banned, had left him feeling rootless. It was at this time that he seriously considered emigrating to Israel. The specifically Jewish component of Vitali's personality was much more trained and conscious of itself than is usually the case among highly educated Soviet Jews, and that part of him hoped to find nurture in Israel. But after a while Vitali began to question whether Israel was the right place to go, after all. Perhaps what was most important was that he make his voice heard, that he speak out about the despotic nature of Soviet society. Surely the place to do that was America. If he could publish sufficiently in English, using America as a base, his voice would be heard much more widely, and he could do much more good. He could actually affect world politics through affecting American public opinion.

Vitali had begun work on a series of sketches of life among Odessan Jews of the Soviet period, which he planned to build into a large-scale novel, though this work could never have been published in the Soviet Union even before the ban. He continued to work on this project in secret—"for his desk drawer," as the Soviets express it—and tried to ward off despair. He had money to live on, for during those few years of prosperity he and Galina had saved much of their income. They could live, though not luxuriously, and Galina continued to work and to earn her salary as a doctor.

But writing for the desk drawer was like shouting in the wind. A writer must have readers, an audience, people who can criticize and respond. The audience, whether loved or loathed, is an anchor to reality, without which even the clearest voice may gradually and unwittingly drift into inconsequence. Vitali did show his works to a few trusted friends, but this was dangerous as well as being far too ingrown to substitute for a real audience. Vitali felt more and more that he was living at the bottom of a well, cut off from all participation in his own life. He led Galina, in their frequent nighttime strolls, past the building that housed the KGB headquarters, in order to demonstrate to himself that he wasn't frightened. In fact, he was terrified, not of being carted off summarily to Siberia, but of choking to death from that steady and irrevocable strangulation of the spirit.

Even after he and Galina finally applied for exit visas, in early 1975, the Party bosses continued to urge him to cooperate. He was assured that it wasn't too late; if he withdrew his application and behaved himself he would still be well treated. But even if he were both able and willing to write for the Party bosses, how could he believe their promises? Look what had happened to his old acquaintance, Arkadi Gorelsky, who had been a Party hack right from the start of his carreer. Arkadi had spent his entire adult life lecturing and writing in strict accord with directives, and then was forced to suffer demotion and public shame when his nephew, Alexandr, applied for a visa. The whole scandal had blown up at the end of 1973, eight or nine months after Vitali had been banned from publishing, and those Party men still persisted in promising Vitali the world if he would cooperate.

Alexandr Gorelsky's case gave the Leonovs plenty of food for thought. At the time Vitali applied for a visa, Alexandr had just received his second refusal from OVIR. Although Alexandr's request was granted only a few months later, the possibility of being refused was very real to the Leonovs, and posed a constant worry.

In fact, although the officials tortured Vitali and Galina by holding their applications for fifteen months without a response, they were not refused their visas. In midsummer of 1976 they received word that their visas would be issued.

Late that following October, on a raw night, a car from Kennedy Airport pulled up to the curb on a side street in midtown Manhattan, several dozen yards west of Broadway in the upper Forties. A few minutes later the Leonovs stood, with their luggage at their feet, in the small, seedy-looking lobby of their hotel. As a short man in his early sixties stepped back toward the car in which he had brought them, he turned and looked at the Leonovs, crinkling his eyes in a kind of smile as he said, in Yiddish, "You'll go up to your own room now, have a nice bite to eat—*a gitten umbaissen*," which turned out to consist of three tiny packets of cheese and crackers.

The man was from NYANA, the New York Association for New Americans, the agency responsible for assisting those emigrés who are sent to New York. NYANA's first act of assistance is to place the emigrés in various inexpensive hotels, where they must live until they find their own apartments. Even long after the Leonovs had left that hotel, Vitali knew that he would someday have to write about it, about his arrival there, but it took a long time. It was a year or more before he could look back on that October night, and on the ensuing six weeks during which they had lived in the hotel, with sufficient calm to hold it all steady in his gaze.

First he had to overcome the experience itself, to get beyond the actual fear, for there is something frightening about dirt, whatever kind of dirt it may be, whether it be the filthy, grease-caked, peeling wallpaper and flaking plaster speckled with roach droppings, or the

246

Part Three: BEGINNINGS

often violent sadomasochistic courtship rituals being enacted in the rooms across from their window. Every evening, when they returned from their apartment hunting, they had to immerse themselves in that crowd, among those parasites who prey upon the crowd, and the shouts, and the sirens; and every morning their eyes were assaulted by those large pornographic posters for all-male "girlie" shows, plastered in every window, so that whenever Vitali took that short walk to the subway entrance with his seven-year-old son, he could feel Sergei's impressionable mind being spattered with filth.

Vitali needed the perspective of time in order to weigh the importance, for his story, of certain peripheral occurrences, such as the response of their caseworker at NYANA. Vitali pleaded with her to move him and his family to one of the other hotels that NYANA was using, but she waved his complaints away and assured him that everything would be fine as soon as he found an apartment. Lots of people would *love* to be so near the theater district, she said.

Yes, that was important. He mustn't forget that caseworker. Not that she was rude: she simply knew that there was not much she could do, that even if NYANA were to decide not to use that hotel again (which they ultimately did), they were not going to move the Leonovs out to another hotel. What was so important to Vitali was not merely that the woman knew all this, but that she had adjusted to it all so well. It didn't bother her, or perhaps it *no longer* bothered her.

By the end of 1976 NYANA had been forced to grow into quite a large organization. With all their caseworkers, employment counselors, interpreters, clerks and administrative workers, their staff had roughly tripled within the past three years. Their crowded suite of rooms in a downtown Manhattan office building now housed dozens of workers of all kinds, and thousands of new emigrés were entered into their files every year. Furthermore, expenses were going up all across the board. In late 1973, when the number of Soviet-Jewish emigrés to America was beginning to increase sharply, it cost NYANA about $1,500 to settle a family of four. By the time Vitali arrived that same family cost about $5,000. For an organization that was supported almost entirely by funds donated by

247

philanthropic organizations such as the United Jewish Appeal, with very little in the way of government grants, this increase posed tremendous problems.

Since New York City has always had a much larger concentration of Jews and of Jewish organizational activity than any other community in the nation, it was felt that New York would be able to absorb far more emigrés than any other city. Therefore NYANA committed itself to accept one-half the emigré population entering the United States. However, by the mid and late 1970s New York City's Jewish population had declined from about three million to about one and a half million through migration to other parts of the country. Thus, with only about one-quarter of the nation's Jews, and with a larger percentage of Jewish poor than any other American city, New York was trying to settle and absorb double its per capita share of the tens of thousands of emigrés entering America each year.

With the necessarily rapid growth of NYANA's staff and organization there was a corresponding increase in the number of complaints. The inherent disease of all bureaucracies, that structure begins to outweigh function, was starting to set in. NYANA's administrators were aware, for example, that in getting bargain rates for hotel rooms they ran the risk of ending up with flophouses, so they established a policy that they would stop using any hotel that slipped too far below standard. Nonetheless, as in Vitali's case, it could take time for the outcry to be heeded. The afflicted emigré was one face among thousands, just one more voice raised in complaint, and it was infinitely easier to let him find his own way out of that hotel, when he finally tracked down an apartment for himself, than to try moving him and his family to a room in a somewhat more bearable hotel. Even as it was, that more bearable room might become vacant only in time to house some other family that was already on its way from Rome.

The woman who had been so blasé about Vitali's hotel was a caseworker in NYANA's Reception and Intake Department, the division responsible for accommodations, maintenance fees for food and incidentals, and basic orientation to life in New York. Their interviews were conducted through interpreters, most of whom were emigrés who had already been in the United States for a year or more. Both caseworkers and interpreters dealt with exhausting case loads, and worked under great pressure. How a caseworker handled that pressure was very much a measure of his or her strength of character.

The true experts on the problems of resettlement in New York were neither the caseworkers nor the administrators of NYANA, they were the interpreters. Vera, the young woman who interpreted for Vitali when he begged his caseworker to find a different hotel, could have predicted what the response would be, for she had watched that particular caseworker change gradually after grappling with the more aggressive of her clients. Though Vera was an emigré herself, she could sympathize with that caseworker's dismay when faced with newcomers who failed to understand the limits of donated funds, or whose only way of overcoming their sense of inferiority as emigrés was to work at squeezing a bit extra out of the agencies. Vera had watched a caseworker become soured by an emigré from Lvov who began to shout and pound the table, cursed the caseworker as a "shark" and a "bloodsucker," and demanded tearfully to be sent back to Lvov. All this because he had just been told that NYANA would not pay for new eyeglasses, since the eye doctor had reported that his old prescription was still good. What Vera found even more depressing was that this man would then go out and instruct all the newest arrivals on the sins of NYANA.

During the past year Vera had interpreted for most of the caseworkers at one time or another. She had seen some who could manage to find the right thing to say or do even in the most difficult of circumstances, and whose clients were defenders of NYANA, but she had also seen callousness and stupidity, caseworkers who managed to alienate even the most highly cooperative emigrés who had asked only for the minimum assistance.

As NYANA grew it was forced to hire caseworkers quickly, usually straight out of social-work school, with the result that they were often young, inexperienced, naive, and were only now about to discover whether they were emotionally fit for this kind of work. Some of them felt abused when their clients lied to them, or when an emigré shouted at them because some service, which may well have been desperately needed, could not be forthcoming. There were those, the best of them, whose naiveté gave way to a worldly skepticism tempered with a bit of sympathy; there were others who could only hide behind a lofty barricade of bureaucratic protocol and procedure, and thus became almost useless to deal with the real needs of their clients.

During any emigré's first months in America, the most far-reaching help that he could be given was in the areas of language instruction and vocational guidance. In most communities the Jewish Family Service was not equipped to teach him English, or even to arrange for others to do so, though in many cities it could refer him to courses that were given by the local public adult schools. NYANA, on the other hand, made arrangements for the emigrés in New York to take either a six-week or a twelve-week English course, depending on the level of competence needed. Their philosophy was that a professional needs a more sophisticated level of English than a worker or a craftsman, and so the professional was usually the one sent to the twelve-week course.

Even after the emigré began to develop some competence in English, vocational help continued to be a serious problem, and one that was handled with a wide variety of results in different communities. In San Francisco, for example, within about a year after Alexandr Gorelsky arrived, the local branch of the Jewish Welfare Federation revamped their Jewish Vocational and Career Counseling Center, and created an Emigré Project that soon showed a high rate of success. Their Job Developers each specialized in a particular area of employment, and they spent time establishing contacts for their clients, calling likely employers on the telephone, writing letters, sending out résumés—in short, selling their clients, much as the better private personnel services do.

In New York, as the weeks of language instruction drew to a close, the emigré was sent to a vocational counselor at NYANA's second major division, the Vocational Services Department. Although this was designed to be a much more comprehensive service than most other communities can offer, NYANA was forced to take on a vastly larger case load than places like the Jewish Vocational Center in San Francisco, and therefore had to handle their clients quite differently.

Galina Leonov had been a physician in Odessa, and now faced

the same problem that Leonid Novogradsky was facing in San Francisco. Foreign doctors must pass a formidable battery of medical qualifying examinations that usually require months or years of full-time study to prepare for. Galina decided not to try studying for those exams until her English, as well as the Leonovs' financial position, was better. Now it would be best to find a job. The Leonovs' employment counselor at NYANA tried to convince Galina to take a job in a factory. She refused. Rather than work in a factory, which would be a dead-end for her, she asked that they find her any job in a hospital, where she would at least have some contact with medical people. She was willing to take any lower-level job, as long as she were in a medical milieu where she could learn about opportunities in paramedical training programs or the like, which she could never hear of if she worked in a factory. However, the employment counselor threw up her hands in despair, and explained that she had no hospital jobs in her file.

Galina held her ground and refused factory work. Several months later, in the late winter of 1977, she managed to enroll in a six-month paramedical training program that led to a hospital job that autumn, about a year after their arrival in New York.

Vitali also concentrated on making contacts of his own. A few of his articles appeared in emigré newspapers in America and in Europe, which brought in some money, and he began to get free-lance script-writing assignments from Western radio stations that beam programs to the Soviet Union, but his main task now was to establish himself as an author. NYANA could not fairly be expected to help him with this except in one small respect. After the Soviets banned Vitali from publishing, he continued to work on a large novel depicting the lives of lower-class Odessans, an entire generation of culturally disenfranchised Jews and their little-known world. Vitali had accumulated many hundreds of typescript pages, and had managed to have them secretly microfilmed.

Vitali literally risked his life to get those microfilms to the West, for his future was invested in them. If he could sell this book to a publishing house, it might mean the rebirth of his devastated career. Vitali was willing to take on the problem of finding a translator himself, but first the microfilms had to be enlarged and reproduced so that they could be read. He didn't have the money for this, but

NYANA routinely prepared, translated, and photocopied emigrés' résumés and qualifying documents, so he didn't expect them to balk at helping him. When he asked his counselor if NYANA would pay to enlarge the microfilms, however, she raised her eyebrows and drew her chin back.

"Mr. Leonov, NYANA can't treat you better than other people just because you're a writer. It's the same to us if you're a writer, a butcher, a shoemaker—"

"But what I'm asking is easier than what you do for a butcher or a shoemaker; I'm a writer; this book is my trade. Just have the microfilms run off for me."

But the counselor only shook her head and sighed. "What would these people want next," she thought. "Enlarging microfilms we should pay for! When our grandparents came here, did they ask for enlarging microfilms?"

Vitali walked down Brighton Beach Avenue and turned south toward the boardwalk. Autumn had come, and the Sunday-evening crowd was thinner than he had seen it in months. The massive dirt-gray steelwork of the elevated subway, spanning almost the entire width of the avenue, gave the whole area a heaviness that seemed to press upon the faces and the bones of the loiterers, who stood around talking in clusters on the street corners. Although it meant riding for over an hour and a half on the subway from his apartment, Vitali sometimes needed this pilgrimage, for Brighton was becoming densely populated with Odessans, people he understood.

Thirty or forty years ago one could live fairly comfortably in Brighton with only a slight knowledge of English. Yiddish would have sufficed. But the youngsters left for college and didn't return, and the old gradually died off or moved to Florida. The thick, square, four- and six-story apartment buildings, interspersed with converted bungalows, seemed more somber as the neighborhood became seedier. Through the 1960s some welfare families drifted in, and the crime rate began to climb as it had been doing all over the city.

The Soviet Jews who came to New York in the mid-1970s flocked to areas that were relatively cheap but not yet devastated.

Part Three: BEGINNINGS

The first place to become a Soviet ghetto was Brighton Beach. Once again English became a secondary language there, but now it was Russian that dominated, especially the Russian of Odessa, though there was a healthy sprinkling of newcomers from other parts of the Ukraine as well as from Byelorussia and Moldavia.

Vitali was going to a certain café, which had become an Odessan hangout, to talk and joke in the familiar old way, though every time he went there it was clearer to him that there no longer was a familiar old way. These gruff, indestructible Odessans had changed; something had faded out of them, or had been bleached out. They still prided themselves on their jokes and their quips, but a veil seemed to hang over them. Perhaps something had been snapped when they exchanged the stately green boulevards of Odessa for the gray girders of New York; perhaps they were being poisoned by steel dust. Or could it be a problem of money? For large numbers of emigrés in New York money was a problem, but Vitali suspected that it wasn't the main problem. That was why he was interested in this particular group in the café. They were people who had been in America for several years, and were among the most economically successful emigrés in Brighton.

Vitali noticed that Sonya was back at the café this evening, so he sat down at her table. Sonya was a proud woman in her forties, with heavy rings on each hand, and large earrings dangling from her earlobes. She was talking with a few others whom Vitali already knew. One was a butcher, who was making a good wage now that he'd been in America for a few years, but even so, something was missing.

"Over there, I was *somebody*," the butcher explained. "I was important. I bought a leather coat once, imported—I traded some meat to a sailor, he sold me the coat—so when I wore that coat, people *looked* at me. Here I have even a better coat—a *better* one, you understand?—and every *putz* in the subway is wearing one. So who am I here! I'm *dreck*. A butcher with a coat—who cares?"

Wherever Vitali had traveled in the Soviet Union, he had run across these latter-day merchant princes who had been elevated to great prestige by the perpetual-shortage economy. They parlayed roasts the way Vanderbilt had parlayed railroads, and treated themselves like court patrons. Many of them surrounded themselves with a coterie of the eager-to-please intelligentsia. The playwright or violinist got some steak, and the butcher had the prestige of being known as a member of the elite, one who hobnobbed with artists, with people of a higher realm. Thus, people who could cash in on the underground economy, whether they sold steaks or Party influence, could create their own salons. As for those who couldn't purchase glittering acquaintanceships, they could at least display the goods they had bought. But in America nobody cared how much money—or steak—even the richest emigré had.

The table conversation turned to the subject of children, and Vitali mentioned that he'd received a scholarship to put his son, Sergei, into a Jewish day school—not one of the Orthodox ones, but a modern place run by the Conservative movement. Before he could begin to describe the school, Sonya interrupted.

"What do you need this for? What will this get you? What?"

Vitali tried to explain that he was sending the boy to a Jewish school because he wanted him to be a Jew, really *be* one. He wanted Sergei to have that available to him as a source of satisfaction and of personal strength, so that it would be more than merely a passive reaction to the next fellow's anti-Semitism, as it had been in the Soviet Union; he wanted it to serve Sergei as a kind of inner treasury. Vitali had been robbed of it, but it wasn't too late for the boy. But it was difficult to talk to Sonya about "inner treasuries" and the like. She sensed the inner vacancy, but what had been stolen from that chamber—that was another question.

Perhaps that was the real nature of Sonya's poverty, and the butcher's too, Vitali thought. There was so much talk about money, yet nobody could quite understand why the problems remained even after the money started to come in. The standard complaint, that they'd lost their Russian culture without having gained a new one, was true enough as far as it went, but it didn't go far enough, which was why Vitali sat at this table and probed and pondered. They had lost more than their Russian culture. Their loss had begun long before they'd left the Soviet Union. It was a poverty that had existed all along, and those other things that had become so important to them all—the butcher's status, another man's "pull"—all of that had been false coin to distract them from the real loss.

Although the butcher now yearned to taste again his former triumphs, he and Sonya and thousands of others must have long understood, however dimly, that they had been paid in counterfeit back in Odessa, for they had dumped it all for the sake of their exit visas. They had exchanged it in hopes of something better, though many of them had failed to imagine what to hope for now, except for a bigger and better version of what they'd once had.

In the Soviet Union, Vitali remembered, people complained bitterly in private, but out in the open air they performed an elaborate act of supporting the official line. It was as though they'd had two distinct personalities, each equipped with its own set of values. This seemed natural and acceptable in an authoritarian society, yet the habit didn't always leave them in America. Several months after that evening in the café, a group of fellow emigrés were at Vitali's place for dinner, and he took the opportunity to read to them a story he had recently completed, in which he re-created his first briefing at the HIAS office in Rome. He had described, in careful detail, how the HIAS man in the front of the room sat half sprawled in an insolent slouch, with one leg up on his table, and calmly devastated the group of emigrés sitting before him.

"We know you; all of us Americans and American Jews know you and know what *liars* you are. We know you and we're *sick* of you . . ."

Vitali had worked to recapture every quirk of that man's posture, his way of speaking Russian, which Vitali could remember almost down to the syllable, down to the last detail of that droning American accent.

When Vitali finished reading there was a moment of embarrassed silence. Then one woman, who had been a journalist in the Soviet Union, bluntly accused Vitali of being pathologically negative. "Why don't you submit it to *Pravda*—they'd love it!"

Many of the other guests took up the same line: "So what? One caseworker was a bastard, insulted everybody; how does that weigh in the balance as compared with what HIAS did for us? Why go scavenging among the corpses?"

Conversational anger about the way the emigration was handled was one thing, but writing those things down and having them published was quite another, and brought many of Vitali's friends to their feet with outraged attacks on his "negativity." "What right do you have to publish those stories?" And Vitali answered quite frankly, "What right do I have to stop?"

It was true, there was a "negative" streak to Vitali. He loved having parties, singing Russian songs, he could tell jokes for hours and also enjoyed laughing at other people's stories, yet he had a dark, critical, melancholic side that sprang from the very same source as his laughter: he was in love with the people he wrote about, those Russians and Jews, and even some of the Americans in his most recent pieces; when he wrote about them he adopted them as his kinsmen, his children. What father could know his children so well and avoid melancholy?

Vitali could always publish in Russian-language emigré journals, but the American market eluded him. Even after a large segment of his new novel was published in translation in Western Europe, with both financial and critical success, he was unable to get very far with the American-Jewish intellectual periodicals. Perhaps they were offended by his emigration stories, by the scenes of that mid-town hotel, or of that first HIAS briefing. What could he do? He was forced to explore his people's lives here just as he had done in Odessa. He did not depict grateful and optimistic emigrés, joyful in their new freedom and their new opportunities; and perhaps the editors were put off by the seediness of some of the "benefactors" in his stories. Old habits die hard; he was again ignoring the general line of the "Party."

Even Mikhail Markov, who was already known to a number of American historians and political scientists, had to live from one visiting lectureship to another, and from grant to grant, and he considered himself lucky to get that much. After being hounded out of the Soviet Union by the KGB, terrified that at the last minute they would send him to Siberia instead of letting him emigrate, and then discovering that his friend, Kleinman, was spying on him in Rome and was writing reports on him to some person or persons unknown, Mikhail finally stumbled onto some good luck. Even before the Markovs left Rome, one of the American professors with whom Mikhail had maintained contact since the mid-1960s was able to arrange a one-semester visiting lectureship for him at a midwestern university. He was to report in January 1975, several weeks after his scheduled arrival in the United States.

The one-semester position in the Midwest carried the Markovs only until the summer of 1975, but Mikhail's luck held out, and he was awarded a one-year teaching position in New York. As nerve-racking as this instability was, he was better off than many of his friends. These teaching positions gave him an opportunity to do his research and writing, and for that he was willing to go from job to job and from grant application to grant application. The important thing was the writing, the work itself. A large microfilmed manu-script that an American professor had smuggled to the West for Mikhail now needed to be rewritten. Once Mikhail began to exam-ine the materials in American libraries—materials unavailable or kept under lock and key in the Soviet Union—he saw the need to rethink his work and to expand various parts of it into separate books and articles.

Mikhail felt no more free to abandon his work than did Vitali Leonov. Whereas Leonov, as a fiction writer, was committed to exploring and revealing the inner worlds and the outer circum-stances of his characters, Mikhail's work—what he called his "life-task"—was to do now what he had once hoped to do inside Russia: as a historian and a journalist he must analyze and map the ways of power, especially Soviet power, in order to create an understanding that would prevent the future from repeating the past. He used to tell his friends that this life task was not merely his job but his fate.

In June 1975, the Markovs went to New York and found an apartment in Queens. By this time the Soviet emigré community in New York was dividing itself into two major settlements, one in Brooklyn and one in Queens. This was reminiscent of an earlier generation of New Yorkers. By the late 1940s upwardly mobile Brooklynites and Bronxites were aspiring to move to the relatively genteel Elysium of Queens, to neighborhoods that bore names rem-iniscent of a more graceful age—Kew Gardens, Forest Hills— neighborhoods that seemed airier than Brooklyn and more gracious, even though they too were becoming massed with six-story apart-ment complexes and miles of connected row houses. That old pop-ulation pattern reasserted itself with these new emigrés. Now that

Brighton Beach and other neighborhoods were filling up with thousands of Odessans, it seemed only natural that the proper Muscovites and Leningraders should find their way to Queens.

Actually, not all the emigrés who lived in Forest Hills, or Foreign Hills, as people were beginning to call it, were big-city sophisticates. A family named Brunner, originally from western Siberia, settled just a few blocks away from the Markovs' apartment in the late summer of 1975, and by the autumn of that year they had become a source of neighborhood gossip. From what Mikhail and Natalya Markov were told by their daughter, Irina, the Brunner father was a Polish Jew who had fallen into the hands of the Soviets when Stalin annexed eastern Poland, at the end of the 1930s. He then spent about sixteen years in Soviet prisons and labor camps. He was ultimately released, along with hundreds of thousands of other innocent people, in the late 1950s, during Khrushchev's so-called "destalinization." He emerged much the worse for wear. He did gradually regain his physical strength—he was a wiry, powerful man, though not very tall—but his personality had been scarred, and he was left with an unpredictable and violent temper. Irina and some of her friends got to know Anatoli, the elder of the two Brunner sons, who, like Irina, was in his late teens, and she came home with stories of Anatoli's father brutalizing him.

Anatoli's mother was quite the opposite sort. She was very quiet, a provincial Russian woman whom the father had met when he settled in Siberia after his release from prison. She had an old-fashioned gentleness as well as an old-fashioned Russian-Orthodox Christian piety. Ironically, it was because of her Christianity that she wanted to remain in Israel after the Brunners emigrated there in late 1973. She considered it a holy land, the scene of Jesus' earthly mission. But her husband, although he was born of Jewish parents, had no religious sympathies—all that had been burned out of him long before—and when his attempt to settle in Israel ran into real trouble, no religious or ethnic sentiments dulled his survivor's instinct to grab his family and run.

In the Soviet Union, Anatoli's father had worked as a truck driver. This was a low-paying job, but one that offered opportunities for making money on the side, such as private hauling for a fee or brokering the sale of used vehicles, both strictly illegal. The Brunners did not do badly, but there was a constant risk. Food in the provinces was scarce, almost unavailable in the government stores and expensive on the black market. Without that side income it would have been hard for the Brunners to feed their two sons, and with it Anatoli's father always ran the risk of being prosecuted for "economic crimes," especially since his internal passport labeled him as a Jew, and he was an ex-prisoner.

When the Brunners arrived in Israel, everything went wrong. Instead of feeling more secure, safer, better able to fend for themselves, they felt abused and defenseless. The chain of misfortunes began when they arrived. In October 1973, at the height of the Yom Kippur War, they found themselves assigned to live in an apartment complex perched in the desert outside a small town. The complex was uninhabited and desolate, for it was still incomplete, the walls unpainted, the floors piled with construction rubble, and most of the utilities not yet turned on.

The Brunners spent most of that night on a bus to Tel Aviv. For the next week they slept in the street by night and beseiged the government ministries by day, petitioning to be reassigned to another apartment. They spent two nights in an *ulpan*, an absorption center, but were ordered out and instructed to return to the unfinished building. Finally an elderly woman who had some extra room in her apartment put them up for a few weeks until they could find work and a place to live.

By selling much of their furniture when it arrived from the Soviet Union, Anatoli's father was able to buy a half ownership of an old truck, which he put in running order. He and his partner were then able to set up a small hauling business, which brought in enough money to live on; with Anatoli's income from his construction job, they were even able to save some money. If it were up to Anatoli's mother they would have forgotten their initial problems, chalked them up to bad luck and wartime confusions, and then settled down, but Anatoli's father was desperate to leave Israel. He felt that he'd been cheated and humiliated, and was frightened that another war with the Arabs would take his two sons from him. From 1939 through the late 1950s, all his kinsmen, as well as practically every friend he'd made, had been killed either on the battle-field or in concentration camps, both Nazi and Soviet. He refused to put up with any further risk to his sons.

In mid-1974, after paying their debt to the Absorption Ministry, the Brunners flew to London, but were forced to return because they had no entry papers for England. They spent the next months planning a way through Western Europe. At this time, thousands of people in the Brunners' situation were beginning to squeeze their way back out of Israel. They had little money left and no place to go. Yakov and Raya Shkolnik and their sick child, who lived across the hall from Alexandr and Zoya Gorelsky in their Vienna hotel, were among these "returnees." By 1974 and 1975 these placeless and poverty-stricken people had begun to crowd into Rome, Vienna, Brussels, and other European capitals. In some cities, such as Rome, their children were not permitted into the public schools, and began to wander the streets in wolf packs. Some of these returnees had been victims of administrative confusion, such as the Brunners; others could not find adequate employment in the Israeli economy of the mid-1970s; still others simply couldn't adjust, blamed Israel for all their problems, and hoped for better in the West. The fact that a large majority of emigrés in Israel did manage to settle and support their families was insufficient to give these people hope.

By the end of 1974 the Brunners were in West Germany. Although HIAS and Joint were unable or unwilling to assist these "returnees," the Brunners were accepted for assistance by the International Rescue Committee. In August 1975, they arrived in New York, and the scramble for work began.

Mikhail and Natalya met Anatoli Brunner in the neighborhood once or twice, and he seemed pleasant enough. There was something lively about him. His body was thin, wiry, almost springy, like that of a young animal. Though he was not a cultivated person, not in the sense in which the upper-crust intelligentsia of Moscow or Leningrad use the word, he was civil, polite, and had native intelligence. Moreover, he seemed not to have picked up his father's thorny behavior. Then, toward the end of the year, Irina mentioned that Anatoli's father had beaten him again, and that the young fellow had left home. For the past week he had been living in basements, eating whatever food his friends could sneak to him. Mikhail and Natalya couldn't stand the idea of the boy living like a stray cat, even though they barely knew him, so they told Irina to bring him home and to let him stay with them for a while.

Though Anatoli's narrow, dark-complected face and limbs seemed always restless, he was very quiet and made as few demands as possible. He was grateful but shy, and embarrassed about his troubles. Mikhail and Natalya were fond of him; it was almost like having a son. Actually, he couldn't really be imagined as their son, because a son of theirs would have been quite a well-educated young man by the end of his teens. But then, there was no guarantee that they would have had any more success in turning a son into their kind of intellectual than they'd had with their daughter. Even in high school Irina did as little work as possible; she showed no interest in her father's writing, nor in the articles and books he and his friends were always trading back and forth and discussing. That was the Markovs' life, their passion, not Irina's. She loved her parents, respected them, but she refused to renounce her own world to join theirs. Natalya sometimes wondered how she and Mikhail could have produced a daughter who shared so few of their values and tastes, but in fact Natalya and Irina were much alike: Irina had inherited Natalya's staunch integrity, her iron will, and her sometimes outrageous straightforwardness—though Natalya had always been nervous, volatile, and sensitive, she was never weak. For the benefit of outsiders she might pretend subservience to Mikhail and do everything to enhance his aura, but in fact she had never been his servant. She was always his energetic partner, and sometimes his manager. From their earliest days together, she went over every word he wrote, criticized it, questioned it, probed it from every possible angle, and thus imposed a rigorous discipline on Mikhail's craft as well as on his argumentation. This bone-thin, blond Russian woman was proud. Though raised under Stalin, she had an independent, determined, and keen mind.

Irina, like her mother, was by no means a follower. On at least one occasion she transcended even Natalya in sheer spunk.

Shortly after the Markovs had applied for their visa, Irina was summoned to a large meeting of all the members of the local branch of Komsomol, the Communist Youth League. There, in front of an audience of seven or eight hundred fellow students and Party members, Irina was to be publicly humiliated, denounced as a traitor, and cast out of the ranks of Komsomol. The man who ran the meeting sat at a table covered in red felt, while Irina was made to stand. It should have been apparent to the Party men that Irina was not the timid kind, since she brazenly wore a Star of David on her necklace, but they took no heed. The presiding Party officer, a hairy, bull-necked man in his mid-forties, began to accuse Irina of treason. When he felt that she had been properly reduced to speechlessness he asked her a question.

"Don't you realize what a crime you're committing by moving to a capitalist country?"

"What capitalist country?"

"Israel! What else!"

"Israel's a socialist country. The Labor Party's in power."

The large man stared at Irina for a moment, reddened, then decided that the moment had come to devastate her with irony.

"Wonderful! And would you please tell us when they plan to achieve the benefits of true communism in Israel?"

"If you can tell me when you'll achieve it here."

Eight hundred students and Komsomol officers sat in silence. The leader of the session leaned forward, flushed and sweaty in the late June heat.

"This tells us everything," he said, half in a whisper. "You're no longer a Komsomol. Give me your badge. Where is it?"

"I can't find it. It's probably been thrown out."

Now he bellowed, "How *could* you . . ."

"What's the difference who throws the thing out, you or me? It ends up in the same garbage dump!"

Now that Mikhail was teaching in New York for the 1975-76 academic year, Irina could have taken advantage of a wide variety of educational opportunities, but she was only interested in courses that could improve her English or could teach her business skills. Mikhail and Natalya tried in every way to push her into a broader curriculum in the university, and hoped that her sound intelligence would take the bait, but she dismissed their tactics with a shrug.

During that year in New York Irina put herself on a demanding schedule. Because she insisted on being at least partly self supporting, she worked from ten in the morning until two in the afternoon as a cashier in a large Manhattan department store. From three to six P.M. she attended classes at the university, and from seven to nine she went to a business college. Her enrollment in the university was a concession to her parents, and the business school, for which she paid half out of her wages, was their concession to her.

Irina quickly learned to speak English with almost no trace of an accent, except a New York accent. On the subway she was almost indistinguishable from any of the young office workers, except that she was more attractive than most. The thin features and very white skin of her mother's Russian forebears were framed by the jet-black hair of her father's side of the family, and her face was lively; it had never quite hardened to that glassy, lacquered look affected by so many young New York women. Nonetheless, it seemed to her parents that she was striving for ordinariness.

That was what so many emigrés complained about in their children: it seemed that the Old-World traditions of striving for excellence to accomplish something special were replaced by conformity to the American adolescent norms. A certain sparkle seemed to be gone. Now, no one would have thought of Irina as the Mata Hari who had once had the gall to flirt with a pair of uniformed Soviet guards, at a certain building in Moscow, in order to distract their attention while her father slipped by with a briefcase full of illicit typescript, which he was then able to have smuggled out of the country. *That* had been a rare sort of girl, a real Markov, a character.

But now Mikhail and Natalya watched her become simply a New York secretary. She didn't even ride the subway like an emigré. She lacked that cringe of the newcomer, for whom the subway distills all the terrors of this place: the sense of menace, the glowering people, the unchained bedlamites. The emigrés, who had been used to cleanliness and order in the public life of a city, were depressed and sickened by the graffiti that covered every car of every train, from top to bottom and from end to end. These were not just initials, names, curse words, or political slogans, as one saw in Rome; these elaborately barbed, calligraphed, and depth-shaded letter forms were abstract, devoid of meaning. It was their meaninglessness, their lack of reference or message, and the way they

angled, grimy and opaque, across every surface to block out destination signs, maps, even windows, that seemed to bespeak something barbaric, something aggressively chaotic pushing through the
surface of things. The emigrés often talked about such impressions,
tried to focus them like a lens to gain some insight into this mad-
deningly obscure new life. Irina hated the dirt and the scrawled-up
subways the way a New Yorker hates them: as simply a damned
unpleasant nuisance.

Emigrés suspect that Americans do not know the meaning of the
word "friend." It almost seems that an American calls anyone a
friend whom he knows well enough to greet and who is not overtly
hostile. To a Russian, or a Russian Jew, a friend is a part of the close
family circle, a small group of intimates that also includes a few
well-loved kinsmen. These intimates are necessary to survival. In a
society that cultivates the habit of informing on one's neighbors and
associates as a virtue, even from early school years, everyone must
find a few people he can trust.

What many emigrés find most puzzling, however, is the American idea that a friendship should be easy. To the emigrés, as to
Russians, real friends are family, and therefore are expected to
squabble like relatives. Americans always want to step back a pace
just when things are getting interesting, when the friendship devel-
ops a bit of thorniness. But to the emigrés, no friction means no
friendship, no relationship, no contact, and is as unthinkable between friends as between lovers or spouses.

What the emigrés call friendship the Americans might call sym-
biosis. For anyone raised in the Soviet Union, one's fellow symbionts are necessary to a person's life, to his emotional nourishment.
He cannot digest the daily joys and troubles without chewing them
over with his friends and passing them back and forth from one to
the other, from mouth to mouth, from heart to heart.

Symbionts must evolve together, they must have interlocking
biochemistries or they cannot feed one another. A morsel of experience will become one thing when absorbed into an emotional
chemistry patterned by Moscow troubles, but quite another, an in-
compatible plasm, in a mind patterned in Chicago. And so, Mikhail
and Natalya sometimes found that even the friendliest Americans

simply did not taste the same tastes that they did; their chemistries failed to match.

The Markovs were able to reconstitute at least a bit of their old Moscow circle in New York, but then, in the late summer of 1976 they had to prepare to leave for California. A research grant that included some part-time teaching there was Mikhail's only offer for the following year. This would give him the opportunity to finish a book within the next year or so, and therefore to begin to reestablish his credentials in America, but it would mean loneliness.

It was Natalya who stood to lose most by the separation from their circle, for her own professional life had ended with their emigration, and she now lived largely through Mikhail's work. When the KGB forced them to emigrate, Natalya had already developed a following as a free-lance editor, or rather, as a book doctor, among a small but notable circle of writers in Moscow. She had an unusual talent for spotting what needed to be done to improve a manuscript, or an author's way of working and thinking, and could stimulate a good writer to be a better writer. This gradually began to grow into a career, though it was one that could never be transplanted to America. In New York, and especially in California, she devoted her talents and her energies almost exclusively to working with Mikhail.

The Markovs had no quarrel with California itself; it was a pretty and comfortable place to live, but they felt lost without their friends. And now, to increase their frustration, more of their Moscow friends were arriving in New York. Lena and Dmitri Rottman were due to arrive there in October, and Natalya could hardly stand the thought of missing them. Lena was almost the only person Natalya had been able to talk with, at any length, at the Markovs' going-away party two years before. Rumor had it that she and Dmitri had been through a very hard time since then. Natalya could remember how confused, how ambivalent Lena had looked that evening as she announced that she and Dmitri had just resigned their jobs to apply for visas. For two years now, Lena had been oceans and continents away, completely out of reach; but now she would be in America, in New York. It was *possible* to see her, and therefore maddening not to.

In California, Mikhail and Natalya filled their time with his research and his writing, and with trying to guide Irina into something more like an educated career. Irina was again attending university classes, and they had hopes that she would complete her degree. Even after the household chores and the day's editorial work with Mikhail were done, Natalya still had time and energy to help Irina with term papers, studying for exams, and so on. Anatoli Brunner had come west with the Markovs, but he took up almost none of their time. He still stayed with them occasionally, though he usually roomed with his brother, who had come out to California after completing high school.

After more than a year in California, Irina still puzzled her parents with her obstinacy, her refusal to take things seriously. Even in a university environment she was still the New York career girl. What's more, there was now a bright and well-bred young man with a degree in mathematics—working nearby as a computer scientist—who was paying a good deal of attention to Irina, but she didn't take him any more seriously than she took anything else. Mikhail and Natalya could easily think of him as a son-in-law, and they had hopes that Irina would realize that young men with his personality and brains don't come along every day. But it seemed Irina was simply not yet ready to be serious about a man.

One evening, in the late winter of 1978, Mikhail and Natalya returned to their apartment from a weekend visit to a friend in a neighboring town. On the kitchen table they found a note from Irina explaining that she and Anatoli had decided to build their lives as they were meant to; they felt that what they were now doing was the only right and honest thing. They had taken a flight together to New York that morning. There they would settle, find work, and set up house together.

In the autumn of 1976, two months after the Markovs had left for California, a young woman named Miriam, who had just joined the staff of NYANA, was leading a newly arrived family of five out of the customs area and through the waiting room of the International Arrivals building in Kennedy Airport. She had volunteered to help HIAS with a batch of emigrés who were coming in on a Swissair flight at six P.M., and the exhausting process of taking those thirty people through Immigrations, locating their luggage, and going through customs with them was almost over.

It was already past nine-thirty at night now, and she only had to get this family and a few last stragglers into the minibus, and then she could relax. As she led the Rottmans through the waiting lounge to the parking area she noticed that the husband, Dmitri Rottman, was striding quite a few yards ahead of her, and was looking around as though expecting someone to meet him, while his wife, Lena, her old parents, and their son, Gennadi, who looked about twenty, were trailing well behind Miriam. Suddenly Dmitri stepped to one side and ducked under the ropes that held back the crowd of waiting friends and relatives from blocking the walkway. Miriam lost sight of him for a moment, then saw him in earnest conversation with a man in the crowd, probably an old friend from Moscow. The rest of the Rottman family had stopped just where they were when Dmitri walked into the crowd, and they stood there as though anchored to the spot.

Miriam walked back toward Lena Rottman, who was looking off toward the glass exit doors with a carefully blank gaze. The son was glaring through the crowd at Dmitri with undisguised anger.

Miriam mustered her courage to try out her little bit of college Russian. "Shall we go, *Gospozha* Rottman?"

"We are no longer together." Her voice was low—contralto, Miriam thought. "My husband and I, we are no longer together. That other man will drop him off . . . where he is staying."

At that point a woman stepped through the crowd, a childhood friend of Lena's from Moscow. She had a car and was planning to take Lena and her parents to the hotel. Miriam gave her the address and then ran back to get the remaining families into the minibus.

Fifteen minutes later Miriam drifted back from the bus and saw Lena sitting just inside the open right-front door of her friend's car, sobbing uncontrollably. Her parents were sitting in the back seat: the mother leaning forward and whispering something to Lena, the father staring out the left-hand rear window at nothing.

Two years earlier, in the autumn of 1974, at Mikhail and Natalya Markov's going-away party in Moscow, Lena and Natalya stood in the middle of the room and talked of their future meeting in the West. Even though Lena and Dmitri had just given up their jobs—

the first step toward applying for a visa—she felt little envy over Natalya's impending departure, though she did envy anyone who had completed that fearful period of waiting. When it came down to leaving, however, Lena still had second thoughts. She had questions about her own and her parents' ability to survive the change.

Dmitri would probably be all right, Lena thought. He had always been the strong one. On the other hand, he did have some weaknesses. He was proud, self-willed; there was something very— was it Russian? No, not so much Russian as Soviet—there was something extremely Soviet about Dmitri, something hard about the way he treated people, something inflexible, demanding.

Lena did wonder how he would handle the inevitable loss of status in the West, but Dmitri himself seemed never to give it a thought. He was enthusiastic about the move, and after trying for over a year to convince Lena that the emigration was necessary, he refused to admit that there might be real problems once they crossed the border. He shrugged off Lena's worries about her parents, though her mother was seventy-seven and her father almost eighty.

So even now, after she and Dmitri had quit their jobs to prepare for filing their visa applications, she admitted to Natalya that her feelings were mixed. The one nightmare that Lena avoided talking about just now was the suspicion she had once entertained that Dmitri might be planning to seek out that American woman, Carol, after they arrived in the United States. Carol Starn had long since completed her second extended research trip to Moscow, and was once again teaching college economics somewhere in New Jersey. Perhaps Gennadi's story, a few years ago, that he had seen his father and Carol strolling down a Moscow street, hand in hand, like lovers, really was a product of adolescent fantasy, as Dmitri had sworn. God knows, that girl was no Helen of Troy. Her squarish physique reflected her strength and determination of mind, and seemed to say, Carol gets what she wants. She was Lena's precise opposite, and Lena had once wondered if that wasn't why they had all become such good friends.

Carol was not a great beauty, but Dmitri was approaching middle age, an unpredictable time. Moreover, Carol was part of the American academic community; Dmitri just might have been considering her as a useful acquisition. But Lena had really stopped thinking of all that now, and the Markovs' going-away party, a celebration of their new life, was no place for such frightening thoughts.

Then again, there always *is* something sad about these parties, Lena thought—not the beginning of the new life, but the ending of the old. She noticed that Mikhail Markov himself looked as though he were experiencing the death of the old much more acutely than the birth of the new. He was pale, and though his lips were shaped into a smile, they were drawn taut at the corners Lena could see that Natalya was right when she said that Mikhail was still afraid that he'd never be allowed to get to Vienna. Certainly some of those men weren't helping to cheer him up with the toasts they were making. It had been all right for the first few drinks. They drank to the Markovs' health and coming success, to freedom, to the many books that Mikhail would soon write, to their daughter Irina's new future, and each toast had been introduced by a long, witty, sometimes sentimental speech, in the grandiose Russian manner. Then one fellow lifted his glass in the traditional toast of the democratic dissidents: "Here's to our hopeless cause," and another guest pledged a toast "to all the sailors still at sea," meaning the political prisoners still in cells or labor camps. Lena could see that the Markovs already had that far-off, preoccupied look; they were hardly conscious of what was going on at the party. But, she thought, these celebrations are really like eulogies, they're lost on the ones in whose honor they are given. This party was not really for Mikhail and Natalya, but for Lena and all the others being left behind—the sailors still at sea.

During the year and a half following the Markovs' departure, Lena Rottman had little time to think about the problems she had discussed with Natalya at that party. She and Dmitri were having trouble at OVIR. Dmitri had once been an assistant to an important figure in the Soviet bureaucracy, and had thus been exposed to the inner workings of the system. The government considered this politically sensitive and was toying with the idea of preventing his emigration. It wasn't until the winter of 1976, a year and a half after the Markovs left and a year after the Rottmans applied, that they were given their exit visas.

EXIT VISA

In Vienna the spring was not yet far enough along to assert itself, and Lena barely had eyes for the dusting of green around the Ringstrasse. She kept her balance, nowadays, by looking straight ahead like a tightrope walker, focusing her gaze only on some slender teetering platform before her, so as not to be distracted from the craft of placing one foot in front of the other. She reminded herself how much better their lives would be when Dmitri could finally revive his sagging career. He was already making plans to meet with officials in the United States, and was outlining some articles about the Soviet system. And perhaps this emigration would do something for Gennadi, she thought. Perhaps it would mature him a bit. He had been unambitious in Moscow, and was never much of a student. Maybe this would help him find himself.

Hope. That was the important thing.

After those first Vienna days of interviews, questionnaires, shopping and cooking, Lena was finally able to spare an afternoon to visit some museums. She had always loved art, but had been shielding herself against the external world, concentrating on getting through without looking to either side for months now, perhaps for years. A walk through the Kunsthistorisches Museum was a kind of adventure after this time of fear, a risk, especially after she had closed herself off for so long from the pain she had felt at Dmitri's growing coldness, which had become worse after their arguments about Carol and about emigration. Lena now moved absentmindedly through the ornate building, through room after room of paintings, vaguely disappointed that having anesthetized herself she now seemed unable to resensitize herself. She stopped, suddenly, in the middle of a room.

Back in Moscow, before all these troubles, Lena had been a lover of Brueghel's paintings, and was always on the lookout for reproductions of his work. In libraries, at the apartments of friends lucky enough to own good art books, she had tracked down photos of certain favorite canvases, and she returned to them often for sustenance. Even in the usual dull reproductions, those crazy-drunk Dutch peasants reeling among their wooden tables of ale and pies and soup, and their fire-yellow harvests, heated her with a kind of lovely hunger.

Quite by chance now, in the midst of her emigration, she was

270

standing in this room, surrounded by eight or ten of those old friends, those Brueghels—the originals. She was startled by the blaze of that roistering *Wedding Scene*, and by the darker fire smoldering below the *Battle of Carnival and Lent*. Lena stood in the middle of the room, almost laughing from the sudden presence of these old friends, and knew by that laugh that she was still alive, or rather, alive again.

But the moment couldn't last forever; finally Lena had to walk across the plaza toward Mariahilferstrasse and the streetcar to her pensione, had to return to that careful, constrained, stingily hopeful getting-by, not only in Vienna, but in Rome, in Ostia—where they finally found what could pass for an apartment. But then, perhaps even Lena's modest hopes for survival and recovery were too optimistic, for Carol Starn turned up at the Rottmans' Ostia apartment one afternoon in June. Carol was staying at a nearby hotel for a bit of a European seaside vacation after the end of the teaching year, to recover from the recent breakup of her marriage.

Several years before, when the Rottmans first met Carol in Mosco, Lena had entertained her royally; she prepared elaborate dinners, and the three of them often sat up talking late into the night. But now, on this first day of Carol's appearance in Ostia, Lena was barely able to be polite to her. After Carol left the apartment, Lena turned on Dmitri and insisted that Carol be put entirely out of their lives. Dmitri swore that he had not been in touch with Carol secretly, that she hadn't come specifically to see him, and that they were just innocent acquaintances.

Even after Carol left for the States, a few weeks later, to attend to a sickness in her family, the chill between Dmitri and Lena worsened. Carol stood between them, and Lena could not exorcise her unless Dmitri were willing to talk honestly about the whole affair; but he showed less and less patience for Lena's questions, and as his protestations became angrier, the breach between them deepened.

By the time another month had passed, in late July, Lena had given up probing and was trying to turn her mind away from her suspicions. One afternoon, as she turned a corner onto a street crowded with shoppers, she saw Dmitri and Carol strolling along, window shopping, holding hands.

Carol happened to glance across the street a moment later, and saw Lena staring at her. She mumbled something to Dmitri, who paused for a moment, turned to smile at Lena, then set off across the street toward her.

"I knew you'd be upset about Carol coming back to Italy, so I didn't mention it . . ." When Lena took a step backward from Dmitri, as he approached her side of the street, he changed his tone.

"Come on, Lena, let's be adults. Let's be civilized. Why act like idiots?"

But Lena was in no mood to pretend. She walked away quickly, wandered through the streets by herself for a few hours, then went back to the apartment to tell Gennadi and her parents what had happened. Even as she sat there in that cramped room, with its crumbling plaster, she wondered why she should be so shocked at this. Was it the image of Dmitri in bed with Carol? Or his lies? Perhaps it was her sudden clear perception of Dmitri, the real Dmitri, and the shoddiness of his pride and of his ambitions, his boast that he would show her the world.

For their remaining three months in Rome Lena was forced to continue to live in the same room with Dmitri, for he refused to look for another apartment, and she had to stay to take care of her parents. Dmitri's constant presence forced her to repeat the same questions over and over in her mind. Why had he dragged her and Gennadi and her parents through this emigration? She had told him long before they applied that if he wanted to be with Carol in America she would divorce him and he could emigrate by himself. Why destroy all of them?

But now that Lena no longer needed to create illusions about Dmitri the answers gradually began to take shape for her. It seemed to Lena, now, that if he had abandoned his family in Moscow, the powers that be would have had one more reason to refuse his visa request, and that one reason might have been one too many. He needed Lena. He also needed Lena's parents' savings account, which had supported all of them during that long wait for a visa. Taking them all had been the only possible strategy for him. He'd needed Lena and her parents in Moscow, and he would need Carol in America for her academic contacts. Such, at any rate, was Lena's understanding of Dmitri's strategy.

Part Three: BEGINNINGS

After many weeks, that moment when Dmitri scurried through the Kennedy Airport crowd to meet Carol's emissary stopped replaying itself in Lena's mind. Her first rage gave way, and Lena began to turn some of her anger against herself for having ever believed in Dmitri and his pretensions, in his "ideals," in anything at all about him.

She recalled how she had always felt superior to women who had no husbands, how she had pitied them for being alone and unable to draw pride and strength from a husband's success. And now, in rejecting that pride, in shedding her attachments to him, she found herself trying to draw away from much that had long been bound up with their life together, in fact, much that had become woven in with the aims and values of that little intellectual subculture that had formed their circle. Lena continued to enjoy the company of these friends, their wit, their talk—it sometimes even seemed indispensable to her survival—and yet she found herself seeking out these people less and less often. Along with that beloved passion and richness of Russian talk, these friends carried with them the old arrogance, the exclusiveness, and a deep attachment to the whole apparatus of status and self-admiration that Dmitri had come to represent in Lena's mind.

Like so many other emigrés, Lena too was told by her NYANA vocational counselor that her past professional life was useless to her here, and that she would have to start at the bottom. Lena suspected that the counselor's aim was not so much to start her on the road to good employment but to get her any job so that she would be off benefits, but she reacted to the situation differently from her friends. She saw employment, even menial employment, not only as a way of bolstering her ego, but as a way of becoming self-sufficient enough to abandon that past to which those others were so attached. It was a way to stop being an emigré, to stop being a former Soviet professional, or a former *anything*. She had to start surviving as an American. She had no choice but to start from the bottom, but she had to start or else there would be no change; she would always be the abandoned wife and the forlorn emigré intellectual.

Lena took the elementary typing course in which NYANA enrolled her, and applied for those menial jobs, but she found that they too were not easy to find. She was "overqualified." It was hard for her to believe that a person could be rejected for being too good for a job; nonetheless, after several rejections she eliminated all mention of her former professional work and much of her education from her résumé. Finally she found a job as an all-around office helper in a small downtown printing shop, at a salary of one hundred dollars per week. She soon realized that she was lucky to have been rejected from those factory jobs that many of the emigrés are sent to. The emigreés in those places forget more English than they learn, and are often unable to rise above their initial level even after a year or more.

After a few months in the print shop Lena was ready to move on to something new. She couldn't support herself on the salary they were able to pay her, but that wasn't all. The menial nature of the work itself didn't bother her, but being condescended to, being accepted in the role of the dumb immigrant was more than Lena could stand. The middle-aged woman who owned the print shop was pleasant enough to Lena, but she was constantly surprised at how quickly the immigrant could master her clerical tasks. She gushed in wonderment at how *fast* Lena had alphabetized the invoices, now *nicely* she had addressed the envelopes. This dowdy shopkeeper had fully and irrevocably accepted Lena as the simpleton her résumé had made her out to be. Lena simply smiled and tried to accept the compliments graciously.

The mathematics that Lena had studied years before now made possible her acceptance into a six-month intensive computer-programming course at one of the local colleges, after which she found work in a large financial office at a far better salary than she had been earning.

Lena and Gennadi settled in a two-bedroom apartment in Queens, and her parents were a few blocks away. The neighborhood was far from posh, but it was quite bearable. The large old apartment houses had not yet become very run-down, and they had the advantage of larger rooms and higher ceilings than many of the newer, more expensive buildings.

Lena began to notice many unexpected changes in the texture of her life. For one thing, she felt freed of the habitual lying that had been normal to daily life in the Soviet Union. There was now no need for the incessant pretense, the recitation of hollow slogans, imprecations against the enemies of socialism, and praises of Soviet power as the bulwark of mankind's hope. Lies in the newspapers, lies at the meetings in her office, lies that had to be acquiesced to, sometimes silently, but often aloud and with an air of conviction. How much easier it was to be rid of all that, and how much energy it left for life!

What was more surprising was that Lena found herself becoming less fascinated with material goods than she had been. Back in Moscow, handsome possessions had been lent a kind of magic, a glamour, by their very scarcity. Because acquiring such possessions often demanded pull as well as cash, they had become emblems of rank. In America simple money would buy the tablecloth or the pretty dress. There was no need for contacts, for status, or the perquisites of rank, so the magic was largely gone. Only now did Lena realize just how much excitement and thought had been devoted to those possessions, how much she and all her friends had treasured them.

Oddly enough, as she became disentangled from the need to pretend and from the hunger to own, she also found herself increasingly detached from thoughts of Dmitri. She hadn't seen him in over a year now, and she had little knowledge of how he was doing. According to the grapevine he wasn't doing too well. People said that he was looking harried, that he had tried to set himself up as an expert Sovietologist, but that nobody had been very impressed by what he'd had to say. When the subject of Dmitri did arise in conversation, she felt only a vast irony. Dmitri had always made it plain that he was the strong one, so she had assumed, and he had agreed, that she must be the weak one who derived what strength she had from him. Then, when he had tried to better his chances by shedding all his encumbrances—his wife, his in-laws, his son—he had turned out to be helpless. He was the weak one, and she discovered her own life and strength. Lena was now much more than merely a busy man's no-longer-young wife. She was a force in others' lives and the dominant force in her own. This became plain when she started to go out with men, Americans as well as emigrés, and found that she could be treated as something far better than a useful household accoutrement.

EXIT VISA

There was even something to be said for the seeming chaos of American society. Lena had heard much theorizing by Soviet analysts, and then by emigrés, to the effect that America was amorphous, that it had no firm structure and therefore must soon crumble. So it appeared at first sight, and yet that seeming formlessness was itself a kind of form. What most Soviets couldn't accept or understand, Lena decided, was that American society was a laboratory, it was a place to experiment, a place where a bright woman could explore her life, if she were willing to.

Lena found herself spending less time with many of her old Moscow friends. She was not anxious to while away entire evenings with a roomful of lonely emigrés who were in a constant state of dismay about the peculiarities of Americans. She knew as well as any the frustration of trying to communicate with Americans. She knew that demon in the Russian tongue, and wondered whether English had its own mad spirit. It was said to be there, but she couldn't hear it. And she also understood that even the most cultivated and sensitive American could never know that lavish code of emotion and inference shared by those who were steeped, marrow and bone, in the poetry of Russia. Yet somehow she had managed to throw in her lot with these odd people, these Americans. Perhaps it was because of this that she was able to discover yet another thing about herself that set her apart from her old friends: she had become an optimist. To the Americans she knew, it seemed an unremarkable thing, being an optimist, but Lena understood that it was a gift as rare as love.

Lena Rottman's optimism was not entirely unique. Irina Markov shared it, or something akin to it. When Lena received a letter from Natalya Markov telling her that Irina had run off, her first instinct was to try to help, but the only one who didn't need her help was Irina. Over the next year and more Irina accomplished much of what she had set out to do. She and Anatoli were living together; she was earning a good salary as an executive secretary, and Anatoli worked as a mechanic, on and off, for his father, who was helping to run an auto repair shop. Periodically the old man would notify his sons that they should come to work—he couldn't afford the rates that American mechanics were charging—and then, after a

276

month or so, he would blow up and order the two of them off his lot. A month or two later he would summon them again. Anatoli also earned a good living by reconditioning and reselling old cars.

The only desire of Irina's that failed to work out was her hope that her parents would come to accept her life as she had arranged it. Irina made weekly telephone calls to her parents, to Mikhail really, since he was usually the one who spoke with her. Natalya couldn't pretend to acquiesce in what she felt was a betrayal. Again and again she asked herself, "Was Antoli in love with Irina?" Then why didn't he declare himself? Why couldn't he come out with it and say, "Look, you've taken me in as a son, but I'm not Irina's brother, and cannot treat her like my sister"? And if he was so afraid of being rejected by us that he had to run away with her, why has he never written to explain himself? Never one word from him to say, "I'm not a traitor; I just didn't know how else to handle it." We'd have accepted that.

Mikhail spoke with Irina every week, but he did not ask about Anatoli, about whether they were still living together, or how long they would live together, whether Irina had plans to marry someday, to have children; and Irina herself did not know the answers to all those questions Mikhail ached to ask her.

It was as though she were still emigrating, still in transit, like Lena Rottman. Both of these women understood that there might or might not be such a thing as arrival, as landfall; that was all right, at least for now. The important thing now seemed to be keeping eyes front. Don't look back.

Chapter Nine:
Orpheus Ascending

For the first five months in America the Levins had felt like helpless children. As long as Grigory had no job, as long as he was dependent on the agency and on whatever encouragement his relatives offered, he could not hold his head up.

After the first few months the Jewish Family Service caseworker began to drop hints that they could theoretically find any kind of job for Grigory and then cut off his benefits if he refused it. One of the volunteer workers was losing patience. She had been helpful in every way she could be, but her frequent visits to the Levins became a problem. Instead of offering advice, she was issuing orders.

"Let him get a job as a bartender," she snapped impatiently one evening, when she had dropped by. "When my father came here after the war, he took *any* job, any job at *all* . . ."

Then, when she began to raise her voice at Grigory, he had the choice either of accepting the insult meekly, and then cursing himself silently for the rest of the night, or of calling on what little pride he still had left. He chose the latter course, stood up, and walked out of the apartment. The visits, the bullying tone, and Grigory's walking out became almost a regular occurrence for a while. But leaving the apartment during the helper's visits was small comfort. He was still like an infant, utterly at the mercy of anybody who thought nothing of simply dismissing all that he had struggled for all his life. "He has to be a chemist? Let him wait on tables . . ."

"No." Tatyana cut the woman off. "Grisha will only work as a scientist. If he has to go to Alaska to do it he'll go, and I'll go too. But he will only work as a scientist, because a scientist is what he is."

At the beginning of June, almost six months after arriving, Grigory found a job doing research in a chemistry laboratory connected with one of the nearby universities. He had gambled that he would get work in his field if he didn't lose hope, if he insisted on devoting all his energy to searching for work, rather than spending his days at some menial stopgap job that would bring in a bit of money in the short term, but might defeat the larger purpose. His position paid about $15,000 per year, enough for a start, and enough to allow Grigory and Tatyana to move to a more pleasant apartment with two bedrooms, a sunny living room, and a basement garage for the old Chevrolet that they had just bought, partly with money borrowed from Volodya.

The troubles between that volunteer worker and Grigory passed, now that he had work. He no longer spent occasional evenings walking through the neighborhood streets to avoid listening to her advice. If the anger and the arguments that broke out when Grigory tried to assert himself resembled a kind of adolescence, then other phenomena even more like adolescence could be seen throughout the emigré communities in America. Old friendships, even marriages, became volatile. Relationships of all kinds began to fragment and reshuffle, just as they do among youngsters at puberty. No one could keep track of the tensions, the shifting alliances, the constant regrouping of ententes and concordats that crystallized and vanished among the emigrés like autumn frost.

There were the geocultural groupings: Odessans on the one hand, Muscovites and Leningraders on the other. Then there were the educated elite versus the commoners, a distinction that cut through all geographic party-lines. Intellectuals from Moscow and Leningrad, however, would reject the credentials of intellectuals from Odessa, since Odessa represents all the mercantile vices, in the minds of the northerners.

But even individuals within a given faction had difficulty getting along for any extended period of time, despite the emigrés' constant glowing reminiscences about the profound and loving friendships they had known back in the Soviet Union. One common statement could be heard, with infinite variations, throughout the emigré communities all over America: "Misha used to be a fine person, but he's changed now. Emigration brought out the worst in him . . ." A friend, who once lived according to the highest principles, might now be accused of being a traitor or a money-grubber; a spouse had suddenly become selfish, demanding, intractable; everybody was changing.

And indeed everybody *was* changing, at least relative to one another. If the emigrés' second infancy, enforced by helplessness, was painful and humiliating, then their adolescence was no less difficult. And that adolescence was often more than simply a metaphor. In modern America, youngsters are expected to become somewhat independent of their parents during or shortly after their teens, and wives cherish the ideal of being equal partners with their husbands. In this environment many emigrés seem, both to Americans and to themselves, to have skipped an entire stage of development: the process of outgrowing dependence upon authority and of becoming one's own authority. Sooner or later, however, the environment wins, and many are forced to go through that stage.

By the time Zoya Gorelsky was fourteen years old she knew that she would never be able to go to the university to study literature. Jews were not being admitted unless they had exceptionally influential contacts. The best she could expect was a place in that engineering institute where her mother knew people. Though the idea of engineering school was utterly unappealing to her, it would never have crossed her mind to refuse, to insist on making her own way. The very concept of that kind of independence would have been almost incomprehensible to Zoya, to almost anybody back in Odessa. Perhaps marrying Alexandr was a way of trying to change her life, though even marriage to Alexandr did not free her. She now depended on him, instead of on her mother, to attend to all practical affairs, and those seizures of anxiety and depression that afflicted her throughout the emigration only made her more dependent.

281

The Gorelskys had moved out of Daly City in the early summer of 1976, in hopes that living closer to their friends in San Francisco, closer to the center of things, would alleviate their sense of isolation, and would bring them in contact with a more interesting group of people. Their move was made easier by the fact that Alexandr had stumbled upon a gold mine of translating work that had to be done for a local firm that was planning to build a factory in the Soviet Union. Once again, just as when he first was hired to teach that one course at a nearby college, he felt for a while that he had managed to launch himself out of confusion and disorientation and into hope. It was becoming apparent to Alexandr that his first temporary teaching job would not lead to another, and that the chances of his finding a place in the academic world were next to nonexistent. But with this newly created translation business, or at least with this one account, Alexandr had been able to make enough money in one summer to last for almost a year. For many weeks Alexandr felt that he might now be onto something that would give him a strong hold on survival, at least until he found a real place for himself in America. Unfortunately, that first account was a stroke of luck rather than an indicator of things to come. Alexandr was unable to find enough customers to keep the translation business alive.

So now Alexandr was still floundering, still trying to decide how to retrain himself to fit into some kind of job. He was willing to compromise, to abandon all hope of an academic career, even to go into business, if possible. In examining his strengths and weaknesses, neither Alexandr nor his friends had ever forgotten that he had been most clearly in his element during those refusenik days in Odessa, when he had helped guide people through the maze of emigration, through conflicts with the Soviet bureaucracy, even with the KGB. That had been Alexandr's finest hour. He had been buoyed up through those hungry days partly by his love of being the canny advisor, of being looked up to by people as a man of affairs and a power in their lives. It was Ella Novogradsky who pointed out the obvious: let Alexandr become a lawyer.

When Ella suggested this, Alexandr pondered carefully for a few moments, nodded, and agreed that it sounded like an interesting alternative. Within him, however, something took fire at the idea, though he could hardly allow himself to hope that he might be admitted to law school. Nonetheless, the next day he made some calls to inquire about application procedures, and found that he had only a bit over a week left before the application deadline expired. He and Zoya went into a fury of activity to fill out forms, get the needed recommendations from members of the American community, since his Odessa professors were beyond reach, to arrange for taking the law-school test, and so on. When everything was complete, Alexandr tried not to let himself become too hopeful. But one morning, in the spring of 1977, while Alexandr was out looking for bargains at a local flea market, Zoya found a letter in their mailbox announcing that he had indeed been admitted to the law school.

Zoya wanted to surprise Alexandr, so when he returned she simply handed him the letter. He looked at it, glanced up at Zoya blankly for a moment, then looked back at the letter, grinning. "Zoyotchka!" He suddenly grabbed Zoya and held her. Since his late teens, certainly since he had begun to think about emigrating, this was Alexandr's first real vindication. He could now be more than the bright kid who'd gone astray. This was the beginning of success, the manly ability to take hold of one's life and set it on course. Now he wouldn't be just another guy on line, just another immigrant.

Between partial scholarships, student loans, and personal loans Alexandr was able to begin law school in the fall of 1977. During the ensuing winter Zoya once again relapsed into her depression, but now she and Alexandr were a bit Americanized, and had developed a touch of Californian sophistication.

"Try to get in touch with your anger . ."

Zoya was sitting cross-legged at one end of a bare mattress on the floor, next to a heap of pillows, in a sparsely furnished apartment. Frank, a former engineer, now a therapist of the eclectic persuasion, who currently leaned toward bioenergetics, was sitting at the other end of the mattress. He was in his late forties, a bit puffy about the chest and belly, and almost bald, though a stringy, untrimmed fringe of grayish-black hair hung down his neck and between his slumped shoulders. For the first part of the hour Frank used to sit across from Zoya on the mattress and have her talk about herself.

Then he would hand her an old, warped tennis racket and make her beat the pillows with broad, menacing, full-arm swings to that she could get in touch with her anger.

"Maybe I'm not angry, Frank."

"You're angry. Just hit that pillow—hard. Feel it!"

Frank stood nearby in his patched, loose Levis, a beatific smile on his heavy lips, and urged her gently.

"Feel it?"

"No . . ."

Frank felt it was essential to see both husband and wife, so one day Alexandr stood there, lean and dapper in his three-piece suit, ready for anything, and slammed away at the pillows. Frank tried to encourage him.

"You're too stiff, Alex, too intellectual. Come down off it for a while and join the rest of the world; feel your anger."

Except for that almost paralyzing depression and withdrawal that Zoya had experienced just after arriving in the United States, this episode during Alexandr's first year of law school was the worst she had experienced. Within a few weeks, however, it began to pass, and by the early spring of 1978 she was feeling well again. She was unable to say whether Frank's therapy had really helped, but both she and Alexandr knew that their initial suspicion of Frank's methods had gradually given way to admiration. Frank had been able to give Zoya one thing that was important to her, that lent her a feeling of personal strength: his unconditional warmth and acceptance.

It wasn't until the following year that the doctors were able to discover that Zoya had been suffering from an endocrine imbalance, which had initially been triggered by the stress of emigration. Ultimately the condition had affected her nervous system so as to increase her anxiety and had damaged her ability to handle stress. Once they were able to identify the condition they were able to treat it with drugs. In cities where Soviet emigrés congregate, doctors had already begun to notice that the emigrés' health seemed to break down either during or just after emigrating, and some medical men began to suspect that a good many of the problems were caused by the fear and confusion these people had passed through,

Part Three: BEGINNINGS

from the day they began to apply until long after they arrived in their new homes.

Zoya was luckier than some others: the pills she was given seemed to help. She never again experienced these episodes, but the correction of her glandular problem was not the only major readjustment in her life. Until now, most of Zoya's friends were really Alexandr's friends. They were people who enjoyed his conversation, his wit, some who had known him in the old days, and had studied English with him in Odessa or in Rome. Now Zoya was beginning to make friends of her own in her classes at the university. These new friends of hers had never met Alexandr, and when Zoya made an end-of-the-year party for them she not only refused to invite Alexandr, but she asked him to leave the apartment for the evening. It was now her turn.

That summer, while Alexandr worked in a law office to gain experience, professional contacts, and enough cash to help them get through the following year, Zoya went off to a part-time job in Los Angeles, where she roomed with some friends and experimented with being on her own. Though she moved back with Alexandr in time to start her final year of studies, she understood now that being there with Alexandr was not absolutely necessary to her survival, nor was it to be taken for granted.

And so, Zoya and Alexandr too were being driven toward change. It was much more than jobs and careers that had to be reestablished on entirely new bases here in America. Most preexisting relationships also had to stand or fall on new and untested foundations, contoured to unexpected needs and to unforeseen desires.

Surrounded as it was by automobile supply shops, laundries, and obscure storefronts, the small facade of the synagogue was easy to miss in the late-afternoon Los Angeles glare. Inside, it was just a plain, one-room *shul*, with a scattering of long tables usually cluttered with books, red and black *tfillin* boxes, and prayer shawls. At the western end of the oblong room was a plain wooden desk—Rabbi Izak Mendelyevitch's "office"—and at the eastern end was the red velvet curtain of the Ark that held the Torah scrolls.

EXIT VISA

But on this Sunday afternoon in early July the room was packed with a dense crowd of emigrés, most of them recent arrivals. Several hundred people were crowded onto benches around the tables, eating chicken, passing paper plates, squeezing by each other, joking in Russian. They were here to honor the start of the Jewish day camp for emigré children, which Izak Mendelyevitch was running.

When Izak left New York in order to help new emigrés in southern California six years earlier, in 1972, American Jews still had little idea that by the end of the decade about 80,000 newcomers would have arrived from the Soviet Union. At that time Jewish organizations all over the Western world had been rallying under the slogan, "Save Soviet Jewry." It would not be for another few years, not until the mid-1970s, that active American Jews would begin to feel disappointed in the lukewarm attitude of many Soviet Jews toward organized forms of Jewish life and religion.

By the late 1970s that attitude had become well known, but Izak also knew that the picture was not so simple. Many of the emigrés occupied an uncomfortable middle ground. The ability to take part in religion had been trained out of them, and yet there were those who would have liked to be able to regenerate that ability, who would certainly have liked their children to possess it. But it wasn't only social pressure from other emigrés that discouraged them. When Izak arrived in southern California he began to wonder if the Jewish philanthropic agencies weren't even less interested in Judaism than the emigrés. His first stop was at the office of a major Jewish philanthropic organization where he asked for a list of the local emigré families. At that time there were still fewer than twenty families in the area; he wanted to contact each of them personally to see what he could do for them, but the agency workers refused to give him the names.

"They're not interested in Jewishness, Rabbi. They only want to be Americans. There's no point giving out names."

Not interested. "Of course they're not interested . . ." Izak tried to explain . . . "of course, everybody wants a job first, money, a house: what else? This is America! But they want more than that. Yes, really. You don't believe me?

"Look. A Jew comes out from Russia, he's like a forest man who was lost in the woods maybe when he was an infant, and was raised by the wolves and the bears. So he thinks he's also a bear. How should he know different? Still, comes one day, he leaves the forest to be with people. Why? Because he's *not* a wolf and *not* a bear. He's a man, a human. You think he knows it? He *doesn't* know it. But he walks away from the woods, and then you have to teach him."

Izak left the office without the list of emigrés. Fortunately, a few weeks later he met one of the new emigrés through some friends, and within a few days he was able to track down most of the others.

Although Izak assisted the emigrés with purely practical problems wherever he could, he considered his most valuable help to lie in bringing them back to being practicing Jews. But both kinds of help are necessary; he'd been trying to preach that to community leaders, rabbis, everybody all over the state. How many synagogues had put up signs with the words, "Save Soviet Jewry," he wondered. Dozens; he could see them on every street. And how many of those rabbis in the fancy synagogues go in person to help a new family, take them to the store, show them around, teach a little *Yiddishkeit* to the children. Few if any. Instead, they set up a committee, and the committee votes to give a *bissel* money, sends out printed announcements of a picnic for the "Russians"; meanwhile, the emigré sits home and feels abandoned. For this he should break a lifelong atheist training? For this he should give up his time to pray? Izak had no patience with it. "You want to save Soviet Jews?" he used to ask. "Fine! Save! But then you have to help them!"

And now, six years after those people refused to give him the list, he was standing on a platform in that *shul*, surrounded by hundreds of emigrés, giving out a boxful of prizes to the boys who ranged in age from six to about thirteen, and who, along with their fathers, had just been circumcised within the past few weeks.

Izak knew how proud the Soviets are that they have practically stamped out Jewish ritual circumcision in the Soviet Union: he had known of cases in which both the father and the *mohel* who performed the circumcision went to prison, though the authorities no longer stopped the Moslems of Soviet Central Asia from performing the same rite. Izak knew that in eliminating the mark of the covenant, the Soviets had hoped to eliminate the people of the covenant, and he knew that they had failed. As these boys and their fathers stood up to receive their prizes and their applause, Izak could see that the Soviets had failed, and never mind all the grumbling from those so-called "Jewish community leaders" that the emigrés were interested only in assimilating.

Early the next morning Izak watched the children sitting around the tables with their counselors, chanting the Hebrew alphabet, singing the morning blessings, each table competing with the other to see who could sing loudest.

Izak stood outside for a few minutes, while the crowd piled into an old school bus in front of the building. The counselors—sparse-bearded yeshiva boys from New York, some from the underground schools in the Soviet Union—loaded canisters of juice and bag lunches onto the bus, and the whole shouting, singing, stamping busload took off, rattling toward the baseball field.

As Izak stepped back into the synagogue and picked up the stack of telephone messages that had already piled up on his desk, he could clearly recall when his work had first begun to make a dent. It was in 1974, about two years after his arrival in California. An emigré tailor asked Izak to help him raise $2,000 so that he could open a small shop. He was already working for a local tailor, an American Jew, but the boss wanted him to work on Saturday. "I didn't come to America to be forced to work on *Shabbes*, like in Russia. . . ."

Izak wanted to help. He could see that the tailor was honest, but how could Izak help him raise $2,000? He went to the bank, but they said he needed a sponsor. One of the old Chassidic rabbis in the area was willing to sponsor the loan, so they got the money. In three months the tailor paid it back.

"That's where it started," he recalled. "And meanwhile another one needs money, so we borrow some more. And then another: and a *mezuzah* for a doorpost, and a *tallis* for a bar mitzvah: and that's how it started—with *tfillin*, with *mezuzahs*, with this, with that, with the other. We spent the money, helped the people, a little here, a little there, a little-little-little-little: until now I owe for the camp ninety-thousand dollars, and for the *shul* ninety-thousand dollars—so all together, in six, seven years' work, a total deficit of a hundred and eighty thousand dollars. It's *takeh* not so bad—some kind of a success!"

The funeral parlor was a simple, square room, with folding chairs for the mourners. The deceased was an emigré in his early fifties, a man of little luck who hadn't a kopeck to his name in Minsk and had little more in America. He left behind a wife and a six-year-old son. The widow, a small, plain woman in her forties, sat on one side with two or three other women. There were only a few mourners besides the black-clad rabbis from Chabad House and a few neighbors of the widow. They barely had a prayer-quorum of ten adult males.

As the funeral party moved toward the doors of the parlor, after the service, Izak stopped and looked around. "Where is the little boy?"

"In school," the mother answered.

"So, we'll stop at the school and pick him up."

An American woman, who lived in the same apartment house as the widow, was a bit taken aback.

"Rabbi, he's only six years old. It'll be a trauma."

"Listen. God took away the boy's papa; soon the boy will forget even his papa's face. Now we should take away from him the funeral? It's all the boy has left of the papa. Call the school, we'll stop off there."

The small group of male mourners acted as pallbearers, helped lower the coffin into the grave, read the prayers, and took turns shoveling the soil over the coffin. The women sat on folding chairs about ten feet away. While the little boy fidgeted and whimpered about the feet of the black-suited Chassidim who were standing around the fresh mound of earth, Izak looked down toward the mound and began to speak quietly. Only those standing close to him could hear him speak, as though they were overhearing a private conversation. He spoke in Yiddish.

"We made your funeral and your burial the only way we know how. If we did anything wrong today it's from our ignorance, not from neglect, so please don't hold it against us. And remember, you're going to the *bessere velt* now, the better world, but your wife and the boy are still here in this world. Intercede for them, for your wife, she should live and find comfort and solace and health, and for your boy, he should grow up to strength and wisdom, to Torah and *mitzvos—*"

One of the other Chassidim interrupted to add: "—and a wedding, and children of his own—"

"Yes." Izak glanced up for a moment, then faced the grave again and continued, "He should grow up to marriage, and children, and a Jewish life. You shouldn't forget them. Help—intercede—don't forget . . ."

In Vitali Leonov's cramped fourth-floor walk-up in New York, as the temperature and the humidity both hovered in the nineties, and decades of thick, yellowing wall paint swelled to jam the windows and the doors, Vitali stood up from his chair and tried to unstick the sweaty clothes from his skin. His guest, an American writer who knew some of the Leonovs' friends on the West Coast, was hunched over a typescript of one of Vitali's stories.

"You know," Vitali interrupted him, "you know, you Americans all believe it is impossible to live in Russia, but I must tell you that it is not impossible to live there. As long as you don't do something stupid, some mistake. Of course, for me the trouble had to happen, but for the usual person it is not impossible to live. And Odessa especially. Odessa is not a gray city with dreary, sad people, as you all believe. No. It is colorful, rich with impressions, with kinds of people. It's full of energy, and cleverness, and also foolishness, but of a special type . . ." Vitali's fair complexion was becoming red with his frustration at the awkwardness of his English, at the impossibility of touching this American with the love that he himself could still feel for the city that would still be home if not for those *svólitchi,* those bastards. "Bastards!" he hissed, "Bastards who drove us out of there!"

Vitali leaned back in his chair for a moment. "I will tell you absolutely the truth. Most are miserable here. The emigrés—I see them in New York—most are without place, without meaning, miserable. And I tell you something else: Americans are also like this. Americans too. No, no, I'm not wrong, I have begun to see very much—" And he shook his head and stopped his guest's objections with a raised forefinger. "Especially the intellectuals, writers. They are an alien species here, maybe even more than in Russia, though here nobody jails them or exiles them. Still, a small, alien nation inside of America. And I feel in the air this sad restlessness. Like exiles, all of them. Not only in New York. I felt it when I was invited to speak in Europe last spring. In Europe too, yes. It is a sadness everywhere, the same sadness, the same—"

The guest allowed his mind to wander, for a moment, back to what the old Kabbalists used to say, that the Jewish exile was only a symbol for the universal exile; that all mankind, in fact, the entire cosmos, is in a state of exile and fragmentation. As he was reminded of this, he wondered momentarily about those, among the settled American Jews, who resented these newly arrived immigrant Jews. There had always been some like that. HIAS had letters on file from American Jews in the 1880s, the 1900s, the 1930s, the post-Nazi period, and now in the 1970s: "Please don't send us any more of these good-for-nothings; they're not like our fathers. They're lazy, arrogant . . ." Perhaps it was because the very presence of these newcomers defied the settled American Jews' security, and seemed to shout in their ears: *"I'm* an immigrant? *You're* an immigrant! You forgot already? I'll remind you! . . ."

As the two of them stood up to walk into the other room, where Galina had set out the dishes for lunch, Vitali stopped his guest for a moment to tell him one of those jokes that had been born out of this emigration, or perhaps reborn from the vast, dormant stock of Yiddish tales.

"A Jew—an Odessan, of course, you understand—a Jew, Rabinovitch, sits in the HIAS office in Rome. He can't decide what country he should go. 'I was thinking,' he says, you know, with this Yiddish kind of singsong, 'I was tinki-i-ing, maybe New Zealand: Eh! Too far from anyplace. Maybe Canada-a-a-a: Eh! Too cold. America-a-a: Eh! Too much crime.' So the HIAS worker says to him, 'Look, Rabinovitch, you're making me crazy. Here's a globe, a globe of the whole world. Take it into that room and look at it. I'm going to lunch. I close the office at five, so by then you should decide.' Hours later, at five, the caseworker is about to leave, he remembers Rabinovitch. 'Rabinovitch!' He calls him in. 'You have that globe?'

"I got the globe.'

"You looked at the globe?'

"I looked the globe.'

"So, Rabinovitch? Your decision?'

(Pause)

"You got maybe another glo-o-obe?' "

Despite the loneliness Tatyana had felt for her old friends back in Leningrad during those first months in America, despite the Levins' isolation and strangeness in that first little apartment in Oakland, Tatyana still used to say that she felt like someone who had been touched by a miracle, like Orpheus. And yet she could not anchor herself here as long as she kept yearning for her old friends in Leningrad, as long as those bonds drew her mind and her heart back there. She tried to make new friends quickly, but her disappointment in those sudden new friendships was as anguished as her hunger for them had been.

About a year after the Levins arrived, however, a small group of friends did begin to emerge. One was a university student whom Tatyana had tutored in Russian, another was a colleague from Grigory's lab; one by one they began to detach themselves from the crowd.

At this time Tatyana wrote to her father. Until now she had addressed all her letters to both her father and her mother, but only her mother answered them. Although Tatyana had insulted her mother terribly at that going-away lunch in Grigory's parents' apartment, she did call her mother on the phone the next morning, that last morning in Leningrad, and, as Tatyana now wrote to her father, She remained my mother . . .

> . . . She remained my mother, she wished me happi-
> ness, she was friendly, she was loving. Since then, only
> she has answered my letters, only she has accepted my
> telephone calls from Rome, from America   . .

Part Three: BEGINNINGS

When I was fifteen, I remember, your old mother had a stroke. You hadn't seen her for many years, but as soon as you heard about it you ran off to the country, hundreds of miles away, to see her. It was midwinter, and you arrived too late, but your brothers told you that she had regained consciousness and mentioned you just before she died. She said, "Sasha will be here for my funeral, so tell him not to take off his hat, because he might catch cold."

You had been her favorite, her firstborn, and she never abandoned her love for you, not through all those decades since you'd run away from the village as a boy. And now I must ask you about that love you once felt for me, whether it is gone without a trace, whether you have nothing of your mother's feelings. I was once your favorite little girl. Is there nothing left of that, or has it all been replaced by cowardice? . . .

It was Tatyana's last letter to her father. Perhaps the fact that he never answered it helped her to climb past the need to look back, made it easier for her to stop yearning for those old loves.

Jobs were now no problem for Alexandr Gorelsky. As his graduation approached, he was being flown to interviews in various cities. Offers were being made, and as he sat on those planes he found himself reminded, with increasing frequency, of one particular emigration joke that had been popular when he was in Rome. A colonel in the KGB summons Abramovitch to his office and starts yelling.

"What's wrong with you, Abramovitch! Three years ago you applied for an exit visa, so we let you go to Israel. A year later you moved to America, and a year after that you begged us to let you come back to Odessa. Now you're in Odessa, and you're applying for another visa! Suddenly you like Israel?"

"Listen, Colonel. Israel? Fooey! America? Also fooey! Russia? Double fooey! Ah, but the *flight*, Colonel! The *flight*!!"

In his own way Alexandr was very fond of America, though

something about it eluded him. His life here seemed to lack a cer
tain flavor, a pungence that he had imagined but had never tasted
So much that he had dreamed of as a refusenik had actually begun t
come true, yet it lacked the savor of the dream. He sometimes sat by
himself, now, and tried to redraw in his mind the image and th
texture of that hope, that goal he had once treasured, but it altered
before the gaze like a distant migrant flock whose contours contin
uously shift. The memory of his goal was changing; Zoya wa
changing; he was changing. And though he had achieved rare suc
cess, he hadn't quite located *his* America, the one that only he had
known of and had sought.

In the small hours of the morning, Tatyana dreams that she i
back there, has never left, may never leave; at these times America i
a bubble, a mirage, a cloud-castle blown to nothing in the wind o
her sleep, and now she is back there, unprotected. And the "bacl
there" of the dream has none of the baroque beauty of the ol
Leningrad architecture, the canals, the bridges with their carve
lions, the green and yellow stone squares and palaces. There is onl
the cold, the damp, the power that peers at her through walls. It i
all she hated and ran from, and it shouts her awake, strangling
cramped, reminding her: Behind, there is nothing; whatever there i
lies ahead.

Appendix A:
Recent Developments

The procedures of the agencies that handle the emigrés once they leave the Soviet Union are in an almost constant state of flux. For example, although the Gorelskys spent only a short time being interviewed by the Sokhnut representative, the problem caused by an ever-increasing percentage of emigrés who decide against going to Israel brought about an important change by the end of the 1970s. It became policy that the emigrés who had initially decided against Israel would be given information about Israel in the form of films, slide shows, and lectures for at least a day or two after their arrival in Vienna. Only then would they be interviewed by the Sokhnut representatives. Until that representative signed a release, no emigré could even enter the building that housed the HIAS and Joint offices. Sokhnut's orientation sessions were being held in several of the hotels and pensiones used by the emigrés. This alteration in procedure was meant to answer the Sokhnut allegation that HIAS and Joint were discouraging people from going to Israel, and that Sokhnut had insufficient time to teach the emigrés about Israel.

The Israeli insistence that pressure be brought to bear on the emigrés to discourage them from avoiding Israel has recently resulted in further plans for modification. As of this time (December 1980), a compromise plan is nearing completion that would send all those not going to Israel to a single site—one near Naples is presently under consideration—where teams from the various agencies would try to convince them to go to Israel rather than to the West. Those who could not be convinced to do so would then be sent to Rome for the usual processing. Theoretically, those who have close relatives in America or other Western countries would be the first to be released to the care of Rome's HIAS and Joint offices. Before leaving the Soviet Union the emigrés would be told by the officers at the Dutch Embassy in Moscow that they will be expected to proceed to Israel rather than to the West.

The details for this so-called "Naples Plan" have not yet been finalized, nor is its implementation an absolute certainty. The American-Jewish philanthropic agencies have gone on record as opposing any plan that restricts emigrés' freedom of choice in the matter of the country of their destination, but the Israeli organizations, such as Sokhnut, have maintained very strong pressure to discourage emigrés from going to the West.

At the beginning of December 1980, an important change was made in the processing of the emigrés in Vienna. Now, instead of separating those going to Israel from those going to the West, all the emigrés are kept together in the special facilities near Vienna, and those proceeding to Italy (and, ultimately, the West) are kept in Vienna only for a few days. One result of this change is that those who are not Jewish, and who must therefore be handled by Caritas, the IRC, or the Tolstoy Foundation, will be turned over to those other agencies in Rome rather than in Vienna. This change has been facilitated by the drastic reduction in the number of emigrés after the disruption of a stable détente between the United States and the Soviet Union, caused by the Soviet invasion of Afghanistan in January 1980.

In the United States itself, the economic difficulties of 1979-80 have hurt the fund-raising capabilities of all Jewish philanthropic organizations, which has cut down on the availability of funds for emigré resettlement. Thus, many local agencies have cut the support period of emigrés from six to three months, and other support services have also been curtailed in some areas.

Appendix B:
Bibliography

Amalrik, Andrei, *Involuntary Journey to Siberia*, New York: Harcourt Brace Jovanovich, 1970.

Berdyaev, Nicolas, *Origin of Russian Communism*, Ann Arbor: University of Michigan Press, 1960.

Bocca, Geoffrey, *Moscow Scene*, New York: Stein and Day, 1976.

Bronfenbrenner, Urie, *Two Worlds of Childhood: U.S. and U.S.S.R.*, New York: Basic Books, 1970.

Chalidze, Valery, *Criminal Russia: A Study of Crime in the Soviet Union*, New York: Random House, 1977.

_____, *To Defend These Rights: Human Rights and the Soviet Union*, New York: Random House, 1975.

Chesler, Evan, *The Russian Jewry Reader*, New York: Behrman House, 1974.

Cole, J. P., *Geography of the U.S.S.R.*, New York: Penguin Books, 1967.

Crankshaw, Edward, *Khrushchev, A Career*, New York: Viking Press, 1976.

_____, *The Shadow of the Winter Palace*, New York: Viking Press, 1976.

Decter, Moshe, ed., *Redemption: Jewish Freedom Letters from Russia*, American Jewish Conference on Soviet Jewry, 1970.

EXIT VISA

Eliav, Arie L., *Between Hammer and Sickle*, Philadelphia, Pa.: Jewish Publication Society and Signet Books, 1969.

Israel, Gerald, *The Jews in Russia*, New York: St. Martins Press 1974.

Kaiser, Robert G., *Russia; The People and the Power*, New York Atheneum, 1976.

Khrushchev, Nikita S., *Khrushchev Remembers*, Boston: Little Brown, 1971.

Kochan, Lionel, ed., *The Jews in Soviet Russia Since 1917*, 3rd ed. New York: Oxford University Press, 1967.

Mandelstam, Nadezhda, *Hope against Hope: A Memoir*, New York Atheneum, 1970.

_____, *Hope Abandoned*, New York: Atheneum, 1972.

Markish, Esther, *The Long Journey*, New York: Random House 1978.

Medvedev, Zhores, A., *Ten Years After Ivan Denisovich*, New York: Vintage Books, 1974.

Navrozov, Lev, *The Education of Lev Navrozov*, New York: Harper & Row, 1975.

Reddaway, Peter, ed., *Uncensored Russia: Protest and Dissent in the Soviet Union*, New York: American Heritage Press, 1972.

Sawyer, Thomas E., *The Jewish Minority in the Soviet Union*, Boulder, Colo.: Westview Press, 1979.

Schroeter, Leonard, *The Last Exodus*, New York: Universe Books 1974.

Shindler, Colin, *Exit Visa: Détente, Human Rights, and the Jewish Emigration Movement in the U.S.S.R.*, Bachman and Turner 1978.

Shragin, Boris, *The Challenge of the Spirit*, New York: Alfred A Knopf, 1978.

Smith, Hedrick, *The Russians*, New York: Ballantine Books 1977.

Smolar, Boris, *Soviet Jewry Today and Tomorrow*, New York: Macmillan, 1971.

Solzhenitsyn, Aleksandr I., *The Gulag Archipelago*, three vols. New York: Harper & Row, 1973-1978.

Stern, August, *The U.S.S.R. Versus Dr. Mikhail Stern*, New York Urizen Books, 1977.

298

Bibliography

Stern, Paula, *Water's Edge: Domestic Politics and the Making of American Foreign Policy*, Westport, Conn.: Greenwood Press, 1979.

Svirsky, Grigory, *Hostages: The Personal Testimony of a Soviet Jew*, New York: Alfred A. Knopf, 1976.

Taylor, Telford, *Courts of Terror: Soviet Criminal Justice and Jewish Emigration*, New York: Alfred A. Knopf, 1976.

Tökés, Rudolf L., *Dissent in the U.S.S.R.: Politics, Ideology and People*, Baltimore, Md.: Johns Hopkins University Press, 1975.

Wiesel, Elie, *The Jews of Silence*, New York: Holt, Rinehart & Winston, 1966.

Yanov, Alexandr L., *The Russian New Right*, Inst. of International Studies, Univ. of Cal., Berkeley, 1978.